CHILTON'S Repair and Maintenance Guide

Travel Trailers

ILLUSTRATED

Prepared by the
Automotive Editorial Department

Chilton Book Company
401 Walnut Street
Philadelphia, Pa. 19106
215—WA 5-9111

managing editor **JOHN D. KELLY;** assistant managing editor **PETER J. MEYER;** senior editor, recreational vehicle department, **KERRY A. FREEMAN;** editor **ROBERT J. BROWN;** technical editor **Philip A. Canal;** copy editor **Eric J. Roberts**

CHILTON BOOK COMPANY   PHILADELPHIA   NEW YORK   LONDON

Copyright © 1973 by Chilton Book Company

First Edition

All rights reserved

Published in Philadelphia by Chilton Book Company
and simultaneously in Ontario, Canada,
by Thomas Nelson & Sons, Ltd.

Manufactured in the United States of America

Library of Congress Cataloging in Publication Data

Chilton Book Co. Automotive Editorial Dept.
  Chilton's repair and maintenance guide travel trailers.

    1. Automobiles—Trailers—Maintenance and repair.
I. Title. II. Title: Repair and maintenance
guide: travel trailers.
TL297.C513   629.28'7'6   73-976
ISBN 0-8019-5841-5
ISBN 0-8019-5853-9 (pbk)

Contents

Chapter 1 General Information 1

    Introduction, 1
    Preparing the Trailer for Use, 3
    Hitching the Trailer to the Tow Vehicle, 3
    Off-Season Storage and Winterizing, 6
    Towing and Parking, 7
    State and Provincial Trailer Laws, 11

Chapter 2 Tow Vehicle 13

    Effects of Pulling on the Tow Vehicle, 13
    Factors Affecting Towing, 13
    Vehicle Safety, 14
    Tow Vehicle Components, 15
    Passenger Car and Stationwagon Tire Load Limits, 21
    Conventional Truck Tire Load Ratings, 25
    High Flotation Truck Tire Load Ratings, 27
    Trailer Tire Load Ratings, 28
    Trailer Towing Information, 35

Chapter 3 Water and Sewage 98

    The Water System, 98
    Water Pump Troubleshooting Chart, 100
    The Sewage System, 101
    Thermasan, 105

Chapter 4 Fuel and Heating 121

    The Liquid Petroleum Gas System, 121
    Heating System, 125
    Heater Troubleshooting Chart, 127

Chapter 5 Electrical, Refrigeration, and Air Conditioning 129

    The Electrical System, 129
    Refrigerator, 130
    Refrigeration Troubleshooting Chart, 135
    Air Conditioning, 136
    Air Conditioning Troubleshooting Chart, 141
    Generators, 144
    Small Appliance Current Requirements, 148

Chapter 6 Running Gear Assembly 149

    Axle Removal, 150
    Axle Alignment, 151
    Trailer Tires and Wheels, 152
    Wheel/Tire Assembly Troubleshooting, 153
    Wheel Bearings, 153
    Bearing Failure Chart, 157
    Electric Brakes, 163
    Surge Brakes, 169
    Brake Troubleshooting Chart, 171

Chapter 7 Routine Maintenance 174

    Canvas Care, 176
    Vinyl Care, 176
    Interior Maintenance, 176
    Exterior Maintenance, 176
    Aluminum Care, 177
    Pop Rivets, 177
    Drilling Solid Rivets, 177
    Fiberglass Repairs, 179

ACKNOWLEDGMENTS

CHILTON BOOK COMPANY expresses appreciation to the following firms for their assistance and technical information:

1. Air Lift Company, Lansing, Michigan.
2. Airstream, Jackson Center, Ohio.
3. American Motors Corporation, Detroit, Michigan.
4. Atwood Vacuum Machine Company, Rockford, Illinois.
5. Bert R. Parker & Sons, Glenolden, Pennsylvania.
6. Boler American Corporation, Wichita, Kansas.
7. Chevrolet Motor Division, General Motors Corporation, Lansing, Michigan.
8. Chrysler Corporation, Detroit, Michigan.
9. Dico, Moline, Illinois.
10. Dodge Division, Chrysler Corporation, Detroit, Michigan.
11. Equal-izer Sales Corporation, South Salt Lake, Utah.
12. Fayette Manufacturing Company, Fayette, Ohio.
13. Flex-a-lite Corporation, Tacoma, Washington.
14. Ford Marketing Corporation, Dearborn, Michigan.
15. French & Hecht; a division of Kelsey-Hayes Company, Davenport, Iowa.
16. Gem Industries, Incorporated, Grand Rapids, Michigan.
17. Generac Corporation, Wankesha, Wisconsin.
18. Intertherm Incorporated, St. Louis, Missouri.
19. Johnson Corporation, Monroeville, Indiana.
20. Kelsey-Hayes Company, Mequon, Wisconsin.
21. Kohler Company, Kohler, Wisconsin.
22. Oldsmobile Division, General Motors Corporation, Lansing, Michigan.
23. Owens-Corning Fiberglass Corporation, Toledo, Ohio.
24. Pontiac Motor Division of General Motors Corporation, Pontiac, Michigan.
25. Recreational Vehicle Institute, Incorporated, Des Plains, Illinois.
26. Serro Travel Trailer Company, Ashburn, Georgia.
27. Tekonsha Engineering Company, Tekonsha, Michigan.
28. The Coleman Company, Incorporated, Somerset, Pennsylvania.
29. Thermasan Corporation, Ann Arbor, Michigan.
30. The Timken Company, Canton, Ohio.
31. Winnabago Industries, Incorporated, Forest City, Iowa.
32. Worthington Cylinders, Columbus, Ohio.

1 · General Information

Introduction

Since there is a tendency to confuse the various classifications of campers and motor homes, a brief definition of each type may be helpful.

The following definitions are those accepted by the Mobile Home Manufacturers Association. They define a Pick-Up Camper as a structure designed primarily to be mounted on a pick-up or truck chassis of one-half ton or larger. There are two types of Pick-Up Campers: the slide-in campers (which are known as portable) and the chassis-mount campers (which are permanently attached). Pick-Up Covers, which are portable units enclosing the bed of pick-up trucks and providing all-weather protection, are very similar although much smaller. Other names for these units are caps or shells.

Motor Homes are self-powered units designed to provide complete living facilities. These include living and dining areas, usually a kitchen, and a full bath with a shower.

Travel trailers measure from 10 to 35 feet in length and average about eight feet in width. They are designed to be towed behind passenger vehicles and may be equipped with single or tandem axles. The trailers within this range do not require special permits when transported on public roads.

Camper trailers are more compact since they are constructed with a collapsible roof and side walls that can be quickly raised and folded out. When collapsed, the

A chassis-mounted camper.

A Slide-in camper.

GENERAL INFORMATION

A Pick-up shell.

A Motor home.

A Travel trailer.

unit forms a neat outline which is ideal for towing and storage. Camper trailers are designed to be towed by a car or light truck and are also known as fold-down campers or tent trailers.

The travel trailer is a unit constructed of light-weight aluminum or fiberglass mounted on a steel frame chassis. It appears to be a miniaturized mobile home from the outside but similarities stop at appearance. A travel trailer is much more durable because it is built to withstand the extra stresses of being towed over the road much of its life, whereas a mobile home might be moved only once or twice during its life. A travel trailer is more self-contained than a mobile home. Many have their own power source which is almost unheard of in mobile homes. Some travel trailers can operate for days completely free from any outside utilities and

Closed

Open

A Camper trailer.

GENERAL INFORMATION

Some travel trailers can be completely self-contained. (© Airstream Corp.)

still satisfy all the occupants' needs. A travel trailer can accommodate four to eight people comfortably, depending on its size.

Preparing the Trailer for Use

If the trailer has been stored for a period of time, it is necessary to make a thorough check of all mechanical components before hitching up and taking to the road. Lack of lubrication, corroded parts, or other malfunctions may cause irreparable damage if not corrected. Beside this, it is simply good common sense to make a thorough check before using the trailer.

The following is a good checklist to be followed when returning a stored trailer to service.

1. Check the condition of both the tires and the tire rims. Also check the lug nuts for the correct (manufacturer's) torque.
2. Make an inspection of the wheel bearings for condition and lubrication. It is a good idea to repack the bearings at least once a season, and more frequently depending upon the severity of use.
3. Check the braking system (if the trailer is so equipped). This must be a thorough check since this is one of the most critical components. Inspect the linings, drums, and hydraulic lines. Check the fluid, line connections, and wheel cylinders for any sign of leaks. Take your time and make a thorough check. On trailers with electric brakes, remember to check for worn magnets, frayed wires, and leaks at the controller.
4. Lubricate all points recommended by the factory with the correct lubricant.

5. Examine the hitch tongue for any stress cracks or tears in the metal.
6. Check the electrical lines for positive connections and for loose or frayed wires which might contact the frame.
7. Fill the tires to the recommended pressure.

Hitching the Trailer to the Tow Vehicle

1. Make sure that all the breakables are secured before the travel trailer is closed for towing. The walkway sections of the trailer can be used for storage. Make sure that all items are secure to prevent breakage and damage to the trailer.
2. Make certain that all cabinet doors are closed and that the door is secured and locked correctly. Also remember to secure the retractable steps if the unit is so equipped.
3. Raise the coupler of the trailer until it is high enough to clear the hitch ball located on the tow vehicle hitch.
4. Back the tow vehicle to the trailer with someone straddling the end of the coupler. (From this position one can tell if the tow vehicle is coming back straight enough to hook up to the trailer before the tow vehicle has to pull up to make a correction.) The large corrections can be made before the tow vehicle comes close; finer corrections can be made just before the ball is in position under the coupler on the trailer. Have the person who is doing the directing establish some kind of communications with the driver of the tow vehicle, whether it be by hand motions or speaking.

(There are mirrors available for mounting on the tongue of the trailer that can be

Back up the car to the trailer until the ball is directly under the coupler. (© Airstream Corp.)

GENERAL INFORMATION

Coupler mirror. (© Airstream Corp.)

adjusted so that you can see the coupler from inside the car while backing up.)

Another method of lining up the trailer and the car is to establish some kind of reference point on the car and the trailer while backing toward the trailer.

The ball has to be centered by at least one-half the width of the ball to slip under the coupler of the trailer. Make sure that the coupler latch is in a position to allow the trailer to drop all the way down onto the ball.

When the trailer has been dropped into position, fasten the lever to secure the latch against the ball. For safety's sake, place a bolt through the hole of the lever and run a nut onto it. This hole can also be used to lock the tongue by putting a lock through the hole when the trailer is not in use or is left unattended over an extended period of time.

Drop the trailer down onto the ball. (© Airstream Corp.)

5. If your trailer is equipped with an equalizing hitch, do not drop the trailer any further than just after the coupler is secure on the ball. Note the height of the hitch ball and raise the trailer and the car to the full height of the hitch jack. Attach the leveling bars and lower the car and

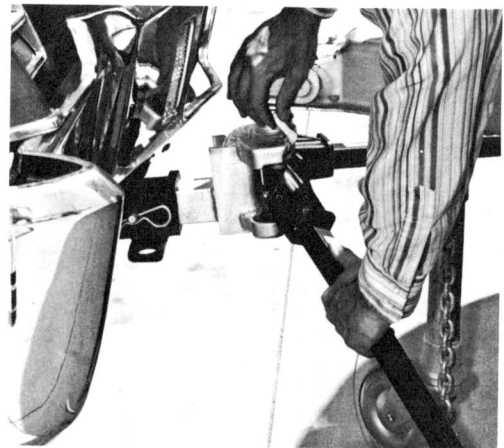

Attach the stabilizer bars to the hitch on the car. (© Airstream Corp.)

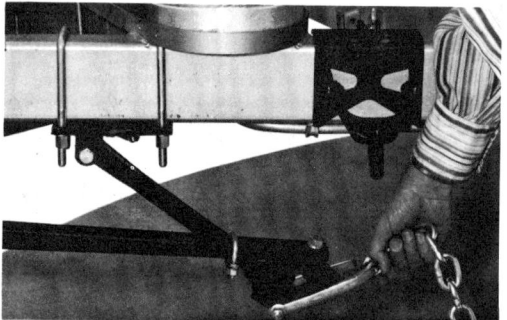

Attach the stabilizer bars to the struts on the tongue of the trailer if so equipped. (© Airstream Corp.)

Attach the stabilizer bars to the tongue of the trailer via the pre-selected link in the chain. (© Airstream Corp.)

the trailer until the hitch jack is just off the ground. Note the height of the hitch ball. The point of all this is to adjust the tension of the load-leveling bars so that the car and the trailer are held up about one inch higher at the hitch ball than before the bars were attached. This will result in the best balance for towing and steering control as the weight-equalizing

GENERAL INFORMATION

hitch transmits the hitch weight of the trailer via the load-leveling bars onto all four wheels of the car. A little practice with your rig will teach you just how far to pull up the bar and you may wish to mark the chain links that match your rig. Always use level ground for checking the correct hook-up.

NOTE: *If your tow vehicle is equipped with load-leveling shocks, you must load typical luggage and passengers and bring it back to level. Attach the trailer and adjust the load-leveling bars or the air shocks on your car will overload the rear wheels.*

Proper adjustment of the equalizer hitch. The hitch ball is slightly higher than it is without the trailer attached. (© Airstream Corp.)

Hitch is too low; need more load on the front wheels; more tension on the load equalizing bars. (© Airstream Corp.)

Hitch is too high; too much load on the front wheels; less tension on the equalizing bars. (© Airstream Corp.)

A low hitch ball increases tailwagging tendencies. If the nose of the trailer is lower than it should be, the center of support for the trailer is changed and reduces the weight on the front wheels of the car.

6. Attach the safety chains and the breakaway switch to the tow vehicle.

7. Turn up the front jack and remove the dolly wheel, if designed to do so.

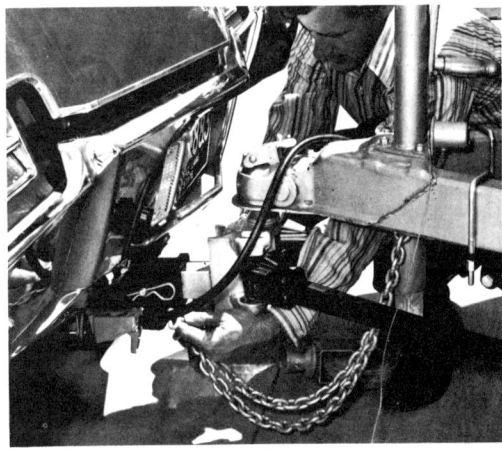

Attach the safety chains. (© Airstream Corp.)

8. Attach the electrical connections from the tow vehicle to the trailer and test the lights to see if all the directional signals, stoplights, and back-up lights work correctly.

Attach the electrical connections. (© Airstream Corp.)

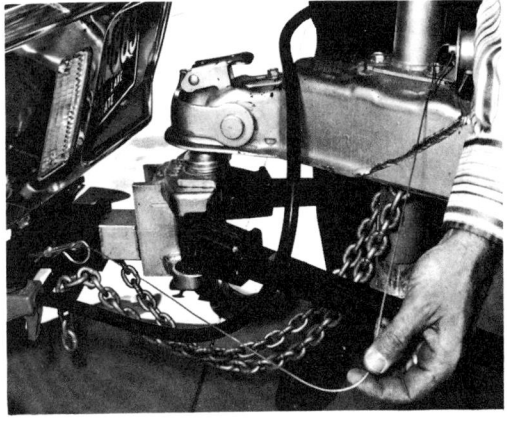

Attach the breakaway switch cable to the tow vehicle. (© Airstream Corp.)

9. Attach the breakaway switch cable to the tow vehicle.

6 GENERAL INFORMATION

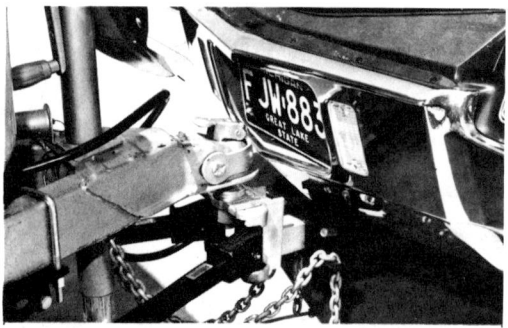

The completed hook-up. (© Airstream Corp.)

When storing, back the trailer onto blocks if jacking is not possible. (© Airstream Corp.)

10. Make a quick test of the trailer brakes to see if they operate correctly and without any drag or noise.

11. Before leaving your trailer site, check the area for lost or forgotten articles. Be sure that you have cleaned your area of trash and have put out all fires.

CHECKLIST FOR THE ROAD

It is impossible to be equipped for every emergency on the road but it is possible to have a reasonable amount of equipment to overcome some of the day-to-day tragedies. The following is a small list of equipment which might be helpful in the event of an emergency.

1. First aid kit
2. Fire extinguisher (dry chemical type)
3. Assortment of common tools (hammers, screwdrivers, assorted wrenches, pliers, electrical tape, etc.)
4. Tow rope (35–50 ft)
5. Jack and correct size lug wrench
6. Spare tire, properly inflated
7. Distress flares and/or reflectors and flags
8. Flashlight
9. Sewer hose with campground connections (if the trailer is equipped with a holding tank)
10. Three-prong electrical extension cord (100 ft) with two prong adaptors
11. Small shovel and axe
12. Bucket
13. Water hose (about 50 ft).

Off-Season Storage and Winterizing

Use the following storage procedures if your camper is not to be used for an extended period.

Raise the trailer so the tires do not touch the ground, and remove the tires and store them in a cool dry place. If this is not possible, jack the trailer wheels individually and place them on wooden blocks so the moisture from the ground will not rot the tires. If jacking the trailer is an inconvenience, all you have to do is back the trailer onto the blocks. The first procedure is the best however, because holding the trailer up by jacks removes all the weight from the suspension, affording the springs and shock absorbers optimum life expectancy.

The main concern in winterizing is to protect your trailer against freezing damage to the hot and cold water systems, including the traps, waste holding tank, the water heater, and the battery. You should use the same precautions that you would use in your home if you were to go away for a long time during the winter. Keep this in mind while following these procedures.

1. Level the trailer from side to side and from front to rear. Open all of the faucets.

2. Turn off the water pump.

3. Open all of the drain valves for the water tank, the hot water heater, and the holding tank. Open any valve that might be located in the middle of a line.

4. While the water is draining from the system, flush the toilet. If you have a hand spray for the toilet, depress the thumb button and hold the nozzle below the rim of the toilet to drain all the water out of the hose. Drain the shower head. If water is allowed to remain in these lines it may freeze and cause damage.

5. Lower the front of the trailer as far as the tongue jack will allow. When water ceases to drain from all of the open valves, crank the tongue jack up as far as it will

GENERAL INFORMATION

go and let the remaining water drain out of the trailer.

6. After the water has stopped flowing from the drains, apply air pressure, if at all possible, to the drain lines with all drain valves and faucets open. This will force any remaining water from the water heater and remove any water which may be laying in low areas.

7. Pour a cup of Glycol type antifreeze into the toilet, sink, and shower drains to prevent water from freezing in the traps.

8. Open the waste holding tank drain and flush the tank thoroughly. Frozen waste in the tank could cause serious damage.

9. Remove the inlet and outlet lines on the water pump and turn the pump by hand until all of the water is removed.

10. Remove the battery from the trailer and store it where it won't freeze, preferably in your house. Do not store the battery on the ground or a concrete basement floor. Instead, place it on wood blocks or a work bench so the battery does not establish a ground and drain itself of all its electrical power. If a battery is allowed to go completely dead, it will not accept a charge and will not return to its original power rating. The battery should be charged at regular intervals throughout the winter months to ensure a full charge in the spring.

11. Remove any food, cosmetics, or other items from the trailer that might be damaged by freezing or might damage the trailer if their containers break.

An aftermarket additive (such as Winterize ®) can be added to the trailer's water system, including the drinking water tank, to prevent freezing. The liquid itself is guaranteed to −60° F and is safe for human consumption as tested by the federal government.

The additive is added to the tank with that amount of water necessary to dilute it to the proper freezing range. This is tested, much the same as car antifreeze, with a suction gauge specially made for the additive. The chart shows the proper mixture of additive to water needed to achieve the proper freezing protection.

Most manufacturers recommend that the tester be used to measure for proper consistency even when the red color of Winterize is present in the water.

Towing and Parking

If you have never towed a trailer before, spend some time in a large empty parking lot with the trailer connected to the car. Practice making turns and backing up.

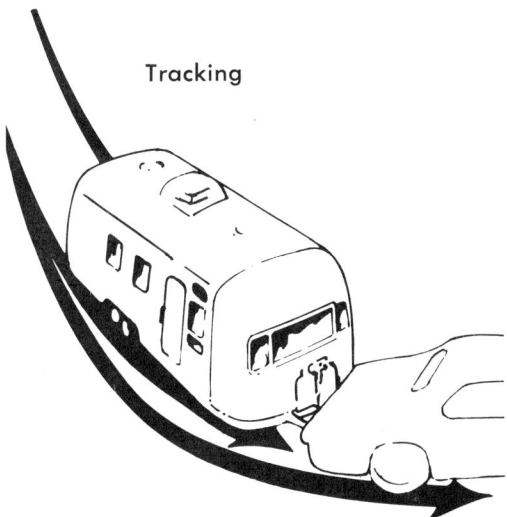

Left turn. Notice the track of the trailer as compared to the tow vehicle's.

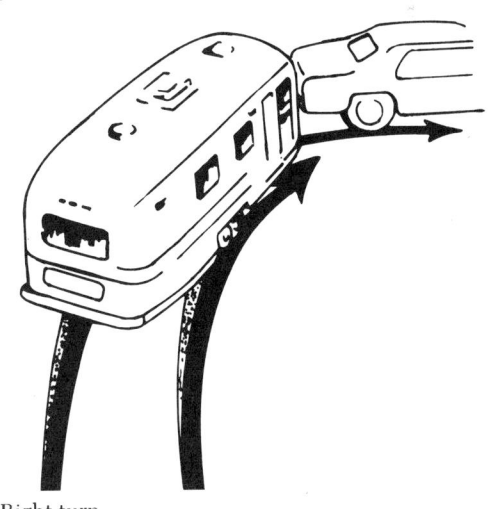

Right turn.

Additive (gal concentrate)	Water (dilution in qt)	Approx Protection (°F)
1	none	−60
1	1	−56
1	2	−50
1	3	−30 to −23
1	4	−20 to −12
1	5	−10 to −4
1	6	−3 to 0
1	7	0 to 4
1	8	5 to 9

GENERAL INFORMATION

Detachable mirror used for extra vision while towing a travel trailer. (© Airstream Corp.)

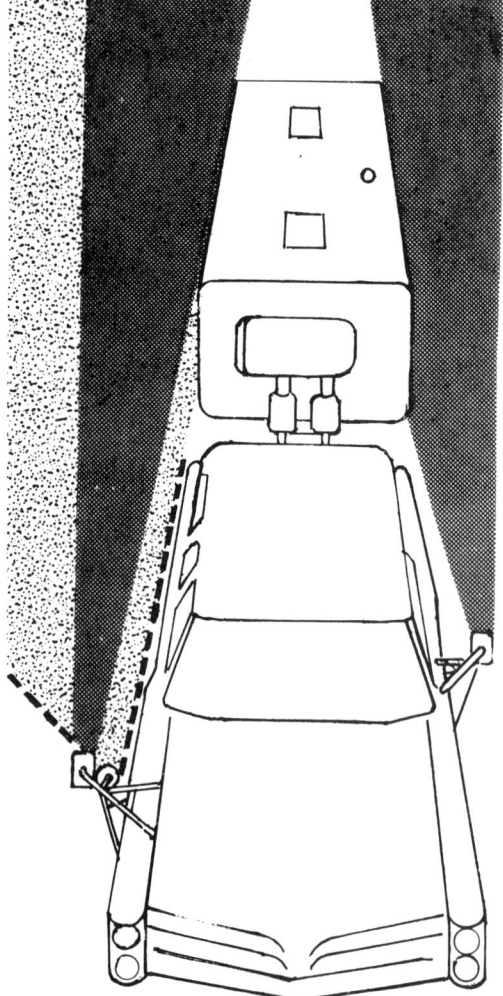

The proper positioning of extra mirrors used for towing trailers and their field of vision. An optional convex mirror is installed on the larger mirror's bracket on the passenger side of the tow vehicle.

Since the trailer wheels do not follow the tow vehicle wheels in the same track, you will have to make allowances in steering when negotiating corners.

Be sure to have your tow vehicle equipped with extra mirrors (fender mounted type) so you can see clearly to the rear of the trailer and far enough to the sides. You should learn how to drive by your mirrors both forward and backward. Use them as often, and even more often, than you use the regular mirrors on your car.

While out on the freeways and highways, try to pick the lane you want to travel in and stay in it. Always maintain a safety margin between you and the car ahead of you. A good rule to remember is at least one length of your rig (car and trailer) for every 10 miles per hour. Also remember that it will take your car longer to accelerate and you will need to allow for the length of the trailer before return-

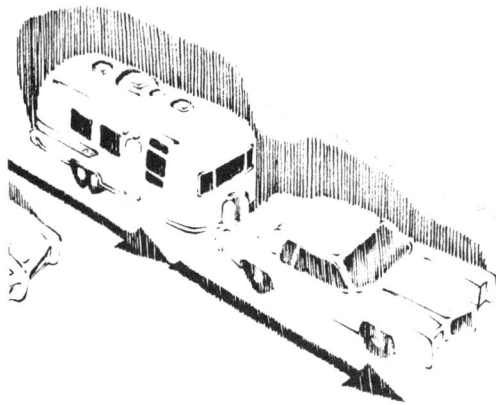

Passing another vehicle, allow a longer distance before returning to the right lane. (© Airstream Corp.)

ing to the right lane. If traffic backs up behind you on a two-lane road, pull over to the shoulder and let the faster-moving traffic pass. This is a common courtesy which should be practiced by all recreational vehicle drivers.

No matter what type of hitch you buy, you cannot eliminate the swaying of the trailer when it is passed by a large truck or bus. The air being displaced by the truck or bus first pushes the back and then the front of the trailer. Do not apply the brakes on either the trailer or the tow vehicle. Steer very slightly and momentarily

GENERAL INFORMATION

When being passed by a large truck or bus, steer slightly toward the passing vehicle to counteract the sway caused by the truck or bus. (© Airstream Corp.)

toward the bus or truck just as the trailer starts to sway.

CAUTION: *In this type of situation, be sure that you do not oversteer, in the direction of the passing vehicle.*

This will compensate for the sway induced by the passing vehicle.

Backing up with your trailer attached to the car may seem quite difficult at first but, as always, practice makes perfect. Practice backing up in that empty parking lot you found, remember to do everything slowly and in small amounts (slow speed and turn the wheel only slightly in any direction). Correct direction immediately if you see that the trailer is heading the wrong way. Turn the wheel only the minimum amount necessary to correct direction. You should concentrate on the rear of the trailer. Turn the bottom of the steering wheel in the direction you want the trailer to go. Watch in the mirror or out the window until the trailer is pointing in the direction you want. Then turn the wheel back in the opposite direction. You will have to turn the wheel faster than when the car and the trailer are in line. When they are in line, straighten the steering wheel. Always try to back into a space from the left side of the two vehicles. This will afford you the maximum visibility. If you don't achieve the desired position on the first try, it will be much easier for you to pull up to your original position and start over again.

SECURING THE TRAILER

Try to pick out as level a parking spot as possible. If you must park on a slope, park facing downhill—it is easier to level the trailer in this position. Place the

Level from side to side first. (© Airstream Corp.)

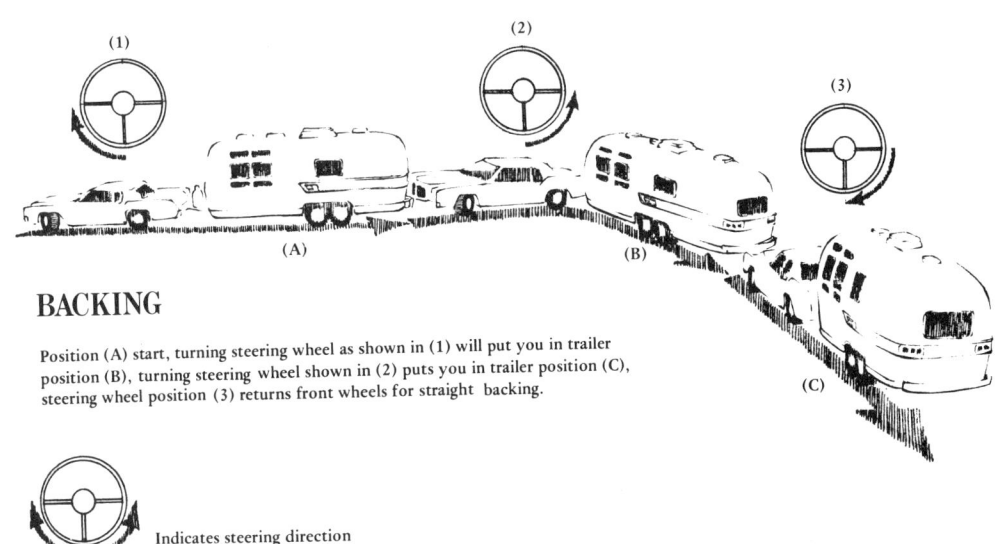

BACKING

Position (A) start, turning steering wheel as shown in (1) will put you in trailer position (B), turning steering wheel shown in (2) puts you in trailer position (C), steering wheel position (3) returns front wheels for straight backing.

Indicates steering direction

Backing up with a travel trailer attached to your car. (© Airstream Corp.)

small fluid level (that you should always carry in the trailer) on the counter top. Correct the tilt from side to side first. This is most easily accomplished by running the wheel up on a ramp made of boards that are tapered at one end. This can also be done through the use of the stabilizing jacks which can be used for minor leveling adjustments. Do not put the full weight of the trailer on the jacks because they are not designed for this purpose; they are just for stabilizing. Don't run your trailer into a hole to make it level because you may not be able to pull it out without help from a tow truck.

Disconnect the car and block the trailer wheels.

Level the trailer from front to back next, through the use of the tongue jack. Once

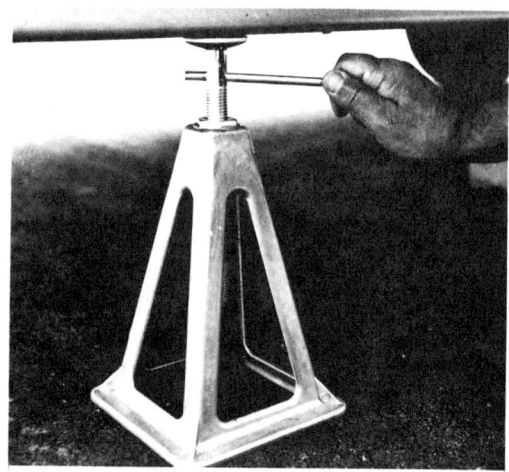

Place the stabilizing jacks in the proper locations. (© Airstream Corp.)

Level from front to rear. (© Airstream Corp.)

the trailer is level from front to back, place the leveling jacks under the prescribed locations. Check your owner's manual for the proper locations.

Hook up your water, electric, and sewage lines. Turn on the gas supply and light all of your pilot lights.

NOTE: *Before hooking up the electric cable, be sure that the electric supply is of the same voltage that your trailer was designed to handle. The line should be properly grounded at both ends.*

Hooking up a sewage drain pipe. (© Airstream Corp.)

GENERAL INFORMATION

State and Provincial Trailer Laws

RULES FOR THE ROAD
FOR TRAVEL TRAILERS AND OTHER RECREATIONAL VEHICLES

Note: Contact State Police for Changes to Laws and Regulations.

State or Province	Speed Limits (mph)① Day	Night	Business	Residential	Max Dim Length⑪	Width	Height	Brakes, if Weight is Over:	Safety Chains	Stop Light	Tail Light	Clearance Light	License Light	Reflectors	Flares	Turn Signals	Other	Riding Permitted in Trailer	Overnight Off-Roadway Parking Allowed⑬
Alabama	60-70	50-60	20	25	55'	8'	13'6"			°	°	°	°	°	°		°	㉒	Yes	②
Alaska	50-70	50-70	25	25	60'	8'	13'6"	3000	°	°	°	°	°	°	°	°			No	Yes
Arizona	65	60	25	25	65'	8'	13'6"	1500	°	°	°	°	°	°					No	Yes
Arkansas	60	60	30	30	60'	8'	13'6"	3000	°	°	°	°	°	°	°	°			No	Yes
California	55	55	25	25	60'	8'	13'6"	1500	°	°	°	°	°	°	°	°			No	Yes⑫
Colorado	60-70	60-70	35	35	65'	8'	13'6"	1500	°	°	°	°		°					No	No
Connecticut	60-70	AP	AP	AP	50'	8'6"	13'6"	3000	°	°	°	°	°	°					No	No
Delaware	AP	AP	AP	AP	65'	8'	13'6"	2000	°	°	°	°	°	°	°	°		㉒	No	Yes
District of Columbia	25	25	25	25	50'	8'	12'6"	3000	°	°	°	°		°					No	No
Florida	AP	AP	AP	AP	55'	8'	13'6"	3000	°	°	°	°	°	°	°				No	Yes⑥
Georgia	60-70	50-65	35	35	55'	8'	13'6"	2500	°	°	°	°	°	°	°	°		㉒	No	Yes
Hawaii	25-65	25-65	25	25	65'	9'	13'6"	1500	°	°	°	°	°	°					Yes	No
Idaho	60	55	AP	AP	60'	8'	14'	3000		°	°		°	°					Yes	Yes
Illinois	55	55	30	30	60'	8'	13'6"	3000	°	°	°	°	°	°	°	°			No	Yes⑫
Indiana	65	65	AP	AP	55'	8'	13'6"	3000	°	°	°	°	°	°	°				Yes	Yes
Iowa	55-75	55-65	20	25	60'	8'	13'6"	⑤		°	°	°	°	°	°	°			Yes	No
Kansas	70	60	20	30	50'	8'	13'6"	⑤	°	°	°	°	°	°	°	°	°	㉒	No	No③
Kentucky	60	50	AP	AP	55'	8'	13'6"	⑤	⑤	°	°		°	°	°				Yes	Yes④
Louisiana	60-70	60-70	AP	AP	60'	8'	13'6"	3000	°	°	°	°	°	°	°	°			No	Yes⑤
Maine	45 AP	45 AP	AP	AP	55'	8'6"	13'6"		°	°	°		°			°			No	No
Maryland	AP	AP	AP	AP	55'	8'	13'6"	1500	°	°	°		°	°					No	No
Massachusetts	50	50	30	30	⑮	8'⑭	13'6"	⑯	°	°	°		°			°			No	Yes⑥
Michigan	50	50	25	25	60'	8'4"	12'6"	1500		°	°	°		°		°			No	No
Minnesota	65	55	30	30	55'	8'	13'6"	1500	°	°	°	°	°	°		°		㉒	Yes	No
Mississippi	65	65	AP	AP	55'	8'	13'6"	2000	°	°	°	°		°					Yes	Yes
Missouri	65-70	60-70	AP	AP	55'	8'	13'6"	No		°	°		°	°					No	Yes
Montana	50	50	AP	AP	60'	8'	13'6"	3000		°	°		°	°	°				Yes	Yes
Nebraska	50	50	20	25	65'	8'	13'6"	All		°	°	°	°	°					No	Yes⑦
Nevada	AP	AP	AP	AP	55'	8'	Any	3000	°	°	°	°	°	°	°				No	No
New Hampshire	45	45	AP	AP	55'	8'	13'6"	3000	°	°	°	⑰	°	⑰	⑰	⑰		㉒	Yes	Yes
New Jersey	50	50	25	25	45'	8'	13'6"	3000	°	°	°	°	°	°					No	Yes⑤
New Mexico	60	50	25	25	65'	8'	13'6"	3000		°	°	°		°		°			No	No
New York	50	50	AP	AP	55'	8'	13'6"	1000		°	°	°	°	°					No	Yes
North Carolina	45	45	20	35	55'	8'	13'6"	1000	°	°	°	°	°	°					No	Yes
North Dakota	60	60	25	25	60'	8'	13'6"	All	°	°	°	°	°	°		°			Yes	No
Ohio	60-70	50	25	35	60'	8'	13'6"	2000	°	°	°	°	°	°					Yes	Yes
Oklahoma	50-70	50	AP	AP	55'	8'	13'6"	3000	°	°	°	°	°	°	°				No	No
Oregon	55	55	20	25	60'	8'	13'6"	⑨	°	°	°	°	°	°					No	Yes
Pennsylvania	55-60	55-60	AP	AP	55'	8'	13'6"	3000	°	°	°	°		°					No	No
Rhode Island	50	45	25	25	55'	8'6"	13'6"	4000		°	°	°	°	°		°			Yes	Yes
South Carolina	55-70	50-65	25	30	60'	8'	13'6"	3000	°	°	°		°	°					Yes	Yes
South Dakota	70	60	30	30	60'	8'	13'6"	3000		°	°		°	°					Yes	No
Tennessee	50-75	50-75	AP	AP	55'	8'	13'6"	1500		°	°	°	°	°	°				Yes	Yes
Texas	⑱	⑱	AP	AP	55'	8'	13'6"	3000	°	°	°	°	°	°	°				Yes	Yes
Utah	AP	AP	25	25	60'	8'	14'	2000		°	°			°				㉓	No	Yes
Vermont	50	50	AP	AP	55'	8'	13'6"	1500	°	°	°		°	°					Yes	No
Virginia	45-55⑲	45-55⑲	AP	AP	55'	8'	13'6"	3000	°	°	°	°	°	°	°	°			No	No
Washington	⑳	⑳	25	25	65'	8'	13'6"	㉑												

State and Provincial Trailer Laws (cont.)

RULES FOR THE ROAD
FOR TRAVEL TRAILERS AND OTHER RECREATIONAL VEHICLES

Note: Contact State Police for Changes to Laws and Regulations.

State or Province	Speed Limits (mph)①				Maximum Dimensions			Required Equipment										Riding Permitted in Trailer	Overnight Off-Roadway Parking Allowed⑬
	Day	Night	Business	Residential	Length⑪	Width	Height	Brakes, if Weight is Over:	Safety Chains	Stop Light	Tail Light	Clearance Light	License Light	Reflectors	Flares	Turn Signals	Other		
Wisconsin	65	55	AP	AP	60'	8'	13'6"	3000	°	°	°	°	°	°	°	°		No	No
West Virginia	55-70	55-70	25	25	55'	8'	12'6"	3000		°	°	°	°	°	°		°		Yes	Yes⑤
Wyoming	65-75	65-75	20	30	65'	8'	13'6"	3000	°	°	°	°	°	°		°	°		Yes	Yes④
Alberta	AP	AP	AP	AP	65'	8'6"	12'6"	2000	°	°	°	°	°	°			°		No	⑩
British Columbia	50	50	AP	AP	60'	8'	12'6"	3000	°	°	°	°	°						No	No
Manitoba	60	60	30	30	65'	8'6"	13'6"	10,000	°	°	°	°							No	Yes
New Brunswick	60	60	30	30	60'	8'6"	13'6"	3000	°	°	°	°					°	㉒	No	Yes
Newfoundland	AP	AP	AP	AP	55'	8'	12'6"	6000		°	°	°	°	°	°					⑩
Northwest Territories	60	60	AP	AP	60'	8'	13'6"	1500	°	°	°	°	°	°	°		°		No	⑩
Nova Scotia	60	60	30	30	65'	8'6"	13'	4000		°	°	°	°	°	°		°		Yes	Yes⑧
Ontario	50	50	30	30	65'	8'6"	13'6"	2999	°	°	°	°	°				°		No	Yes⑫
Prince Edward Island	60	55	30	40	80'	8'6"	14'6"	8000		°	°	°	°				°		Yes	Yes
Quebec	50	45	30	30	60'	8'6"	12'6"	3000	°	°	°	°	°	°	°	°	°	㉒	No	No
Saskatchewan	65	60	AP	AP	65'	8'6"	13'6"	3000		°	°	°		°			°		No	Yes④
Yukon	60 AP	60 AP	AP	AP	70'	8'6"	13'6"	1500	°	°	°	°	°	°	°		°	㉒	No	Yes

Notes:
AP As Posted
① Posted speed limits always take precedence over statutory speed limits
② Not at roadside parks
③ Yes in rest areas with toilets
④ Not at roadside parks and rest areas
⑤ Recommended but not required
⑥ Not on limited access or state highways
⑦ In rural areas, not on state highways
⑧ At rest areas
⑨ Trailers over 45'
⑩ Only in designated areas
⑪ Trailer and towing vehicle without permit
⑫ Except when otherwise posted
⑬ Parking never allowed along limited access expressways or freeways, except when indicated above at rest areas
⑭ Additional 6" is allowed for mirrors
⑮ Maximum length for travel trailer without permit is 33'
⑯ Brakes not required if towing vehicle foot brakes will stop from 20 mph within 30', and hand brake within 80'
⑰ Required on vehicles 80" or more in width
⑱ 60 mph day and 55 mph night if overall length is 32' or less, excluding tow bar or weight less than 4500 lbs; otherwise 45 mph
⑲ Same as passenger cars if trailer weight does not exceed 2500 lbs
⑳ Truck speed limits when towing, generally 10 mph less than passenger cars
㉑ Required if weight of trailer exceeds 3000 lbs or 40 per cent of towing vehicle
㉒ Safety glass
㉓ Fire extinguisher

2 · Tow Vehicle

With the epidemic growth of trailers—especially the less expensive travel trailers—car manufacturers have recently offered an option known as the "Trailer Package." This group of options, which the manufacturers believe to be advantageous, includes such components as a larger engine, oversized alternator and radiator, heavy-duty shock absorbers and springs, heavy-duty transmission and transmission oil cooler, larger radiator fan, and a radiator shroud. Instead of adding all of the aftermarket trailer components to the car, the vehicle can now be ordered with these items as factory equipment.

The total weight-to-horsepower ratio is very important when buying a car that is not fitted with a trailer package. The most practical upper limit for the ratio is approximately 60 pounds per horsepower while the average is 30–40 lbs/hp. This ratio is calculated by adding the trailer and the tow vehicle weight and then dividing this weight by the rated engine horsepower. One must remember that the weight of the provisions must be considered.

Effects of Pulling on the Tow Vehicle

As you can imagine, the increased weight of the trailer being pulled will have effects on the tow vehicle. One can only estimate the exact relationship between driving with the trailer and without it, but certain points are certain; the acceleration time of the car is lengthened along with a reduction in gas mileage. The grade climbing ability and the top speed of the vehicle are also reduced.

It is important to remember that you need more time to accelerate when you wish to pass another car if you are towing a trailer. You must also remember to allow for the increased length of the trailer when returning to the right-hand lane.

Factors Affecting Towing

It is important to keep in mind the approximate vicinity in which the trailer will be used *before* buying a tow vehicle since both climate and temperature greatly affect the performance of the average tow vehicle. For example, a unit which was set to run on the eastern coast of the United States would have to be modified to run correctly in the mountainous areas of the West where the air is thinner. Furthermore, the advantages of oversized radiators and transmission coolers are apparent if the unit is to be used in a warm climate as opposed to a colder climate.

No one is expected to stay at home with

his trailering rig so the best plan is to equip the vehicle with warm-weather as well as cold-weather components and to deal with thin-air problems as they arise. Any qualified service mechanic can make the proper adjustments when the rig is to be driven through mountainous thin-air regions.

Vehicle Safety

SAFE ROUTES AND SPEEDS

The key words are "plan ahead." There are some individuals who like surprises but most of us don't. When planning a camping trip, sit down with up-to-date maps and plan the safest and most convenient route. It is no fun getting lost. Also calculate the distance to be covered each day so that the approximate location of each night's campsite can be found. This will enable you to make reservations ahead of time. It will also save time and trouble searching for campsites after a full day of driving.

When it comes to speed recommendations, the figures are always relative. They are dependent on the size and weight of the trailer and the tow vehicle, and the braking and acceleration ability of the entire unit. Actually common sense comes into play a great deal. Remember that you are towing a trailer, the stability of which decreases as speed increases. This in turn causes increased control problems. The trailers manufactured today advertise cruising speeds equal to most driving needs but there are so many variables (e.g., wind and terrain) that maintaining a reasonable speed is important. Also, the faster you go, the more power is needed just to overcome the greater wind resistance created by the trailer. Thus, the fewer miles per gallon you receive from the tow vehicle. Your most economical cruising speed can be determined only through trial and error.

TRAILER SAFETY CHAINS

The safety chain is a type of link between the trailer frame and the bumper or frame of the car. The reason for these chains is to keep the trailer from separat-

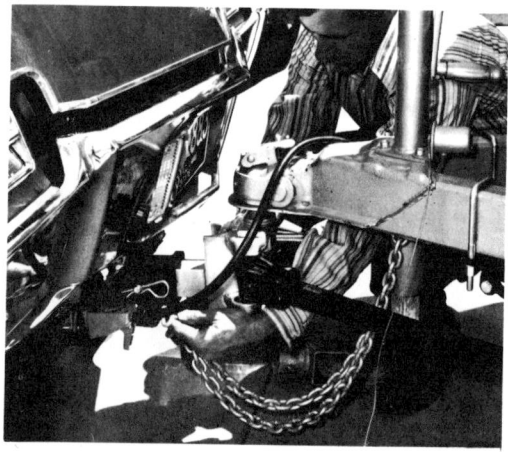

Safety chains.

ing from the car if the hitch or the hitch connection breaks. These chains are required equipment in some states.

The safety chain should be attached to the trailer frame and to the car bumper or frame with a tight connection. Make sure the connection is tight; if the hitch connection breaks, the chain will keep the hitch tongue from striking the ground. The safety chain is a good precaution against a breakaway trailer and the damage that could be caused.

PERIODIC INSPECTION OF THE TOW VEHICLE

It is a good practice to examine the tow vehicle before it is used for towing the trailer any great distance. Follow the paragraphs below in checking the car components.

Make an inspection of the hitch assembly. Check for any stress cracks in the hitch supports or any loose welds or broken bolts. In short, make certain that the hitch is still securely attached to the tow vehicle.

A common—and troublesome—mistake made by trailer owners is the attempt to use the same old hitch on a new, larger trailer. The result can be permanent damage to the car, as well as the trailer, and the possibility of an accident. See that the new trailer and its hitch are compatible (within the same weight classification).

Check the car's shock absorbers by pushing on that part of the body of the vehicle over the shock. Continue pushing until the car is moving briskly in the vertical direction, then stop the pressure. If the vehicle keeps moving up and down, the shock is bad. The car should return to the rest position within one bounce. Also check the shocks to see if any leakage is present. If so, replace them.

The tow vehicle's shock absorbers should be replaced every 10,000 miles, at a maximum. Faulty shocks can greatly increase the twisting motion of the car body causing harder handling and magnifying the possibility of an accident.

Make an inspection of the tow vehicle's tires before any trip. They all should be in good condition and have equal pressure. Using recapped tires or snow tires in the summer is only asking for trouble. Alternating an old tire and a new one on the rear of the car may also cause trouble in stopping and may even cause jackknifing.

These checks, as simple as they might seem, are of great importance. This is, however, not the end of the inspection. Inspect all the mechanical components of the car yourself or have this done by a qualified mechanic. Such things as lubricant in the crankcase and transmission should be checked along with the level of the cooling system and the front-end alignment. Have these things attended to so that a breakdown will not hamper your free time.

Tow Vehicle Components

SPRINGS

Overload springs are added to the stock equipment of the tow vehicle to raise the rear of the vehicle to the normal, level, driving position of the car after the trailer is attached. Overload springs come in a variety of models ranging from the coil type to leaf spring sets which are added to the factory equipment.

With the advent of air-lift shock absorbers and air bag spring inserts, overload springs are rarely used except on older vehicles. They do, however, give the correct position to the car which otherwise, because of the weight, would be sitting with its nose high in the air. This nose-up angle

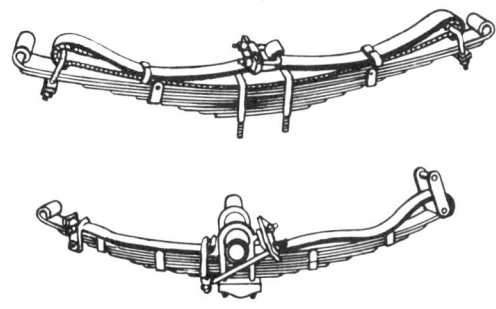

Overload springs.

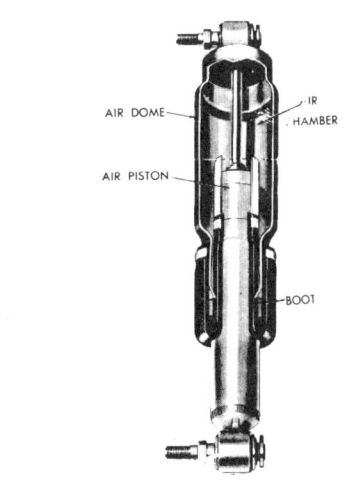

Air shock absorber.

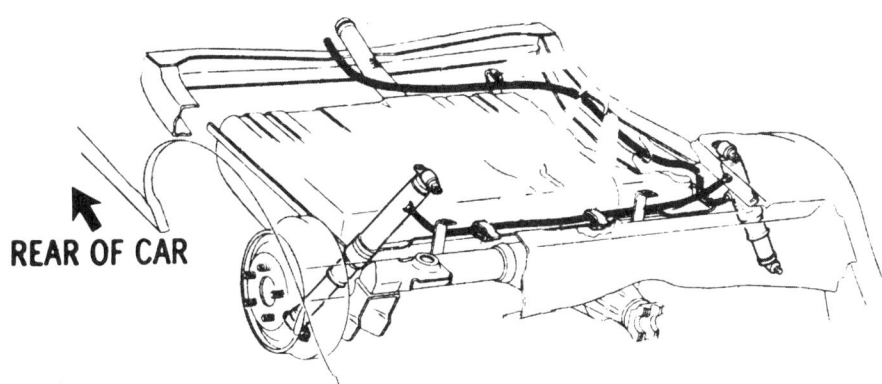

Routing of air lines for air shocks.

16 TOW VEHICLE

Air bag spring inserts.

leads to hazardous driving since all the weight is transferred to the rear axle, leaving none on the front suspension for steering. Such a condition will result in unpredictable handling and extreme tire wear at the rear wheels. Driving at night with the car in a nose-up position is especially dangerous because your headlights are, in effect, improperly aimed. They are pointed too high and will shine into the eyes of oncoming drivers, making it difficult for them to see properly. You also won't be able to see the road surface the way you should.

LIMITED-SLIP DIFFERENTIAL

Since the traction of the tow vehicle plays an important part in the car-trailer package, anything to help traction is an asset. The limited-slip or positive-traction rear axle falls into this category.

The conventional "open" differentials have a tendency to transfer the torque of the engine to the rear wheel with the least resistance. When a vehicle is positioned with its left rear wheel on ice and the right rear wheel on a dry surface, the force of the engine is applied to the left rear wheel causing it to spin freely, never gaining traction. The limited-slip differential has an internal clutching system which transfers the torque from the spinning wheel to the wheel which has the *best* traction, thus enabling the vehicle to move forward.

This type of differential is a definite advantage in foul weather situations such as snow or rain where traction is a problem. One must remember that the traction of the tow vehicle is of utmost importance for safety. Limited-slip or positive-traction rear axles were available for many years as an option on standard cars. Today they are standard equipment on most cars or trucks fitted with a trailer package. To check for this locking type of differential, just jack the rear of the car until both rear wheels clear the ground. Spin either tire in the direction of forward movement and watch the rotation of the other tire. If the other tire turns in the same direction as the one you are turning, the differential is a clutch type differential; if the other tire turns in the reverse direction, the axle is an open type.

TRANSMISSIONS

Manual

The manual, or "stick," transmission was for years the "most reliable" type of transmission for towing. The positive contact of the clutch disc to the flywheel makes a sure engagement. A closer examination of the clutch mechanism for towing has come about in recent years. When you think about the situation and about how the clutch works, you can see its disadvantages.

The idea of a clutch type transmission is positive engagement with a limited amount of slip. However, when towing a reasonably large trailer with a medium-sized engine, the driver must slip the clutch greatly to start the car moving. Once moving, positive engagement is allowable but one can see this problem magnified by a slippery surface. In order to set the vehicle and trailer in motion, the clutch must be slipped drastically; if not, the wheel will turn freely because of the sudden application of torque on the slippery surface.

Automatic

With the advent of the new type Turbo-Hydromatic ® transmission, and other modern three-speed transmissions, old wives' tales about automatics for towing have fallen by the wayside. In fact, the large manufacturers offering the current trailer towing packages recommend the automatic transmission.

Older automatics lived up to the fears of trailer towers mainly because the car itself was not "set up" for towing. Either the differential was of the incorrect ratio or the car wasn't driven correctly. To function correctly, the vehicle must be geared for towing. This point will be discussed in the "Rear Axle Ratio" section.

The advantage of the automatic transmission, as opposed to the manual, is that the torque may be applied gradually without any slipping. The slip of the torque converter accomplishes this action. This is not the same type of slip as in a clutch set-up because there is no wear to any component. This gradual starting procedure allows the transfer of torque to the rear wheels slowly and, consequently, lessens the chance of the wheels breaking free of the road surface.

AUTOMATIC TRANSMISSION OIL COOLING

Transmission oil coolers are usually offered in the new trailer towing packages since the extra load of a trailer forces the transmission to work harder than under normal conditions. The extra load causes the transmission to create more heat due to increased friction. This extra heat is transferred to the transmission oil and, if the oil is allowed to become too hot, it will change its chemical composition or become burnt. When this occurs, valve bodies become clogged and the transmission doesn't operate as efficiently as it should. Serious damage to the transmission can result. Thus the need for the extra transmission oil cooling capacity.

You can tell if the transmission fluid is burnt by inspecting it for a burnt smell and discoloration. Burnt transmission fluid

Transmission oil cooling kit.

dipstick out and place the end on a tissue or paper towel. Particles of sludge can be seen more easily this way. If any of the above conditions do exist, the transmission fluid should be completely drained, the filtering screens cleaned, the transmission inspected for possible damage, and new fluid installed.

The solution to these problems, as mentioned previously, is the installation of a transmission oil cooler. If your tow vehicle is not equipped with an oil cooler and it becomes evident that you need one, you can purchase one at any well-supplied auto parts store or trailer service center. Do not install the oil cooling radiator in front of the water cooling radiator since it will restrict the flow of air through the

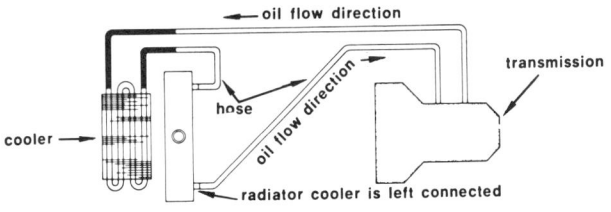

Diagram of a transmission oil cooler.

is dark brown or black as opposed to its normal bright clear red color. If the transmission fluid is burnt it will also have a distinct burnt odor. Since transmission fluid "cooks" in stages, it may develop forms of sludge or varnish. It is also possible for a leak to develop inside the radiator oil cooler and contaminate the transmission fluid. Pull the transmission

water cooling radiator. Install it off to the side. An additional benefit of installing a transmission oil cooler is that the engine block will also run cooler since some of the cooling load is removed from the water cooling radiator.

Proper driving techniques can also help keep the transmission oil cool while towing a trailer. Never lug the engine in high gear at low speeds (e.g., climbing a hill). Instead, downshift into the next lower gear. This reduces the heat produced in the transmission by increasing the mechanical efficiency of the torque convertor. Also the engine cooling capacity is increased due to higher fan and water pump speed.

REAR AXLE RATIO VARIATIONS

The rear axle ratio, as pointed out above, is very important to a vehicle which is used to tow a trailer. The average car, as it comes equipped from the factory, has a rear axle ratio suited to normal load conditions. Such vehicles are equipped with differential ratios in the high twos, such as a 2.73 ratio.

The axle ratio is the relationship between the number of turns the driveshaft makes as compared to the number of turns of the drive axles. For example, if the car is equipped with a 2.73 differential, the driveshaft will turn 2.73 times for each time the drive axles turn once. It would be then said that this car has a 2.73 differential. The drive axle ratio, combined with the size of the engine, determines the pulling power of the car.

There is no set differential ratio recommended for all trailers. A 3.63 ratio can be used with a six-cylinder engine effectively while a 3.23 can be used with a V8 with the same amount of success. The trailer packages offered by the vehicle manufacturers recommend specific axle ratios for each engine. These can be checked at your local dealer.

A small class in axle ratios is in order at this point. The axle ratio is based on the direct relationship between the turning of the driveshaft and the turning of the drive axles. The higher the numerical ratio of the differential, the lower the gearing of the axle. For example, a differential with a ratio of 4.11 will cause the engine to turn faster to maintain a 50 mph speed than will an axle with a ratio of 3.23.

The object in choosing a rear axle ratio is to properly combine the torque curve of the engine with the appropriate ratio—keeping in mind the type of pulling which is to be done and formulating the correct ratio. As you can see this is a complicated task. Thankfully, the large car and truck manufacturers calculate the ratios and publish them in the trailer towing packages available for new vehicles.

Concentrate on the correct ratio for towing; the harmful side effects are many at both extremes. If the ratio is too low (numerically), it will require a greater slipping of the clutch mechanism to get the unit moving initially, thus causing wear to the clutch mechanism. On the other hand, if the ratio is too high (numerically), the top speed of the rig is greatly lowered. The tendency with a very high differential ratio is to run the engine above the acceptable rpm range which will cause great damage to the engine. The importance of the correct ratio is evident.

WHEELS AND TIRES

There are so many variables and possibilities in today's tire market that outfitting a rig can become quite confusing.

Wheels and tires.

Selecting tires for your tow vehicle is perhaps the more confusing. Consider exactly what type of driving you will be doing and over what kind of terrain. Will you be traveling at high speeds for long periods of time? Will you be traveling off the road very much? Will there be snow or mud where you will be going? Will your tires be subjected to extremely high road temperatures? There are many factors to be taken into consideration. First, let's discuss the different types of tires.

There is a growing trend away from the conventional bias tires and toward the bias-belted and radial ply tires.

The conventional bias tires are constructed so that the cords run from one wire bead to the other at an angle. Alternate plies run at an opposite angle. This type of construction gives rigidity to both the sidewall and the tread surface.

The construction of the radial tire differs from that of a conventional bias tire in that the cords run from bead to bead at an approximate angle of 90 degrees. This type of construction gives the tread a great

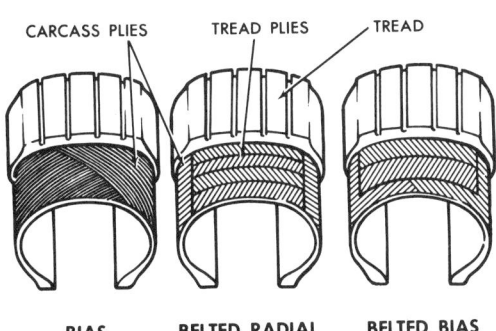

The three types of tires. (© Chevrolet Div. G.M. Corp.)

amount of rigidity and the side walls a great amount of flexibility. The belts restrict the amount of "squirm" when the tread comes in contact with the pavement, thus improving the tread life.

The bias-belted tire is constructed in much the same manner as the conventional bias tire. There are belts running at an angle and also at a 90° angle to the bead as in the radial ply tire. This type of construction gives rigidity to the tread and the sidewalls of the tire. Tread life is improved over the conventional bias tire but the objectional feeling of instability sometimes found in the flexible sidewalls of the radial is eliminated.

It is true that there is greater safety and longer tread life with tires of a higher load rating. But to achieve this, one must sacrifice the soft ride that original equipment tires provide.

WARNING: *Heavy-duty suspensions are a must for the application of radial ply tires. Coupled with a standard, "mushy" suspension, radial tires will "cup" and wear unevenly. Never mix radial ply tires with any other type of tire on the same axle. If you decide to put wide, flotation type tires on your tow vehicle, remember that they must not be installed on narrow rims. Extra-wide rims or wheels must be used.*

Tread design should be taken into consideration when selecting the tires for your tow vehicle. Decide what kind of driving you will be doing most often. Will you be driving off the road frequently? Will you be doing a lot of high-speed driving for long periods of time? A combination of both maybe or strictly one or the other? For strictly off-the-road traveling, you will want a heavy-duty tread design that will

A tread design for strictly off-road use.

A tread design for highway use.

A tread design for both off-road on-road use.

give you lots of traction and protect the tire against severe road conditions. For strictly highway use, you want a tread that will run quietly, give good mileage, and stay cool while running at high speeds. There are tires available that are designed for both off-road and on-road use. They have a traction type tread design that stays relatively cool and runs quietly. Radials are not recommended for strictly off-the-road use because the stiff tread will cause the sidewall to bulge out when the tire travels over an obstacle such as a rock. The sidewalls will bulge so much that they become susceptible to cuts or punctures.

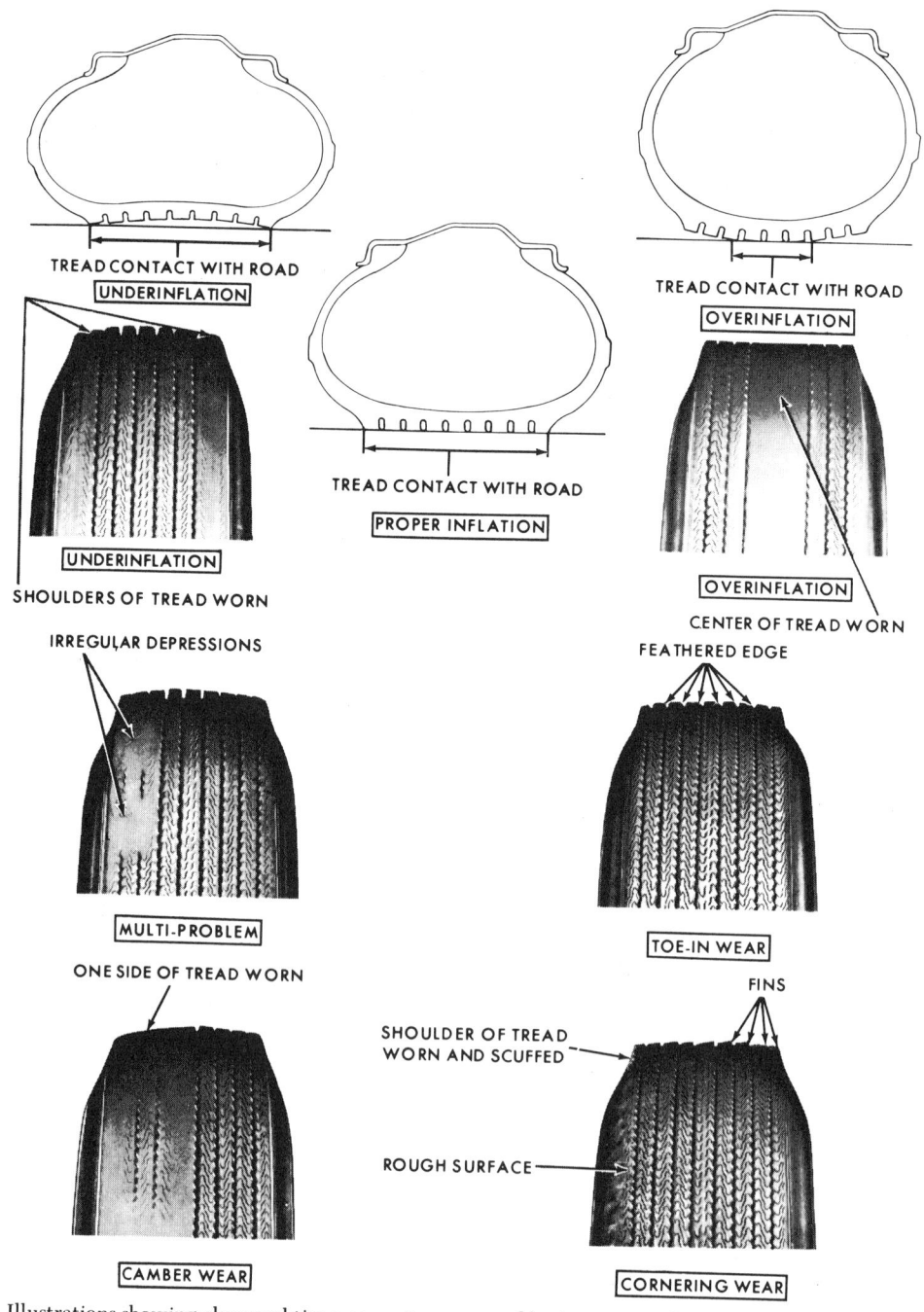

Illustrations showing abnormal tire wear patterns caused by improper inflation, misalignment, improper balance, or suspension neglect. (© Chevrolet Div. G.M. Corp.)

Passenger Car and Stationwagon Tire Load Limits

Load Range B (4-ply rating)
Load Range C (6-ply rating)
Load Range D (8-ply rating)

TIRE SIZE OR DESIGNATION								Cold Inflation Pressures—Pounds Per Square Inch											
Bias 1965 On	Pre 1965	78 Series (Bias)	70 Series (Bias/Belted)	60 Series	Radial 78 Series	Radial 70 Series	Metric	20	22	24	26	28	30	32	34	36	38	40
6.00-13							165 R 13	770	820	860	900	930	970	1010	1040	1080	1110	1140
		A78-13	A70-13		AR 78-13	AR 70-13		810	860	900	940	980	1020	1060	1090	1130	1160	1200
6.50-13		B78-13	B70-13		BR 78-13	BR 70-13	175 R 13	890	930	980	1030	1070	1110	1150	1190	1230	1270	1300
		C78-13	C70-13		CR 78-13	CR 70-13		950	1000	1050	1100	1140	1190	1230	1270	1320	1360	1390
7.00-13							185 R 13	980	1030	1080	1130	1180	1230	1270	1310	1360	1400	1440
			D70-13		DR 78-13	DR 70-13		1010	1070	1120	1170	1220	1270	1320	1360	1410	1450	1490
			E70-13		ER 78-13	ER 70-13	195 R 13	1060 1070	1110 1130	1170 1190	1220 1240	1280 1300	1320 1350	1370 1400	1440	1490	1540	1580
			A70-14			AR 70-14	155 R 14	780 810	820 860	860 900	900 940	940 980	970 1020	1010 1060	1090	1130	1160	1200
6.45-14	6.00-14	B78-14	B70-14		BR 78-14	BR 70-14	165 R 14	860 840 890	910 900 930	960 930 980	1000 980 1030	1040 1020 1070	1080 1060 1110	1120 1100 1150	1160 1130 1190	1200 1170 1230	1240 1210 1270	1270 1240 1300
6.95-14	6.50-14	C78-14	C70-14		CR 78-14	CR 70-14	175 R 14	950 950 930	1000 1000 990	1050 1050 1030	1100 1100 1080	1140 1140 1130	1190 1190 1170	1230 1230 1210	1270 1270 1250	1310 1320 1300	1350 1360 1330	1390 1400 1370
		D78-14	D70-14		DR 78-14	DR 70-14		1010	1070	1120	1170	1220	1270	1320	1360	1410	1450	1490

Passenger Car and Stationwagon Tire Load Limits (cont.)

Load Range B (4-ply rating)
Load Range C (6-ply rating)
Load Range D (8-ply rating)

TIRE SIZE OR DESIGNATION							Cold Inflation Pressures—Pounds Per Square Inch									
Bias		Bias and Belted Bias		Radial												
1965 On	Pre 1965	78 Series	70 Series 60 Series	Metric	78 Series	70 Series	20	22	24	26	28	30	32	34	36	38	40
7.35-14	7.00-14	E78-14	E70-14	185 R 14	ER 78-14	ER 70-14	1040 1030 1070	1100 1100 1130	1160 1140 1190	1210 1190 1240	1260 1240 1300	1310 1290 1350	1360 1340 1400	1400 1380 1440	1450 1430 1490	1490 1470 1540	1540 1520 1580
7.75-14	7.50-14	F78-14	F70-14	195 R 14	FR 78-14	FR 70-14	1150 1150 1160	1210 1230 1220	1270 1280 1280	1330 1340 1340	1390 1390 1400	1440 1450 1450	1500 1500 1500	1550 1550 1550	1600 1600 1610	1650 1650 1650	1690 1700 1700
8.25-14	8.00-14	G78-14	G70-14	205 R 14	GR 78-14	GR 70-14	1250 1240 1250	1310 1320 1310	1380 1380 1380	1440 1440 1440	1500 1500 1500	1560 1560 1560	1620 1620 1620	1670 1670 1680	1730 1730 1730	1780 1780 1780	1830 1830 1830
8.55-14	8.50-14	H78-14	H70-14	215 R 14	HR 78-14	HR 70-14	1360 1330 1360	1430 1420 1440	1510 1480 1510	1580 1550 1580	1640 1610 1650	1710 1670 1710	1770 1740 1770	1830 1790 1830	1890 1850 1890	1950 1910 1950	2000 1960 2010
8.85-14	9.00-14	J78-14	J70-14	225 R 14	JR 78-14	JR 70-14	1430 1430	1510 1500	1580 1580	1660 1650	1730 1720	1790 1790	1860 1860	1920 1920	1990 1980	2050 2040	2100 2100
			K70-14			KR 70-14	1460	1540	1620	1690	1770	1830	1900	1970	2030	2090	2150
	9.50-14		L70-14			LR 70-14	1540 1520	1640 1600	1700 1680	1780 1750	1850 1830	1930 1900	2000 1970	2060 2040	2130 2100	2200 2170	2260 2230
	6.00-15			165 R 15	BR 78-15		870 890 890	910 930 940	960 980 980	1000 1030 1030	1050 1070 1070	1090 1110 1110	1130 1150 1150	1190	1230	1270	1300
6.85-15	6.50-15	C78-15	C70-15	175 R 15	CR 78-15	CR 70-15	950 950 980	1000 1000 1040	1050 1050 1080	1100 1100 1130	1140 1140 1180	1190 1190 1230	1230 1230 1270	1270 1270 1320	1320 1320 1360	1360 1360 1400	1390 1400 1440

Size	Alpha-Numeric	Radial	Metric	1010	1070	1120	1170	1220	1270	1320	1360	1410	1450	1490
7.35-15	D78-15	DR 78-15		1070	1130	1180	1240	1290	1340	1390	1440	1480	1530	1570
	D70-15	DR 70-15	185 R 15	1070	1130	1190	1240	1300	1350	1400	1440	1490	1540	1580
7.75-15	E78-15	ER 78-15		1150	1210	1270	1330	1380	1440	1490	1540	1590	1640	1690
	E70-15	ER 70-15		1110	1190	1230	1290	1340	1400	1450	1500	1550	1590	1640
	E60-15		195 R 15	1160	1220	1280	1340	1400	1450	1500	1550	1610	1650	1700
6.70-15	F78-15	FR 78-15		1240	1300	1370	1430	1490	1550	1610	1660	1720	1770	1820
	F70-15	FR 70-15		1190	1270	1320	1380	1440	1500	1550	1600	1660	1710	1760
	F60-15		205 R 15	1250	1310	1380	1440	1500	1560	1620	1680	1730	1780	1830
7.10-15	G78-15	GR 78-15		1250	1310	1380	1440	1500	1560	1620	1670	1730	1780	1830
	G70-15	GR 70-15		1340	1410	1480	1550	1620	1680	1740	1800	1860	1920	1970
	G60-15		215 R 15	1310	1400	1450	1520	1580	1640	1710	1760	1820	1880	1930
8.25-15	H78-15	HR 78-15		1360	1440	1510	1580	1650	1710	1770	1830	1890	1950	2010
7.60-15	H70-15	HR 70-15		1360	1430	1510	1580	1640	1710	1770	1830	1890	1950	2000
8.55-15	J78-15	JR 78-15	225 R 15	1430	1510	1580	1650	1720	1790	1860	1920	1980	2040	2100
8.85-15	J70-15	JR 70-15		1380	1470	1530	1600	1670	1730	1800	1860	1920	1980	2040
8.00-15				1430	1500	1580	1650	1720	1790	1860	1920	1980	2040	2100
9.00-15		KR 70-15		1460	1540	1620	1690	1760	1830	1900	1970	2030	2090	2150
8.20-15	K70-15			1470	1570	1630	1710	1780	1850	1920	1980	2050	2110	2170
			235 R 15	1460	1540	1620	1690	1770	1830	1900	1970	2030	2090	2150
9.15-15	L78-15	LR 78-15		1510	1600	1680	1750	1830	1900	1970	2030	2100	2160	2230
	L70-15	LR 70-15		1520	1600	1680	1750	1830	1900	1970	2040	2100	2170	2230
	M78-15			1610	1700	1780	1860	1940	2020	2090	2160	2230	2300	2370
8.90-15	N78-15			1700	1790	1880	1970	2050	2130	2210	2280	2360	2430	2500
				1700	1810	1880	1970	2050	2130	2210	2290	2360	2430	2500
6.00-16				1075	1135	1195	1250	1300	1350	1400	1450	1500		

Passenger Car and Stationwagon Tire Load Limits (cont.)

Load Range B (4-ply rating)
Load Range C (6-ply rating)
Load Range D (8-ply rating)

TIRE SIZE OR DESIGNATION							Cold Inflation Pressures—Pounds Per Square Inch									
Bias Pre 1965	Bias 1965 On	Bias and Belted Bias 78 Series	Bias and Belted Bias 70 Series	60 Series	Metric	Radial 78 Series	70 Series	20	22	24	26	28	30	32	34	36	38	40
6.50-16								1215	1280	1345	1405	1465	1525	1580	1635	1690		
7.00-15								1310	1380	1450	1515	1580	1640	1700	1760	1820		
7.00-16								1365	1440	1515	1585	1650	1715	1780	1840	1900		

NOTES:
1. Ply Rating While there is no industry-wide definition of ply rating, passenger car tires marked "4-ply rating/2-ply" have the same load carrying capacity as a current or most recent 4-ply tire of the same size at the same inflation. Passenger car tires marked "8-ply rating/4-ply" have the same load carrying capacity as 8-ply rating tires of the same size at the same inflation, regardless of the actual number of plies.

2. Load Range The "load range" system is now being used in tire marketing with letters (e.g., Load Range B, C, D, etc.) to identify tires with their particular load and inflation limits and service requirements. While the ply rating system is being gradually phased out, both designations may be used on tire sidewalls and are shown in the tables above. During their interim period Load Range B tires may be marked 4-ply rating/2-ply or 4-ply; Load Range C tires, 6-ply rating/4-ply or 6-ply and Load Range D tires, 8-ply rating/4-ply, 8-ply rating/6-ply or 8-ply.

Conventional Truck Tire Load Ratings

Load Limits (lbs per tire) at Various Cold Inflation Pressures

Size	Load Range	Ply Rating	20	25	30	35	40	45	50	55	60	65	70	75	80	85	90	95	100
4.10-6	B	4	185	210	235	260	280	300	320	335	350	370							
4.80-8	A	2	305	345	385														
4.80-8	B	4	305	345	385	425	455	490	520	550	580	610							
4.80-8	C	6	305	345	385	425	455	490	520	550	580	610	635	660	685	710	735		
4.80-9	A	2	330	375	415														
4.80-9	B	4	330	375	415	455	495	530	560	595	625	655							
4.80-12	B	4	405	465	515	565	610	655	695	735	775	810							
4.80-12	C	6	405	465	515	565	610	655	695	735	775	810	845	880	915	950	980		
5.30-6	A	2	310	355	395	430	465	500	530	560									
5.30-6	B	4	310	355	395	430	465	500	530	560									
5.30-12	B	4	485	550	615	670	725	780	825	875									
5.70-8	B	4	420	480	535	585	630	675	720										
5.70-8	C	6	420	480	535	585	630	675	720	760	800	835	875	910					
5.70-8	D	8	420	480	535	585	630	675	720	760	800	835	875	910	945	980	1015	1045	
6.50-10	C	6	685	775	865	945	1020	1100	1170	1230	1300								
6.50-10	E	10	685	775	865	945	1020	1100	1170	1230	1300	1360	1420	1480	1540	1590	1650	1700	1759
6.90-9	B	4	580	655	730	800													
6.90-9	C	6	580	655	730	800	865	925	985	1045	1095								
6.90-9	E	10	580	655	730	800	865	925	985	1045	1095	1150	1200	1250	1300	1345	1400	1435	1480
6.90-12	B	4	690	785	875	955	1035												
6.90-12	C	6	690	785	875	955	1035	1105	1175	1245	1310								
7.00-10	D	8	765	870	970	1060	1140	1230	1300	1380	1450	1520	1590						
7.00-10	E	10	765	870	970	1060	1140	1230	1300	1390	1450	1520	1590	1650	1720	1780			
7.50-10	E	10	825	935	1040	1140	1230	1320	1400	1490	1560	1640	1710	1780					
9.00-10	E	10	1110	1260	1400	1530	1650	1770	1890	2000	2100	2200							

Conventional Truck Tire Load Ratings (cont.)

Load Limits (lbs per tire) at Various Cold Inflation Pressures

Size	Load Range	Ply Rating	20	25	30	35	40	45	50	55	60	65	70	75	80	85	90	95	100
6.50-13 ST	B	4	705	800	895	980													
6.50-13 ST	C	6	705	800	895	980	1060	1130	1200	1275									
7.75-14 ST	B	4	895	1020	1140	1240													
7.75-14 ST	C	6	895	1020	1140	1240	1340	1440	1530										
7.75-15 ST	B	4	895	1020	1140	1240													
7.75-15 ST	C	6	895	1020	1140	1240	1340	1440	1530										
16.5 x 6.5-8	A	2	415	475	525	570	615												
16.5 x 6.5-8	B	4	415	475	525	570	615	655	695	735	770								
16.5 x 6.5-8	C	6	415	475	525	570	615	655	695	735	770								
20.5 x 8.0-10	B	4	655	745	820	895	965	1030	1090										
20.5 x 8.0-10	C	6	655	745	820	895	965	1030	1090	1150	1210	1270	1320						
20.5 x 8.0-10	D	8	655	745	820	895	965	1030	1090	1150	1210	1270	1320	1370	1420	1470			
20.5 x 8.0-10	E	10	655	745	820	895													
18.5 x 8.5-8	B	4	560	630	700	760	820	875	930										
18.5 x 8.5-8	C	6	560	630	700	760	820	875	930										
23.5 x 8.5-12	B	4	805	910	1010	1100	1180	1260	1340										
23.5 x 8.5-12	C	6	805	910	1010	1100	1180	1260	1340										

High Flotation Truck Tire Load Ratings

Size	Load Range	Ply Rating	30	35	40	45	50	55	60	65	70	75	80	85	90
						Maximum Tire Loads (pounds) at Various Cold Inflation Pressures (psi)									
8.00-16.5	B	4	1360												
8.00-16.5	C	6	1360	1490	1610	1730									
8.00-16.5	D	8	1360	1490	1610	1730	1840	1945	2045						
8.00-16.5	E	10	1360	1490	1610	1730	1840	1945	2045	2145	2240	2330			
8.00-16.5	F	12	1360	1490	1610	1730	1840	1945	2045	2145	2240	2330	2420	2500	2590
8.75-16.5	B	4	1570												
8.75-16.5	C	6	1570	1720	1850	1990									
8.75-16.5	D	8	1570	1720	1850	1990	2110	2240	2350						
8.75-16.5	E	10	1570	1720	1850	1990	2110	2240	2350	2470	2570	2680			
9.50-16.5	B	4	1860												
9.50-16.5	C	6	1860	2030	2190	2350									
9.50-16.5	D	8	1860	2030	2190	2350	2500	2650	2780						
9.50-16.5	E	10	1860	2030	2190	2350	2500	2650	2780	2920	3050	3170			
10-16.5	B	4	1840												
10-16.5	C	6	1840	2010	2170	2330									
10-16.5	D	8	1840	2010	2170	2330	2480	2620	2750						
10-17.5	C	6	1910	2095	2265	2425									
10-17.5	D	8	1910	2095	2265	2425	2580	2730	2870						
10-17.5	E	10	1910	2095	2265	2425	2580	2730	2870	3010	3140	3270			
10-17.5	F	12	1910	2095	2265	2425	2580	2730	2870	3010	3140	3270	3395	3520	3640
12-16.5	D	8	2370	2590	2800	3000									
12-16.5	E	10	2370	2590	2800	3000	3190	3370	3550						
14-17.5	C	6	3210												
14-17.5	D	8	3210	3500	3790	4060									
14-17.5	E	10	3210	3500	3790	4060	4320	4570	4800						
14-17.5	F	12	3210	3500	3790	4060	4320	4570	4800	5030	5260	5470			
14-17.5	G	14	3210	3500	3790	4060	4320	4570	4800	5030	5260	5470	5680	5890	6090
10-15	B	4	1760												
10-15	C	6	1760	1930	2080	2230									
10-15	D	8	1760	1930	2080	2230	2370	2510	2640						
10-16	B	4	1840												
10-16	C	6	1840	2010	2170	2330									
10-16	D	8	1840	2010	2170	2330	2480	2620	2750						
11-14	B	4	1820												
11-14	C	6	1820	1990	2150	2300									
11-14	D	8	1820	1990	2150	2300	2450	2590	2730						
11-15	B	4	1900												
11-15	C	6	1900	2080	2250	2410									
11-15	D	8	1900	2080	2250	2410	2560	2710	2850						
11-16	B	4	1980												
11-16	C	6	1980	2160	2330	2500									
11-16	D	8	1980	2160	2330	2500	2650	2810	2950						

NOTE: For the tire sizes not listed, consult your tire supplier, or write Rubber Manufacturer's Assoc. for load and inflation information.

Trailer Tire Load Ratings

Size	Load Range	Ply Rating	30	35	40	45	50	55	60	65	70	75	80	85	90	95	100
								Load Limits (lbs per tire) at Various Cold Inflation Pressures									
6.00-16 LT	C	6	1130	1230	1330	1430											
6.50-16 LT	C	6	1270	1390	1500	1610											
6.70-15 LT	C	6	1210	1320	1430	1530											
7.00-13 LT	C	6	1000	1090	1170	1260	1340										
7.00-13 LT	D	8	1000	1090	1170	1260	1340	1420	1490								
7.00-14 LT	C	6	1030	1130	1220	1310											
7.00-14 LT	D	8	1030	1130	1220	1310	1390	1470	1550								
7.00-14 LT	E	10	1030	1130	1220	1310	1390	1470	1550	1620	1700	1770					
7.00-15 LT	C	6	1350	1480	1610	1720											
7.00-15 LT	D	8	1350	1480	1610	1720	1830	1940	2040								
7.00-16 LT	C	6	1430	1560	1680	1800											
7.00-16 LT	D	8	1430	1560	1680	1880	1910	2030	2130								
7.10-15 LT	C	6	1320	1440	1560	1670											
7.50-15 LT	D	8	1560	1710	1840	1980	2100	2220	2330								
7.50-15 LT	E	10	1560	1710	1840	1980	2100	2220	2330	2450	2560	2660					
7.50-16 LT	C	6	1620	1770	1930	2060											
7.50-16 LT	D	8	1620	1770	1930	2060	2190	2310	2440								
7.50-16 LT	E	10	1620	1770	1930	2060	2190	2310	2440	2560	2670	2780					
8.25-16 LT	D	8	1980	2160	2330	2500	2660	2820	2960								
8.25-16 LT	E	10	1980	2160	2330	2500	2660	2820	2960								
9.00-16 LT	D	8	2250	2460	2660	2850	3030	3210	3370								
9.00-16 LT	E	10	2250	2460	2660	2850	3030	3210	3370								
7-14.5	D	8	1140	1240	1350	1440	1530	1620	1710	1790							
7-14.5	E	10	1140	1240	1350	1440	1530	1620	1710	1790	1870	1940	2020	2090	2160	2230	2300
7-14.5	F	12	1140	1240	1350	1440	1530	1620	1710	1790	1870	1940	2020	2090	2160	2230	2300
8-14.5	E	10	1380	1510	1630	1750	1860	1970	2070	2170	2270	2360	2450	2540	2620	2710	2790
8-14.5	F	12	1380	1510	1630	1750	1860	1970	2070	2170	2270	2360	2450	2540	2620	2710	2790

Tire Pressure

Even pressure in the tow vehicle's tires plays an important part in the stability of the car-trailer unit. Low or uneven tire pressure can result in hard handling, erratic braking, and possible swerving which may result in an accident. Overinflated tires have the tendency to wear in the center and suffer a reduction in overall traction. Do not trust a gas station tire pressure gauge. Surveys have shown such gauges to be as much as 10 psi incorrect. Carry your own tire pressure gauge so each tire can be set at the correct amount.

Wheels

The tire rim forms the direct union between the car and the tire. It absorbs the direct stress which the tire encounters and transfers it to the steering mechanism. Rims are usually maintenance-free and require little or no service. If a high-speed blowout or any other accident where rim damage is possible occurs, the rims should be checked and replaced if found defective.

It is advisable to have your tires mounted on wheels by a qualified mechanic. Damage to the wheel and the tire might otherwise result.

If it is necessary to install larger tires onto the tow vehicle, do not attempt to install these tires on the narrow rims. Oversized or wider rims should be used for these tires.

AIR SHOCK ABSORBERS

Air shocks are a relatively new addition to the camping field. These are conventional shock absorbers with internal power pistons which expand and contract when air pressure is applied to them. They were first used in racing autos, the suspensions of which had to be raised or lowered to compensate for varying track conditions.

These can be a welcome solution to the rear-end sag problem of tow vehicles. Since the travel trailer has a relatively low hitch height, the installation of the air shock assembly, with no other suspension changes, can regain the normal riding height of the car.

Installation is relatively simple; merely replace the conventional shock absorbers using the same mounting brackets. The only addition is the placement of the air line (which is used to fill the shocks). This line is usually mounted in the trunk of the auto. When the hitch is in place, the shocks can be filled to the proper level so that the car is horizontal; when the trailer is removed they can be deflated to give the car a smoother, more even ride.

Check with your trailer dealer when purchasing the shocks regarding the correct models for your trailering needs and the correct procedures for installing and using the air shock package.

DEALER TRAILER PACKAGES

Since more and more towing is being done with the conventional automobile, the auto manufacturers have offered cars directly from the factory with the heavy-duty equipment necessary for trailer towing. In the past these components had to be added once the conventional auto was purchased.

Mechanical engineers have investigated and calculated which drive train components are necessary to produce a car capable of towing the different classes of trailers with no particular problem. Such components as heavy-duty battery, transmission, cooling system, electrical system, suspension, and engine are already included.

When a new vehicle is to be purchased to tow a trailer, consult the dealer and he will have you look at a special brochure which will present an orderly arrangement of the packages available with each model of car. The charts in this book will provide most of the same information.

4 WHEEL DRIVE

Four-wheel-drive (4wd) vehicles have recently gained popularity in the recreation field. The idea started with those who bought surplus Jeeps and found a new area of fun in off-road driving. Manufacturers gradually entered the 4wd market; today there is a wide variety of four-wheel-drive models on the market.

A 4wd vehicle is basically the conventional two-wheel rear-drive model which has been combined with a front-drive axle. The front axle has a power drive to pull the vehicle while the rear axle pushes it. One can easily see the tremendous increase in traction with the addition of a front-drive axle. Driving a 4wd vehicle in the early days was hazardous and anything but comfortable since the front axle was always engaged and the front suspen-

TOW VEHICLE

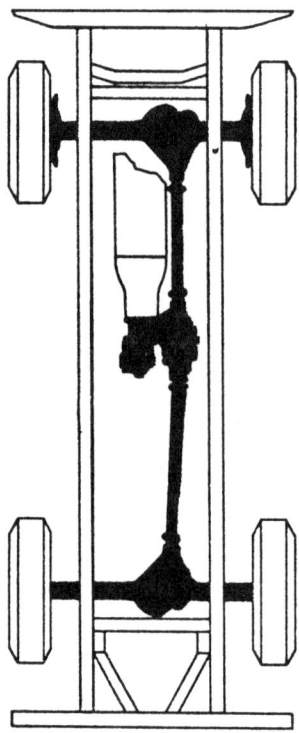

A four-wheel-drive chassis.

sion was rigid and hard. Today, however, this is all changed. The front differential can be disengaged while the vehicle is on a paved highway and then engaged when off-road traction is necessary. The suspension has also been modified so that comfort will not suffer to any great extent.

Just looking at the added traction of *two* drive axles, and knowing that traction is the key word when pulling a trailer, shows a 4wd unit to be an excellent tow vehicle. This is not to say, "run out and buy" on the merits shown here. It should be considered however, if you plan to do a great deal of off-road camping. Your local dealer can tell you which vehicles are equipped with the 4wd option and will give you the information regarding the different components.

TOW HITCHES

Before beginning to classify tow hitches into groups, let's break down the hitch into two basic components: the tow bar and the coupler. The tow bar is the unit which is fastened to the car whether it be to the frame or bumper. The coupler is the portion containing the hitch ball which connects to the tongue of the trailer.

There are basically three types of hitches: the frame-mounted; the axle-mounted; and the equalizing type hitch. These will be discussed further under their own headings.

It is important for any tow hitch to be strong but this becomes doubly important when a heavy trailer is to be towed. A custom hitch is rarely necessary with light travel trailers but, as the tongue weight of the trailer increases, the need for such a hitch also increases.

All well-mounted hitches should be fastened at three points on the tow vehicle body. This three-point attachment achieves both stability and strength which is necessary in towing. When buying or installing any type of tow hitch, consult a qualified hitch dealer if you are a novice. This is an important piece of equipment, with an expensive car in front of it and an expensive trailer behind it, so consult a reputable dealer for his advice with regard to the hitch.

Frame and Axle Tow Hitches

Frame hitches are the least expensive to buy. They are usually straight or slightly offset beams which are attached to the frame and the rear bumper of the tow ve-

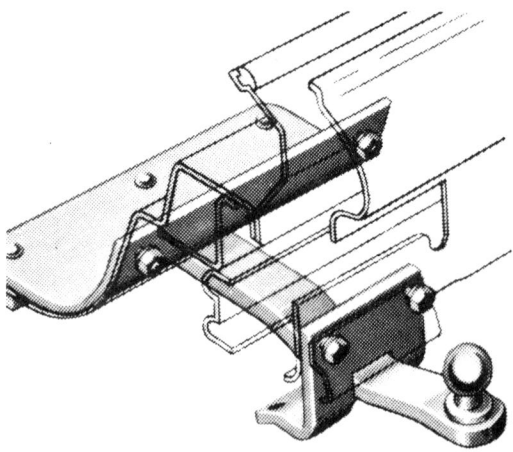

A typical non-equalizing hitch.

hicle. The trailer hitch ball is on the other end of the support beam and engages the coupler of the trailer. This type of hitch is not generally used with any type of trailer above 2000 lbs gross vehicle weight and a tongue weight over 200 lbs.

The axle hitch is fastened on either side of the axle housing with two support rods which intersect at the rear bumper and are

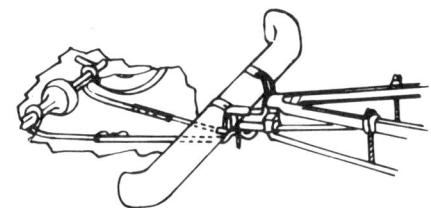

An axle hitch with equalizing bars.

fastened there. The axle support hitch centers the pulling power of the car on the stable rear axle housing.

This type of hitch is not recommended for towing modern heavier trailers such as travel trailers. Even though the hitch is fastened to the tow vehicle's bumper or frame at the very rear of the car, there is a certain amount of forward-backward flexing and strain put on the axle housing where the other end of the hitch is fastened. A certain amount of forward-backward flexing movement is present with all types of trailer hitches, even if they are properly installed. With types other than the axle hitch, the flexing occurs at points where the least amount of harm is done, such as the frame and the bumper. With the axle hitch, however, the flexing is present on the rear axle housing of the tow vehicle. This can cause bent or cracked axle housings, bent or broken U-bolts that attach the axles to the leaf springs, and (on cars with rear coil springs) damage to the upper and lower control arms.

Trailer Equalizing Hitches

The object of a trailer equalizing hitch is to keep the tow car in a reasonably level condition despite the added weight at the rear. The physics behind the equalizing hitch distributes the hitch weight of the trailer between the front and rear wheels of the car and the trailer's wheels.

It is easy to see in the following example. Placing a weight of 200 lbs in the trunk of a conventional auto results in the downward slope of the vehicle toward the rear. Suppose we weld two five-foot pieces of metal beam a foot equidistant from the center of the rear bumper. A man applying pressure in the upward direction can raise the car to its original height.

Now we take the 200 lbs of weight out of the car trunk and place a travel trailer with a hitch weight of 200 lbs onto the trailer hitch. The rear of the car will once again slope to the rear but, again, a man can restore the car to level by exerting the same upward pressure on the two beams.

Suppose we fasten the beam supports to the trailer tongue with chains while the man is exerting pressure. With this done, the manual pressure can be released and neither the car nor the trailer will move downward. What has happened? The weight has distributed itself: one-third has been placed on the front wheels of the car; one-third has been placed on the rear wheels. The remaining third has been positioned on the trailer wheels. This is how a weight distribution hitch works.

The solid beams extending from the tow vehicle are usually made of spring steel to flex when severe vertical pressure is applied—as might happen if the tow vehicle happens to hit a deep hole. When the equalizing hitch is properly hooked up, both the trailer and the car are level.

Installation of a Trailer Hitch

Installing a trailer hitch is no job for a novice, if the trailer to be towed is a fairly large one (class II, III). Class I hitches can be installed by almost anyone with common hand tools. Hitch installation should be done by an experienced, competent trailer service center with mechanics who are trained for this operation. This is also no place for penny pinching. The difference in cost between a corner-cutting installation and one done correctly should not be more than a few dollars. This is not to say that you shouldn't shop around to get the best price on a hitch installation, however. You must simply put the emphasis on the quality of the work and not on the price.

There are a lot of companies that design and make prefab trailer hitches to fit each make of car. These can be trusted to be strong enough if the hitch is installed correctly and you do not tow anything heavier than is recommended by the hitch manufacturer.

If by chance you have to have a hitch custom made to fit your car properly, inspect the material that the hitch is to be made of. Check to be sure that the steel is made of a sufficiently heavy gauge, strong enough to carry the load of your trailer. Remember to look for quality and not price. Check around among your trailering

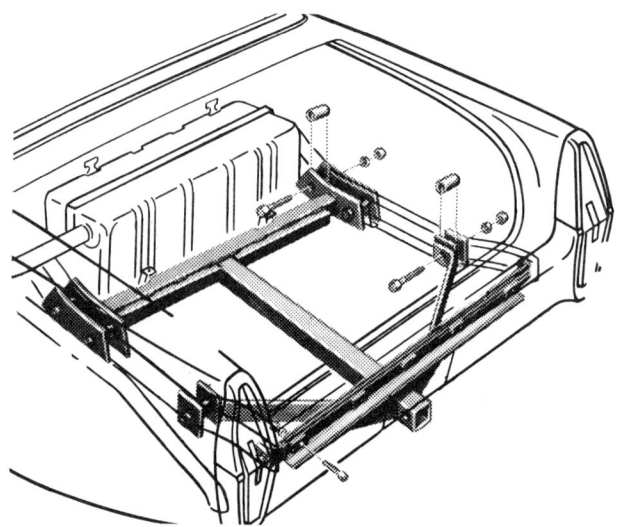

Installation of an equalizing hitch.

friends to find shops that install trailer hitches and have a reputation for good work. Maybe you would like to visit a few of the shops you had in mind and look them over. A certain amount of equipment is essential to installing and fabricating hitches. Metal-bending and cutting tools, welders, hoists, power-impact wrenches, and jackstands to hold parts into place for cutting and fitting should be readily visible. Check over some of the installer's work. You don't have to be an expert to be able to see poor workmanship which indicates indifference, as opposed to pride of a job well done. Examine the welds carefully to see if the beads are of even width; they should look like a line of evenly spaced crescent shapes. Pockmarks, large lumps of burnt material, or otherwise interrupted beads are a sign of poor welding.

The tow vehicle might require reinforcement of the frame before the hitch is installed. This is particularly true of cars with the unit body frame construction. An experienced hitch installer should be able to tell if the frame on your car needed extra reinforcement. (See figure 43.)

There seems to be a bit of discrepancy about how a trailer hitch should be attached to a tow vehicle. Some say to bolt it on and others say to weld it. All that can be done here is to give the drawbacks and advantages of both.

The advantages of having the hitch welded on are:

1. Gives a better bond to the frame of the tow vehicle.
2. Spreads the load over a wider area.
3. Will not work loose as bolts might do.

Disadvantages:

1. Welded job is only as good as the person who does the welding.
2. Welds can break without warning.
3. Heat created by welding could warp or distort the frame of the tow vehicle and could even change the properties of the metal, making it softer or more brittle.

The advantages of having the hitch bolted on are:

1. Squeaks and rattles will let you know if the bolts do work loose.
2. Bolted-on hitches are easier to remove for switching over to another vehicle or to just store for the winter.
3. Easier to install.

Disadvantages:

1. The bolts can work loose.
2. Some car manufacturers recommend that holes not be drilled in the frame of the car.
3. Should a bolt fall out, it cannot be replaced with an average bolt; they must be made of a harder grade of steel.
4. The stress is placed on one small area, right where the bolt is placed through the frame.

When installing a trailer hitch, check to make sure that the height of the hitch ball is the same as the height of the coupler on your trailer when it is level. Also allow at least ¼ in. gap between the gas tank and the floor of the car, and all bars and brackets of the installed hitch. The reason for this is that friction from vibration could wear a hole.

Hitch Maintenance

Most people think that installation is all the attention a hitch requires. Not so. To give long years of dependable service, the hitch should be properly maintained. Here are a few pointers on hitch maintenance:

1. Keep the hitch ball tight. Never install a hitch ball without the correct lockwasher and shank nut.

2. Keep all of the nuts and bolts tight that attach the hitch to the car.

3. Lubricate the ball occasionally. Use a light lubricant; a heavy grease will attract and hold harmful abrasives that could do more damage than the grease could help.

4. Check all levers, pins, and working joints for signs of wear. Lubricate them with a light lubricant. Replace them if they show signs of extreme wear and the possibility of breakage.

5. Spray the hitch and tongue of the trailer with a rust-inhibiting paint from time to time. This should help retard corrosion and extend useful hitch life.

6. Examine the safety chains regularly. Sometimes chains drag on the ground and wear to a point of possible failure if the trailer ever becomes disconnected from the tow vehicle. Replace the chains if they are worn to a point that you think is unsafe.

BRAKES

The tow vehicle serves as the major portion of the braking system of the car-trailer unit. With the new, optional trailer package equipment, manufacturers have kept this fact in mind. Either heavy-duty shoe brakes or disc brakes are offered.

Although heavy-duty shoe brakes offer maximum stopping power, disc brakes are worth the extra money. Their resistance to fade and the excess buildup of heat which causes brake failure is an asset which cannot be overlooked.

If the vehicle is not equipped with a towing package, the stock, factory equipment brake linings can be replaced with center metallic bonded linings. These are harder than the factory linings and will increase the braking power of the car

Disc brake.

greatly—especially when the brakes are warm.

FLEXIBLE AUTO FANS

A frequent hazard of towing a trailer is the tendency for the cooling system to overload and overheat. This generally happens with cars which are not equipped with trailer towing packages. To alleviate this problem, either a larger fan or fan shrouding, or a combination of both, are in order. Today, however, a few companies (the best known being Flex-a-lite®) are producing light-weight fiberglass fans for recreational vehicles. The idea was first initiated in racing cars where maximum cooling was needed at low engine speed with a limited amount of component weight.

A flex fan.

The fan is composed of a fiberglass-reinforced material which is relatively pliable. This construction provides a unit which is light (approximately one-fourth of the weight of the stock unit) and produces twice the cooling capacity at low engine speed.

The fan works in the following manner: At the idle speed or low engine rpm, the blades of the fan extend at a severe angle, cutting the air at a greater degree and causing a greater amount of air to be sucked through the radiator. As the engine speed increases, the centrifugal force of the fan, which is turning at greater speed, causes the blades to bend, thus decreasing the angle of the blades and also decreasing the amount of air being moved. This lowering of the fan's function is desirable because, as the forward speed of the tow vehicle is increased, more air is channeled through the radiator without the help of the fan. Another advantage of the flex type fan is that at higher engine rpm, there is a limited amount of fan noise which is a characteristic of the large-bladed, stock fans.

CLUTCHING FANS

Newer models, equipped with either trailer packages or air conditioning, are fitted with clutch type fans for engine cooling. This sort of unit has a heat-sensing mechanism built into the center shaft of the fan itself. If the engine is relatively cold, the mechanism will allow the fan to "free-wheel" until the sensor's heat mechanism reacts to the engine approaching running temperature. At this temperature the clutch engages inside the fan and the fan turns again at a one-to-one ratio with the fan shaft.

A clutch fan.

Trailer Towing Recommendations

Note: Up to 2000 LBS—Class I (Light)
2000–3500 LBS—Class II (Medium)
3500–5000 LBS—Class III (Heavy)

N.A.—Not Available
———Not Applicable
Std.—Standard
H.D.—Heavy Duty

UNDER NO CIRCUMSTANCES SHOULD A FRAME TYPE HITCH BE INSTALLED ON A 1973 COLLAPSIBLE BUMPER.

1972 Trailer Towing Information
Matador & Ambassador

Equipment	Class I	Class II	Class III
Trailer Type	Any	Any	Any
Tongue Load Limit (lbs)	250	350	500
Engine Requirement	360 cu in., 2 bbl.	360 cu in., 2 bbl.	360 cu in., 2 bbl.
Exhaust System	Std.	Std.	Std.
Engine Cooling	Std.	H.D.	H.D.
Transmission Requirement	"Torque-Command" Automatic	"Torque-Command" Automatic	"Torque-Command" Automatic
Trans. Aux. Oil Cooler	———	Required	Required
Axle Ratio Recommended	Std.	Highest-Numerical Ratio for particular Engine/Transmission combination	Highest-Numerical Ratio for particular Engine/Transmission combination
Differential Type	Std.	"Twin-Grip"	"Twin-Grip"
Wheels Recommended	Std.	Std.	Std.
Tires	Next size option for particular Model/Engine combination		
Brakes Recommended	Power	Power	Power
Front	Drum or Disc	Drum or Disc	Drum or Disc
Rear	Drum	Drum	Drum
Springs	H.D.②	H.D.②	H.D.②
Shock Absorbers	H.D.②	Air shocks②	Air Shocks②
Sway Bar	———	———	———
Steering Recommended	Power	Power	Power
Battery Recommended	Std.	70 Amp	70 Amp

1972 Trailer Towing Information (cont.)
Matador & Ambassador

Equipment	Class I	Class II	Class III
Alternator	Std.	Std.	Std.
Turn Signal Flasher	Std.	Std.	Std.
Type Hitch Required①	Body Mounted or Equalizer	Equalizer	Equalizer

① Not available as factory options.
② H.D.—Heavy Duty American Motors

1972 Trailer Towing Information
Gremlin & Hornet

Equipment	Class I	Class II	Class III
Trailer Type	Low Silhouette①	—	—
Tongue Load Limit (lbs)	Up to 150	—	—
Engine Requirement	Any	—	—
Exhaust System	Std.	—	—
Engine Cooling	Std.	—	—
Transmission Requirement	Any	—	—
Trans. Aux. Oil Cooler	—	—	—
Axle Ratio Recommended	Std.②	—	—
Differential Type	Std.	—	—
Wheels Recommended	Std.	—	—
Tires	Std.	—	—
Brakes Recommended	Std.	—	—
Front	—	—	—
Rear	—	—	—
Springs	Std.	—	—
Shock Absorbers	Std.	—	—
Sway Bar	—	—	—

1972 Trailer Towing Information (cont.)
Gremlin & Hornet

Equipment	Class I	Class II	Class III
Steering Recommended	Std.	——	——
Battery Recommended	Std.	——	——
Alternator	Std.	——	——
Turn Signal Flasher	Std.	——	——
Type Hitch Required ③	Body Mounted or Equalizer	——	——

① Low Silhouette—defined as level with car top height.
② Recommended minimum of 2.73:1 ratio with 232 cu in. engine.
③ Not available as factory options.

1968–'69 Trailer Towing Information
American Motors

Equipment	Class I	Class II	Class III
Trailer Type	Any	Any	Any
Tongue Load Limit (lbs)	250	350	500
Engine Requirement	232 cu in. Six	290 cu in. V-8	343 cu in. V-8
Exhaust System	Std.	Std.	Std.
Engine Cooling	H.D.	H.D.	H.D.
Transmission Requirement		Shift Command Automatic	
Trans. Aux. Oil Cooler	Required	Required	Required
Axle Ratio Recommended	3.15:1 ①	3.15:1	3.15:1
Differential Type	Twin-Grip	Twin-Grip	Twin-Grip
Wheels Recommended	Std.	Std.	Std.
Tires	Std.	Std.	Std. size 8 Ply rated Extra size 4 Ply rated
Brakes Recommended	Power	Power	Power
Front	——	——	——
Rear	——	——	——

1968–'69 Trailer Towing Information (cont.)

American Motors

Equipment	Class I	Class II	Class III
Springs	H.D.②	H.D.②	H.D.②
Shock Absorbers	H.D.②	H.D.②	H.D.②
Sway Bar	—	—	—
Steering Recommended	Power	Power	Power
Battery Recommended	Std.	Std.	Std.
Alternator	Std.	Std.	Std.
Turn Signal Flasher	Std.	Std.	Std.
Type Hitch Required	Body Mounted	Equalizer	Equalizer

① 3.31:1 ratio with six cylinder
② American Motors Handling Package

1971 Trailer Towing Information

Matador & Ambassador

Equipment	Class I	Class II	Class III
Trailer Type	Any	Any	Any
Tongue Load Limit (lbs)	250	350	500
Engine Requirement	232 cu in. Six	304 cu in. V-8	360 cu in. V-8
Exhaust System	Std.	Std.	Std.
Engine Cooling	H.D.	H.D.	H.D.
Transmission Requirement	Shift Command Automatic		
Trans. Aux. Oil Cooler	Required	Std.	Std.
Axle Ratio Recommended	Highest numerical ratio for particular Engine/Transmission combination		
Differential Type	Twin-Grip	Twin-Grip	Twin-Grip
Wheels Recommended	Std.	Std.	Std.
Tires	Largest size option for particular Model/Engine combination		

1971 Trailer Towing Information (cont.)

Matador & Ambassador

Equipment	Class I	Class II	Class III
Brakes Recommended	Power	Power	Power
Front	Drums or Disc	Drums or Disc	Drums or Disc
Rear	Drums	Drums	Drums
Springs	H.D.①	H.D.①	H.D.①
Shock Absorbers	H.D.①	H.D.①	Air shocks
Sway Bar	—	—	—
Steering Recommended	Power	Power	Power
Battery Recommended	H.D.	H.D.	H.D.
Alternator	H.D.	H.D.	H.D.
Turn Signal Flasher	H.D.	H.D.	H.D.
Type Hitch Required	Body Mounted	Equalizer	Equalizer

① American Motors Handling Package

1971 Trailer Towing Information

Gremlin & Hornet

Equipment	Class I	Class II	Class III
Trailer Type	Up to 1000 lbs	—	—
Tongue Load Limit (lbs)	Up to 150	—	—
Engine Requirement	Any	—	—
Exhaust System	Std.	—	—
Engine Cooling	Std.	—	—
Transmission Requirement	Any	—	—
Trans. Aux. Oil Cooler Std. V-8s Opt 6s	Required	—	—
Axle Ratio Recommended	Std.	—	—
Differential Type	Std.	—	—
Wheels Recommended	Std.	—	—

1971 Trailer Towing Information (cont.)
Gremlin & Hornet

Equipment	Class I	Class II	Class III
Tires	Std.	——	——
Brakes Recommended	Std.	——	——
Front	Std.	——	——
Rear	Std.	——	——
Springs	Std.	——	——
Shock Absorbers	Std.	——	——
Sway Bar	Std.	——	——
Steering Recommended	Std.	——	——
Battery Recommended	Std.	——	——
Alternator	Std.	——	——
Turn Signal Flasher	Std.	——	——
Type Hitch Required	Body Mounted	——	——

1970 Trailer Towing Information
American Motors

Equipment	Class I	Class II	Class III
Trailer Type	Any	Any	Any
Tongue Load Limit (lbs)	250	350	500
Engine Requirement	232 cu in. Six	304 cu in. V-8	360 cu in. V-8
Exhaust System	Std.	Std.	Std.
Engine Cooling	H.D.	H.D.	H.D.
Transmission Requirement	Shift Command Automatic Transmission		
Trans. Aux. Oil Cooler Std V-8s Opt 6s	Required	Std.	Std.
Axle Ratio Recommended	Highest-Numerical Ratio for Particular Engine/Transmission combination		
Differential Type	Twin-Grip	Twin-Grip	Twin-Grip

TOW VEHICLE

1970 Trailer Towing Information (cont.)

American Motors

Equipment	Class I	Class II	Class III
Wheels Recommended	Std.	Std.	Std.
Tires		Largest size option for particular Model/Engine combination	
Brakes Recommended	Power	Power	Power
Front	Disc or drums	Disc or drums	Disc or drums
Rear	Drums	Drums	Drums
Springs	H.D.①	H.D.①	H.D.①
Shock Absorbers	H.D.①	H.D.①	H.D.①
Sway Bar	—	—	—
Steering Recommended	Power	Power	Power
Battery Recommended	H.D.②	H.D.②	H.D.②
Alternator	H.D.②	H.D.②	H.D.②
Turn Signal Flasher	H.D.②	H.D.②	H.D.②
Type Hitch Required	Body Mounted	Equalizer	Equalizer

① H.D.—Heavy duty; American Motor Handling Package.
② H.D.—Heavy duty; Electrical system.

1972 Trailer Towing Information

Jeep Truck 6000 and 7000 GVW Models

Equipment	Class I	Class II	Class III
Trailer Type	Any	Any	Any
Tongue Load Limit (lbs)	300	500	750
Engine Requirement	6000 GVW 304 cu in. V-8	360 cu in. V-8	360 cu in. V-8
	7000 GVW 360 cu in. V-8	360 cu in. V-8	360 cu in. V-8
Exhaust System	Std.	Std.	Std.
Engine Cooling	H.D.	H.D.	H.D.
Transmission Requirement	Automatic	Automatic	Automatic

1972 Trailer Towing Information (cont.)

Jeep Truck 6000 and 7000 GVW Models

Equipment	Class I	Class II	Class III
Trans. Aux. Oil Cooler	N.A.	N.A.	N.A.
Axle Ratio Recommended	Std.	Std.	Std.
Differential Type	Std.	Std.	Std.
Wheels Recommended	Std.	Std.	Std.
Tires	Std.	Std.	Std.
Brakes Recommended	Power	Power	Power
Front	Std.	Std.	Std.
Rear	Std.	Std.	Std.
Springs	H.D.	H.D.	H.D.
Shock Absorbers	H.D.	H.D.	H.D.
Sway Bar	N.A.	N.A.	N.A.
Steering Recommended	Power	Power	Power
Battery Recommended	Std.	Std.	H.D.
Alternator	Std.	Std.	H.D.
Turn Signal Flasher	Std.	Std.	H.D.
Type Hitch Required	Frame	Equalizer	Equalizer

Note: Prior to 1972 Jeep did not publish any trailer towing information.

1972 Trailer Towing Information

Jeep—8000 GVW Camper Special

Equipment	Class I	Class II	Class III
Trailer Type	Any	Any	Any
Tongue Load Limit (lbs)	300	500	750
Engine Requirement	304 cu in. V-8	360 cu in. V-8 Std.	360 cu in. V-8 Std.
Exhaust System	Std.	Std.	Std.
Engine Cooling	H.D. Std.	H.D. Std.	H.D. Std.

1972 Trailer Towing Information (cont.)

Jeep—8000 GVW Camper Special

Equipment	Class I	Class II	Class III
Transmission Requirement	Std.	Automatic	Automatic
Trans. Aux. Oil Cooler	N.A.	N.A.	N.A.
Axle Ratio Recommended	Std.	Std.	Std.
Differential Type	Std.	Std.	Std.
Wheels Recommended	Std.	Std.	Std.
Tires	7.50 x 16-E Range 10 Ply (Std.)		
Brakes Recommended	Power	Power	Power
Front	Std.	Std.	Std.
Rear	Std.	Std.	Std.
Springs	H.D. Std.	H.D. Std.	H.D. Std.
Shock Absorbers	H.D. Std.	H.D. Std.	H.D. Std.
Sway Bar	N.A.	N.A.	N.A.
Steering Recommended	Power	Power	Power
Battery Recommended	H.D.	H.D.	H.D.
Alternator	H.D.	H.D.	H.D.
Turn Signal Flasher	H.D.	H.D.	H.D.
Type Hitch Required	Frame	Equalizer	Equalizer

Note: Prior to 1972 Jeep did not publish any towing information.

1972 Trailer Towing Information

Jeep Wagoneer

Equipment	Class I	Class II	Class III
Trailer Type	Any	Any	Any
Tongue Load Limit (lbs)	300	500	750
Engine Requirement	304 cu in. V-8	360 cu in. V-8	360 cu in. V-8
Exhaust System	Std.	Std.	Std.

1972 Trailer Towing Information (cont.)
Jeep Wagoneer

Equipment	Class I	Class II	Class III
Engine Cooling	H.D.	H.D.	H.D.
Transmission Requirement	Automatic	Automatic	Automatic
Trans. Aux. Oil Cooler	N.A.	N.A.	N.A.
Axle Ratio Recommended	Highest-Numerical Ratio for particular Engine/Transmission Combination		
Differential Type	Std.	Std.	Std.
Wheels Recommended	Std.	Std.	Std.
Tires	Oversize	Oversize	Oversize
Brakes Recommended	Power	Power	Power
Front	Std.	Std.	Std.
Rear	Std.	Std.	Std.
Springs	H.D.	H.D.	H.D.
Shock Absorbers	H.D.	H.D.	H.D.
Sway Bar	—	—	—
Steering Recommended	Power	Power	Power
Battery Recommended	Std.	Std.	H.D.
Alternator	Std.	Std.	H.D.
Turn Signal Flasher	Std.	Std.	H.D.
Type Hitch Required	Equalizer	Equalizer	Equalizer

1972 Trailer Towing Information
Jeep (5000 GVW Models)

Equipment	Class I	Class II	Class III
Trailer Type	Any	Any	Any
Tongue Load Limit (lbs)	300	500	750
Engine Requirement	304 cu in. V-8	360 cu in. V-8	360 cu in. V-8

1972 Trailer Towing Information (cont.)
Jeep (5000 GVW Models)

Equipment	Class I	Class II	Class III
Exhaust System	Std.	Std.	Std.
Engine Cooling	H.D.	H.D.	H.D.
Transmission Requirement	Automatic	Automatic	Automatic
Trans. Aux. Oil Cooler	N.A.	N.A.	N.A.
Axle Ratio Recommended	Highest-Numerical Ratio for particular Engine/Transmission Combination		
Differential Type	Std.	Std.	Std.
Wheels Recommended	Std.	Std.	Std.
Tires	Oversize	Oversize	Oversize
Brakes Recommended	Power	Power	Power
Front	Std.	Std.	Std.
Rear	Std.	Std.	Std.
Springs	H.D.	H.D.	H.D.
Shock Absorbers	H.D.	H.D.	H.D.
Sway Bar	—	—	—
Steering Recommended	Power	Power	Power
Battery Recommended	Std.	Std.	H.D.
Alternator	Std.	Std.	H.D.
Turn Signal Flasher	Std.	Std.	H.D.
Type Hitch Required	Equalizer	Equalizer	Equalizer

1972 Trailer Towing Information
Jeep CJ-5, CJ-6, Commando Standard GVW

Equipment	Class I	Class II	Class III
Trailer Type	Any	Any	Any
Tongue Load Limit (lbs)	300	500	750

1972 Trailer Towing Information (cont.)

Jeep CJ-5, CJ-6, Commando Standard GVW

Equipment	Class I	Class II	Class III
Engine Requirement	258 cu in. Six	304 cu in. V-8	304 cu in. V-8
Exhaust System	Std.	Std.	Std.
Engine Cooling	H.D.	H.D.	H.D.
Transmission Requirement	4-speed①	Std.①	Std.①
Trans. Aux. Oil Cooler	N.A.	N.A.	N.A.
Axle Ratio Recommended	Highest-Numerical Ratio for particular Engine/Transmission Combination		
Differential Type	Std.	Std.	Std.
Wheels Recommended	Std.	Std.	Std.
Tires	Oversize	Oversize	Oversize
Brakes Recommended	Power	Power	Power
Front	Std.	Std.	Std.
Rear	Std.	Std.	Std.
Springs	H.D.	H.D	H.D.
Shock Absorbers	H.D.	H.D.	H.D.
Sway Bar	H.D.	H.D.	H.D.
Steering Recommended	Power	Power	Power
Battery Recommended	Std.	H.D.	H.D.
Alternator	Std.	H.D.	H.D.
Turn Signal Flasher	Std.	H.D.	H.D.
Type Hitch Required	Equalizer	Equalizer	Equalizer

① Automatic transmission in the Commando

1972 Trailer Towing Information
CJ-5, CJ-6, & Commando with Optional Heavy-Duty Package ▲

Equipment	Class I	Class II	Class III
Trailer Type	Any	Any	Any
Tongue Load Limit (lbs)	300	500	750
Engine Requirement	258 cu in. Six	304 cu in. V-8	304 cu in. V-8
Exhaust System	Std.	Std.	Std.
Engine Cooling	H.D.	H.D.	H.D.
Transmission Requirement	4 speed	Std.	Std.
Trans. Aux. Oil Cooler	N.A.	N.A.	N.A.
Axle Ratio Recommended	Highest-Numerical Ratio for particular Engine/Transmission Combination		
Differential Type	Std.	Std.	Std.
Wheels Recommended	H.D.	H.D.	H.D.
Tires	H.D.	H.D.	H.D.
Brakes Recommended	Power	Power	Power
Front	Std.	Std.	Std.
Rear	Std.	Std.	Std.
Springs	H.D.	H.D.	H.D.
Shock Absorbers	H.D.	H.D.	H.D.
Sway Bar	H.D.	H.D.	H.D.
Steering Recommended	Power	Power	Power
Battery Recommended	Std.	H.D.	H.D.
Alternator	Std.	H.D.	H.D.
Turn Signal Flasher	Std.	H.D.	H.D.
Type Hitch Required	Equalizer	Equalizer	Equalizer

▲ Optional GVW Package includes Extra Duty Front and Rear Suspension and 6.00 x 16-C Load Range 6-Ply All Service Tires on 16 in. Wheels with 4.5 in. E Rims.

1968–72 Trailer Towing Information

Cadillac ●

Equipment	Class I	Class II	Class III
Trailer Type	Any	Any	Any
Tongue Load Limit (lbs)	200	500	600
Engine Requirement	Std.	Std.	Std.
Exhaust System	Std.	Std.	Std.
Engine Cooling	Std.	H.D.	H.D.
Transmission Requirement	Std.	Std.	Std.
Trans. Aux. Oil Cooler	——	Required	Required
Axle Ratio Recommended	Std.	3.15:1	3.21:1
Differential Type	Std.	Std.	Std.
Wheels Recommended	Std.	Std.	H.D.
Tires	Std.	Std.	H.D.①
Brakes Recommended	Power Std.	Power Std.	Power Std.
Front	Std.	Std.	Std.
Rear	Std.	Std.	Std.
Springs	②	②	②
Shock Absorbers	②	②	②
Sway Bar	——	——	——
Steering Recommended	Std.	Std.	Std.
Battery Recommended	H.D.	H.D.	H.D.
Alternator	Std.	61 amp	61 amp
Turn Signal Flasher	H.D.	H.D.	H.D.
Type Hitch Required	Frame	Equalizer	Equalizer

●Eldorado is capable of towing a Class I trailer only.
① Load Range D
② Automatic Level Control for Class I, Automatic Level Control without A.L.C. Springs for Class II, A.L.C. with H.D. Springs for Class III

1972 Trailer Towing Information

Chevrolet ●

Equipment	Class I	Class II	Class III ▲
Trailer Type	Any	Any	Any
Tongue Load Limit (lbs)	200	350	500
Engine Requirement	350 cu in. V-8①	402 cu in. V-8	402 cu in. V-8⑤
Exhaust System	Std.	Std.	Std.
Engine Cooling	H.D.	H.D.	H.D.
Transmission Requirement	Turbo-Hydro②	Turbo-Hydro②	Turbo-Hydro
Trans. Aux. Oil Cooler	N.A.	N.A.	N.A.
Axle Ratio Recommended	3.08:1③	3.42:1④	3.42:1⑥
Differential Type	Positraction	Positraction	Positraction
Wheels Recommended	Std.	Std.	Std.
Tires	Std.	Std.	Std.
Brakes Recommended	Power	Power	Power
Front	Disc	Disc	Disc
Rear	Drum	Drum	Drum
Springs	H.D.	H.D.	H.D.
Shock Absorbers	H.D.	H.D.	H.D.
Sway Bar	—	—	—
Steering Recommended	Power	Power	Power
Battery Recommended	H.D.	H.D.	H.D.
Alternator	H.D.	H.D.	H.D.
Turn Signal Flasher	Std.	Std.	Std.
Type Hitch Required	Frame	Equalizer	Equalizer

● Except Camaro, Corvette and Vega
▲ Nova not recommended to tow Class III trailers
① 307 cu in. V-8 in Nova, Chevelle and El Camino.
② Standard Transmission in models other than full size.
③ 3.31:1 in models other than full size; 3.42:1 in Nova.
④ 2.73:1 in Chevelle and El Camino.
⑤ 454 cu in. in full size sedans.
⑥ 3.08:1 with 454 cu in. engine, 3.31:1 in Chevelle and El Camino.

1972 Trailer Towing Information

Camaro, Corvette, Vega

Equipment	Class I ▲	Class II ●	Class III ●
Trailer Type	Any	②	②
Tongue Load Limit (lbs)	100	②	②
Engine Requirement	Corvette 350 cu in. V-8 Camaro 307 cu in. V-8 Vega 140 cu in. 4 cyl	② ② ②	② ② ②
Exhaust System	Std.	②	②
Engine Cooling	Std.	②	②
Transmission Requirement	Turbo-Hydro	②	②
Trans. Aux. Oil Cooler	—	②	②
Axle Ratio Recommended	Corvette 3.42:1 Camaro 3.08:1 Vega 3.36:1	② ② ②	② ② ②
Differential Type	Std.	②	②
Wheels Recommended	Std.	②	②
Tires	Std.	②	②
Brakes Recommended	Power	②	②
Front	Std.	②	②
Rear	Std.	②	②
Springs	Std.	②	②
Shock Absorbers	Std.	②	②
Sway Bar	Std.	②	②
Steering Recommended	Power	②	②
Battery Recommended	Std.	②	②
Alternator	Std.	②	②
Turn Signal Flasher	Std.	②	②
Type Hitch Required	Frame	②	②

▲ Up to 1,000 lbs.
● It is not recommended the Classes II and III type trailers be towed by these cars.
② Vehicle not recommended to tow Class II or Class III trailers.

1971 Trailer Towing Information

Chevrolet Trucks ▲

Equipment	Class I	Class II	Class III
Trailer Type	Any	Any	Any
Tongue Load Limit (lbs)	250	350	500
Engine Requirement		See Charts Next Page	
Exhaust System	Std.	Std.	Std.
Engine Cooling	Std.	Std.	Std.
Transmission Requirement	Turbo-Hydro	Turbo-Hydro	Turbo-Hydro
Trans. Aux. Oil Cooler	—	—	—
Axle Ratio Recommended		See Charts Next Page	
Differential Type	Std.	Std.	Std.
Wheels Recommended	Std.	Std.	Std.
Tires	①	①	①
Brakes Recommended	Power	Power	Power
Front	—	—	—
Rear	—	—	—
Springs	Std.	Std.	Std.
Shock Absorbers	Std.	Std.	Std.
Sway Bar	—	—	—
Steering Recommended	Std.	Std.	Std.
Battery Recommended	80 amp-hr	80 amp-hr	80 amp-hr
Alternator	42 amp	42 amp②	61 amp
Turn Signal Flasher	Std.	Std.	Std.
Type Hitch Required	Frame	Equalizer	Equalizer

▲ Suburban C-10, C-20, Pickup C-10, C-20, Blazer (AH), Sportvan G-10, G-20, G-30.
① Blazer, Pickup and Suburban C-10, H78 x 15B
Sportvan G-30, Pickup and Suburban C-20, 8.75 x 16.5C
Blazer K-10, G78 x 15B
Sportvan G-10, F78 x 14B
Sportvan G-20, 8.00 x 16.5C

1971 Trailer Towing Information (cont.)

Chevrolet Trucks

Suburban, Pickup Engine and Rear Axle Chart
Recommended Engine, Rear Axle Ratios and GCW for Trailer Towing
GCW—Combined Weight of Loaded Truck and Trailer—Lbs

Engine C10	4000	5000	6000	7000	GCW 8000	9000	10,000	11,000	12,000
250 cu in. Six	3.07	3.73	4.11						
292 cu in. Six		3.07	3.73	4.11					
307 cu in. V-8		3.07	3.73	4.11					
350 cu in. V-8				3.07		3.73	4.11		
400 cu in. V-8						3.07			
Engine C20									
250 cu in. Six		4.10	4.57						
292 cu in. Six		4.10	4.57						
307 cu in. V-8			4.10	4.57					
350 cu in. V-8						4.10	4.57		
400 cu in. V-8							3.54	4.10	

Blazer Engine and Rear Axle Chart
Recommended Engine, Rear Axle Ratios and GCW for Trailer Towing
GCW—Combined Weight of Loaded Truck and Trailer—Lbs

Engine C10	4000	5000	6000	7000	GCW 8000	9000	10,000	11,000	12,000
250 cu in. Six	3.07	3.73	4.11						
307 cu in. V-8		3.07	3.73	4.11					
350 cu in. V-8				3.07		3.73	4.11		
Engine K10									
250 cu in. Six		3.73							
307 cu in. V-8				3.73					
350 cu in. V-8				3.07		3.73			

Sportvan Engine and Rear Axle Chart
Recommended Engine, Rear Axle Ratios and GCW for Trailer Towing
GCW—Combined Weight of Loaded Truck and Trailer—Lbs

Engine G10	4000	5000	6000	7000	GCW 8000	9000	10,000	11,000	12,000
250 cu in. Six		3.36	3.73						
307 cu in. V-8		3.07	3.36	3.73					
Engine G20									
250 cu in. Six	3.36	3.73	4.11						
350 cu in. V-8				3.36		3.73			
Engine G30									
250 cu in. Six		4.10	4.57						
350 cu in. V-8							4.10	4.57	

1971 Trailer Towing Information

Chevrolet ▲

Equipment	Class I	Class II ●	Class III ■
Trailer Type	Any	Any	Any
Tongue Load Limit (lbs)	250	350	500
Engine Requirement	350 cu in. V-8 ①	402 cu in. V-8 ②	402 cu in. V-8
Exhaust System	Std.	Std.	Std.
Engine Cooling	H.D.	H.D.	H.D.
Transmission Requirement	Turbo-Hydro	Turbo-Hydro	Turbo-Hydro
Trans. Aux. Oil Cooler	—	—	—
Axle Ratio Recommended	3.08:1 ③	2.73:1 ④	3.42:1 ⑤
Differential Type	Positraction	Positraction	Positraction
Wheels Recommended	Std.	Std.	Std.
Tires	Std.	Std.	Std.
Brakes Recommended	Power	Power	Power
Front	Disc	Disc	Disc
Rear	Drum	Drum	Drum
Springs	H.D.	H.D.	H.D.
Shock Absorbers	H.D.	H.D.	H.D.
Sway Bar	—	—	—
Steering Recommended	Power	Power	Power
Battery Recommended	H.D.	H.D.	H.D.
Alternator	H.D.	H.D.	H.D.
Turn Signal Flasher	Std.	Std.	Std.
Type Hitch Required	Frame	Equalizer	Equalizer

▲ Except Vega, Camaro, Corvette.
● Monte Carlo is recommended only for Class I trailer towing.
■ Nova should not tow Class III trailers.
① 400 cu in. V-8 in full size sedans, 307 cu in. V-8 in Chevelle, El Camino and Nova.
② 350 cu in. V-8 in Nova.
③ 3.31:1 in Chevelle, El Camino and Monte Carlo, 3.36:1 in Nova.
④ 3.31:1 in Nova.
⑤ 3.31:1 in Chevelle and El Camino.

1971 Trailer Towing Information
Camaro, Corvette, Vega

Equipment	Class I ▲	Class II ●	Class III ●
Trailer Type	Any	—	—
Tongue Load Limit (lbs)	100	—	—
Engine Requirement	Camaro 307 cu in. V-8	—	—
	Corvette 350 cu in. V-8	—	—
	Vega 140 cu in. 4 cyl	—	—
Exhaust System	Std.	—	—
Engine Cooling	Std.	—	—
Transmission Requirement	Turbo-Hydro	—	—
Trans. Aux. Oil Cooler	—	—	—
Axle Ratio Recommended	3.08:1 ①	—	—
Differential Type	Std.	—	—
Wheels Recommended	Std.	—	—
Tires	Std.	—	—
Brakes Recommended	Power	—	—
Front	Std.	—	—
Rear	Std.	—	—
Springs	Std.	—	—
Shock Absorbers	Std.	—	—
Sway Bar	Std.	—	—
Steering Recommended	Power	—	—
Battery Recommended	Std.	—	—
Alternator	Std.	—	—
Turn Signal Flasher	Std.	—	—
Type Hitch Required	Frame	—	—

▲ Up to 1000 lbs.
● It is not recommended that Class II and III trailers be towed with Camaro, Corvette or Vega.
① 3.36:1 in Vega.

1971–'72 Trailer Towing Information

Charger, Coronet, Polara and Monaco

Equipment	Class I	Class II	Class III ▲
Trailer Type	Any	Any	Any
Tongue Load Limit (lbs)	250	350	500
Engine Requirement	318 cu in. V-8①	318 cu in. V-8①	318 cu in. V-8①
Exhaust System	Std.	Std.	Std.
Engine Cooling	H.D.	H.D.	H.D.
Transmission Requirement	TorqueFlite	TorqueFlite	TorqueFlite
Trans. Aux. Oil Cooler	—	—	—
Axle Ratio Recommended	3.23:1	3.23:1	3.23:1
Differential Type	Std.②	Std.②	Std.②
Wheels Recommended	H.D.	H.D.	H.D.
Tires	③	③	③
Brakes Recommended	Power	Power	Power
Front	Disc	Disc	Disc
Rear	Drum	Drum	Drum
Springs	H.D.	H.D.	H.D.
Shock Absorbers	H.D.	H.D.	H.D.
Sway Bar	Yes	Yes	Yes
Steering Recommended	Power	Power	Power
Battery Recommended	H.D. 70 amp	H.D. 70 amp	H.D. 70 amp
Alternator	H.D.	H.D.	H.D.
Turn Signal Flasher	H.D.	H.D.	H.D.
Type Hitch Required	Equalizer	Equalizer	Equalizer

▲ Up to 4,000 lbs gross.
① 383 cu in. 2 bbl and 4 bbl; 400 cu in. 2 bbl and 4 bbl in 1972 and 440 cu in. 4 bbl in 1971 are recommended options. 360 cu in. 2 bbl in Polara and Monaco.
② Sure Grip is a recommended option.
③ Charger G70 x 14; Coronet Wagons, H78 x 14; Polara and Monaco Wagons L84 x 15.

Chrysler—1968-1972

All Chryslers can be equipped with the following:
1. A larger radiator and a larger transmission oil cooler.
2. A seven-bladed fan and fan shroud and a radiator yoke-to-hood air seal (standard on air-conditioned models).
3. Heavy-duty suspension with larger front torsion bars and additional rear leaf springs.
4. An anti-sway bar and heavy-duty shock absorbers.
5. Heavy-duty stop lamp switch.
6. Heavy-duty turn signal flasher.
7. Heavy-duty drum brakes with 11 x 3 in. drums. Disc brakes are available on the New Yorker and the Town and Country Wagon.
8. Wider rims are also included.
9. Heavy-duty rear axle with a 3.23:1 ratio.

NOTE: *This package is mandatory for tow vehicles pulling trailers weighing 2500–5500 lbs.*

For 1973, Dodge offers three trailer towing packages which may be ordered separately or in combination with each other depending on the intended usage. The Wiring Package is available for pulling the camper type trailers or others of a reasonable light gross weight while the Heavy-Duty package may also be ordered.

The Trailer Towing Package basically consists of all the items in the Heavy-Duty and the Wiring Packages, plus an externally-mounted transmission oil cooler and a 3.23:1 ratio rear axle.

The Heavy-Duty package consists of a Cooling Package (larger radiator, fan shroud, and a coolant reserve system); Heavy-Duty Suspension (larger front sway bar, larger torsion bars, higher rear leaf spring rate), and extra wide wheel rims.

The Wiring Package includes a 60 ampere heavy-duty alternator and a heavy-duty stop lamp switch, a variable-load turn signal flasher, and a trailer wiring harness. This is a seven-wire harness with wires for ground, right stop and turn signal; left stop and turn signal; taillights, license and side marker lights, back-up lamp, electric trailer brake, and auxiliary.

Dodge offers a variety of class I and II hitches for towing light and medium trailers and they are available for all Dodge vehicles. It should be noted that all the hitches are dealer-installed items.

Trailer Towing Information
1972 Ford (Mustang, Maverick, Pinto)

Equipment	Class I	Class II	Class III
Trailer Type	°	—	—
Tongue Load Limit (lbs)	200 lbs.	—	—
Engine Requirement	° °	—	—
Exhaust System	Std.	—	—
Engine Cooling	Std.	—	—
Transmission Requirement	Cruise-o-matic	—	—
Trans. Aux. Oil Cooler	—	—	—

Trailer Towing Information (cont.)

1972 Ford (Mustang, Maverick, Pinto)

Equipment	Class I	Class II	Class III
Axle Ratio Recommended	Std. for Mustang & Pinto Mustang: 3.25:1 Maverick: 3.00:1	—	—
Differential Type	Std.	—	—
Wheels Recommended	Std.	—	—
Tires	Std.	—	—
Brakes Recommended	Power front for Mustang Std. for others	—	—
Front	Std.	—	—
Rear	Std.	—	—
Springs	Std.	—	—
Shock Absorbers	Std.	—	—
Sway Bar	Std.	—	—
Steering Recommended	Power Steering Recommended for Mustang	—	—
Battery Recommended	Std.	—	—
Alternator	Std.	—	—
Turn Signal Flasher	Std.	—	—
Type Hitch Required	Non-Equalizing ①	—	—

* Trailers with frontal area less than 25 sq. ft.
** Maverick uses a 200 cu in. 6 cyl.
Pinto uses a 2000 cc. engine
Mustang uses a 302 cu in. V-8 for Trailers with less than 250 sq ft of frontal area and a 351 cu in. V-8 for over 25 sq ft in frontal area.
① Never use a bumper mounted hitch on these units.

1972 Trailer Towing Information

Torino, Ranchero

Equipment	Class I	Class II	Class III
Trailer Type	Any	Any	Any
Tongue Load Limit (lbs)	200	500	700
Engine Requirement	302 cu in. V-8①	351 cu in. V-8①	400 cu in. V-8①
Exhaust System	Std.	Std.	Std.
Engine Cooling	H.D.	H.D.	H.D.
Transmission Requirement	Cruise-O-Matic	Cruise-O-Matic	Cruise-O-Matic
Trans. Aux. Oil Cooler	—	—	—
Axle Ratio Recommended	Std.	Std.	3.25:1
Differential Type	Std.	Std.	Std.
Wheels Recommended	Std.	Std.	Std.
Tires	Std.	F78 x 14	G78 x 14
Brakes Recommended	Std.	Power	Power
Front	Std.	Disc	Disc
Rear	Std.	Drum	Drum
Springs	Std.	H.D.	H.D.
Shock Absorbers	Std.	H.D.	H.D.
Sway Bar	—	—	—
Steering Recommended	Std.	Power	Power
Battery Recommended	Std.	Std.	H.D.
Alternator	Std.	Std.	H.D.
Turn Signal Flasher	Std.	Std.	Std.
Type Hitch Required	Frame	Equalizer	Equalizer

① Mountainous driving, it is recommended that the larger engines be used (400 cu in. V-8 and 429 cu in. V-8).

1972 Trailer Towing Information

Ford

Equipment	Class I	Class II	Class III
Trailer Type	Any	Any	Any
Tongue Load Limit (lbs)	200	500	900
Engine Requirement	351 cu in. V-8	351 cu in. V-8	351 cu in. V-8
Exhaust System	Std.	Std.	Std.
Engine Cooling	Std.	H.D.	H.D.
Transmission Requirement	Std.	Std.	Std.
Trans. Aux. Oil Cooler	—	—	—
Axle Ratio Recommended	Std.	Std.	Std.
Differential Type	Std.	Std.	Std.
Wheels Recommended	Std.	Std.	H.D.
Tires	Std.	Std.	Std.
Brakes Recommended	Power	Power	Power
Front	Std.	Std.	Std.
Rear	Std.	Std.	Std.
Springs	Std.	H.D.	H.D.①
Shock Absorbers	Std.	H.D.	H.D.
Sway Bar	—	—	—
Steering Recommended	Std.	Power	Power
Battery Recommended	Std.	Std.	H.D.
Alternator	Std.	Std.	H.D.
Turn Signal Flasher	Std.	Std.	Std.
Type Hitch Required	Frame	Equalizer	Equalizer

① Heavy-duty frame.

Trailer Towing Information

1972 (Mercury Monterey, Marquis)

Equipment	Class I	Class II	Class III
Trailer Type	Any	Any	Any
Tongue Load Limit (lbs)	to 200 lbs	200 to 500 lbs	350 to 900 lbs
Engine Requirement	Std.	400 V-8	400 V-8
Exhaust System	Std.	Std.	Std.
Engine Cooling	Extra cooling package	Std.	Std.
Transmission Requirement	Std.	Std.	Std.
Trans. Aux. Oil Cooler	—	—	—
Axle Ratio Recommended	Std.	Std.	Std.
Differential Type	Std.	Std.	Std.
Wheels Recommended	Std.	Std.	Std.
Tires	Std.	Std.	Std.
Brakes Recommended	Std.	Std.	Std.
Front	Std.	Std.	Std.
Rear	Std.	Std.	Std.
Springs	Std.	Std.	Std.
Shock Absorbers	Std.	Std.	Std.
Sway Bar	Std.	Std.	Std.
Steering Recommended	Std.	Std.	Std.
Battery Recommended	Std.	Std.	Std.
Alternator	Std.	Std.	Std.
Turn Signal Flasher	Std.	Std.	Std.
Type Hitch Required	Frame①	Equalizer	Equalizer

Trailer Towing Information

1972 Mercury Cougar

Equipment	Class I	Class II	Class III
Trailer Type	Any	—	—
Tongue Load Limit (lbs)	to 200 lbs	—	—
Engine Requirement	Recommend 351-2V	—	—
Exhaust System	Std.	—	—
Engine Cooling	Std.	—	—
Transmission Requirement	Select-Shift is recommended	—	—
Trans. Aux. Oil Cooler	Recommended	—	—
Axle Ratio Recommended	3.00:1	—	—
Differential Type	Std.	—	—
Wheels Recommended	Std.	—	—
Tires	Std.	—	—
Brakes Recommended	Std.	—	—
Front	Std.	—	—
Rear	Std.	—	—
Springs	Std.	—	—
Shock Absorbers	Air shocks are available	—	—
Sway Bar	—	—	—
Steering Recommended	Power	—	—
Battery Recommended	Std.	—	—
Alternator	Std.	—	—
Turn Signal Flasher	Std.	—	—
Type Hitch Required	Non-equalizing	—	—

Trailer Towing Information
1972 Mercury Comet

Equipment	Class I	Class II	Class III
Trailer Type	Any	——	——
Tongue Load Limit (lbs)	to 200 lbs	——	——
Engine Requirement	*	——	——
Exhaust System	Std.	——	——
Engine Cooling	Std.	——	——
Transmission Requirement	Select-Shift Automatic	——	——
Trans. Aux. Oil Cooler	——	——	——
Axle Ratio Recommended	3.00:1	——	——
Differential Type	Std.	——	——
Wheels Recommended	Std.	——	——
Tires	Std.	——	——
Brakes Recommended	Std.	——	——
Front	Std.	——	——
Rear	Std.	——	——
Springs	**	——	——
Shock Absorbers	**	——	——
Sway Bar	**	——	——
Steering Recommended	Power	——	——
Battery Recommended	55 amp	——	——
Alternator	Std.	——	——
Turn Signal Flasher	Std.	——	——
Type Hitch Required	Non-equalizing	——	——

* 200 cu in. engine is sufficient for trailer with frontal area less than 25 sq. ft.; 302 cu in. engine is sufficient for trailer with frontal area more than 25 sq. ft.
** A handling package is available.

Trailer Towing Information
1972 Thunderbird

Equipment	Class I	Class II	Class III
Trailer Type	Any	Any	Any
Tongue Load Limit (lbs)	up to 200 lbs	200 to 350 lbs	350 to 700 lbs
Engine Requirement	429 4V V-8	429 4V V-8	429 4V V-8
Exhaust System	Std.	Std.	Std.
Engine Cooling	Special cooling system is available		
Transmission Requirement	Std.	Std.	Std.
Trans. Aux. Oil Cooler	——	——	——
Axle Ratio Recommended	3.25:1	3.25:1	3.25:1
Differential Type	Std.	Std.	Std.
Wheels Recommended	Std.	Std.	Std.
Tires	Std.	Std.	Std.
Brakes Recommended	Std.	Std.	Std.
Front	Std.	Std.	Std.
Rear	Std.	Std.	Std.
Springs	*	*	*
Shock Absorbers	*	*	*
Sway Bar	——	——	——
Steering Recommended	Std.	Std.	Std.
Battery Recommended	Std.	Std.	Std.
Alternator	Std.	Std.	Std.
Turn Signal Flasher	*	*	*
Type Hitch Required	Frame	Equalizing	Equalizing

* Trailer Towing Package Includes:
(1) Extra Cooling Components
(2) Wiring Harness
(3) Heavy Duty Suspension
(4) 3.25:1 Rear Axle Ratio

Trailer Towing Information
1972 Mercury Montego

Equipment	Class I	Class II	Class III
Trailer Type	Any	Any	Any
Tongue Load Limit (lbs)	to 200 lbs	200 to 500 lbs	500 to 900 lbs
Engine Requirement	Std.	351 cu in.	400 cu in.
Exhaust System	Std.	Std.	Std.
Engine Cooling	Std.	Std.	Std.
Transmission Requirement		Select-Shift Automatic	
Trans. Aux. Oil Cooler	—	—	—
Axle Ratio Recommended	Std.	3.25:1	3.25:1
Differential Type	Std.	Std.	Std.
Wheels Recommended	Std.	Std.	Std.
Tires	Std.	Std.	G78-14
Brakes Recommended	Std.	Power Disc	Power Disc
Front	Std.	Std.	Std.
Rear	Std.	Std.	Std.
Springs	*	**	***
Shock Absorbers	*	**	***
Sway Bar	*	**	***
Steering Recommended	Std.	Power	Power
Battery Recommended	Std.	Std.	Std.
Alternator	Std.	Std.	Std.
Turn Signal Flasher	Std.	Std.	Std.
Type Hitch Required	Frame	Equalizer	Equalizer

* Cross country ride package is recommended for Class I trailers.
** Medium Duty Towing Package.
*** Optional Trailer Towing Package.

1971 Trailer Towing Information

Thunderbird

Equipment	Class I	Class II	Class III
Trailer Type	Any	Any	Any
Tongue Load Limit (lbs)	200	350	700
Engine Requirement	429 cu in. V-8	429 cu in. V-8	429 cu in. V-8 ①
Exhaust System	Std.	Std.	Std.
Engine Cooling	Std.	H.D.	H.D.
Transmission Requirement	Std.	Std.	Std.
Trans. Aux. Oil Cooler	—	—	—
Axle Ratio Recommended	2.75:1	3.25:1	3.25:1
Differential Type	Traction-Lok	Traction-Lok	Traction-Lok
Wheels Recommended	Std.	Std.	Std.
Tires	Std.	Std.	Std.
Brakes Recommended	Power	Power	Power
Front	Disc	Disc	Disc
Rear	Drum	Drum	Drum
Springs	Std. ②	H.D. ③	H.D. ③
Shock Absorbers	Std.	H.D.	H.D.
Sway Bar	—	—	—
Steering Recommended	Std.	Std.	Std.
Battery Recommended	H.D.	H.D.	H.D.
Alternator	H.D.	H.D.	H.D.
Turn Signal Flasher	Std.	Std.	Std.
Type Hitch Required	Frame	Equalizer	Equalizer

① 4 bbl carburetor recommended.
② With Automatic ride control.
③ Without Automatic ride control.

1971 Trailer Towing Information

Maverick

Equipment	Class I	Class II	Class III
Trailer Type	Any	①	①
Tongue Load Limit (lbs)	200	①	①
Engine Requirement	200 cu in. Six	①	①
Exhaust System	Std.	①	①
Engine Cooling	Std.	①	①
Transmission Requirement	Cruise-O-Matic	①	①
Trans. Aux. Oil Cooler	—	①	①
Axle Ratio Recommended	3.00:1	①	①
Differential Type	Std.	①	①
Wheels Recommended	Std.	①	①
Tires	Std.	①	①
Brakes Recommended	Std.	①	①
Front	Std.	①	①
Rear	Std.	①	①
Springs	Std.	①	①
Shock Absorbers	Std.	①	①
Sway Bar	—	①	①
Steering Recommended	Std.	①	①
Battery Recommended	Std.	①	①
Alternator	Std.	①	①
Turn Signal Flasher	Std.	①	①
Type Hitch Required	Frame	①	①

① It is not recommended that the Maverick tow Class II or III trailers.

1971 Trailer Towing Information

Mustang, Comet

Equipment	Class I	Class II	Class III
Trailer Type	Any	④	④
Tongue Load Limit (lbs)	200	④	④
Engine Requirement	351 cu in. V-8①	④	④
Exhaust System	Std.	④	④
Engine Cooling	Std.	④	④
Transmission Requirement	Cruise-O-Matic	④	④
Trans. Aux. Oil Cooler	—	④	④
Axle Ratio Recommended	3.00:1	④	④
Differential Type	Std.	④	④
Wheels Recommended	Std.	④	④
Tires	Std.	④	④
Brakes Recommended	Std.	④	④
Front	Std.	④	④
Rear	Std.	④	④
Springs	Std.②	④	④
Shock Absorbers	Std.②	④	④
Sway Bar	—	④	④
Steering Recommended	Std.	④	④
Battery Recommended	Std.③	④	④
Alternator	Std.	④	④
Turn Signal Flasher	Std.	④	④
Type Hitch Required	Frame	④	④

① 250 cu in. Six in Comet.
② H.D. in Comet.
③ 55 Amp in Comet.
④ Not recommended for Class II or Class III trailers.

1971 Trailer Towing Information

Ford

Equipment	Class I	Class II	Class III
Trailer Type	Any	Any	Any
Tongue Load Limit (lbs)	200	500	700
Engine Requirement	240 cu in. Six	400 cu in. V-8	400 cu in. V-8
Exhaust System	Std.	Std.	Std.
Engine Cooling	Std.	H.D.	H.D.
Transmission Requirement	Cruise-O-Matic	Cruise-O-Matic	Cruise-O-Matic
Trans. Aux. Oil Cooler	—	—	—
Axle Ratio Recommended	2.75:1	3.25:1	3.25:1
Differential Type	Traction-Lok	Traction-Lok	Traction-Lok
Wheels Recommended	Std.	6.5 x 15	6.5 x 15
Tires	Std.	H78 x 15①	H78 x 15①
Brakes Recommended	Std.	Power	Power
Front	Std.	Disc	Disc
Rear	Std.	Drum	Drum
Springs	Std.	H.D.	H.D.
Shock Absorbers	Std.	H.D.	H.D.
Sway Bar	—	—	—
Steering Recommended	Std.	Power	Power
Battery Recommended	Std.	80 amp	80 amp
Alternator	Std.	55 amp	55 amp
Turn Signal Flasher	Std.	Std.	Std.
Type Hitch Required	Frame	Equalizer	Equalizer

① Standard size on wagons.

1971 Trailer Towing Information

Torino

Equipment	Class I	Class II	Class III
Trailer Type	Any	Any	①
Tongue Load Limit (lbs)	200	350	①
Engine Requirement	351 cu in. V-8	351 cu in. V-8	①
Exhaust System	Std.	Std.	①
Engine Cooling	Std.	H.D.	①
Transmission Requirement	Cruise-O-Matic	Cruise-O-Matic	①
Trans. Aux. Oil Cooler	—	—	①
Axle Ratio Recommended	3.00:1	3.25:1	①
Differential Type	Traction-Lok	Traction-Lok	①
Wheels Recommended	Std.	Std.	①
Tires	Std.	F78 x 14	①
Brakes Recommended	Power	Power	①
Front	Disc	Disc	①
Rear	Drum	Drum	①
Springs	Std.	H.D.	①
Shock Absorbers	Std.	H.D.	①
Sway Bar	—	—	①
Steering Recommended	Std.	Power	①
Battery Recommended	Std.	70 amp	①
Alternator	Std.	55 amp	①
Turn Signal Flasher	Std.	Std.	①
Type Hitch Required	Frame	Equalizer	①

① Vehicle is not recommended to tow Class III trailers.

1971 Trailer Towing Information

Montego, Cyclone

Equipment	Class I	Class II	Class III ●
Trailer Type	Any	Any	—
Tongue Load Limit (lbs)	200	350	—
Engine Requirement	302 cu in. V-8	351 cu in. V-8	—
Exhaust System	Std.	Std.	—
Engine Cooling	Std.	H.D.	—
Transmission Requirement	Select-Shift	Select-Shift	—
Trans. Aux. Oil Cooler	—	—	—
Axle Ratio Recommended	3.00:1	3.25:1	—
Differential Type	Std.	Std.	—
Wheels Recommended	Std.	Std.	—
Tires	Std.	Std.	—
Brakes Recommended	Power	Power	—
Front	Disc	Disc	—
Rear	Drum	Drum	—
Springs	Std.①	H.D.	—
Shock Absorbers	Std.	H.D.	—
Sway Bar	—	—	—
Steering Recommended	Power	Power	—
Battery Recommended	Std.	70 amp	—
Alternator	Std.	55 amp	—
Turn Signal Flasher	Std.	Std.	—
Type Hitch Required	Frame	Equalizer	—

● It is not recommended that these cars tow a Class III trailer.
① Air springs recommended without Equalizer hitch.

1971 Trailer Towing Information

Marquis, Marauder, Monterey

Equipment	Class I	Class II	Class III
Trailer Type	Any	Any	Any
Tongue Load Limit (lbs)	200	500	700
Engine Requirement	400 cu in. V-8	400 cu in. V-8	400 cu in. V-8
Exhaust System	Std.	Std.	Std.
Engine Cooling	H.D.	H.D.	H.D.
Transmission Requirement	Select-Shift	Select-Shift	Select-Shift
Trans. Aux. Oil Cooler	—	—	—
Axle Ratio Recommended	3.25:1	3.25:1	3.25:1
Differential Type	Std.	Std.	Std.
Wheels Recommended	Std.	Std.	Std.
Tires	H78 x 15	H78 x 15	H78 x 15
Brakes Recommended	Power	Power	Power
Front	Disc	Disc	Disc
Rear	Drum	Drum	Drum
Springs	Std.	H.D.	H.D.
Shock Absorbers	Std.	H.D.	H.D.
Sway Bar	—	—	—
Steering Recommended	Power	Power	Power
Battery Recommended	Std.	80 amp/hr	80 amp/hr
Alternator	Std.	55 amp	Std.
Turn Signal Flasher	Std.	Std.	Std.
Type Hitch Required	Frame	Equalizer	Equalizer

1971 Trailer Towing Information

Cougar

Equipment	Class I	Class II ●	Class III ●
Trailer Type	Any	—	—
Tongue Load Limit (lbs)	200	—	—
Engine Requirement	351 cu in. V-8	—	—
Exhaust System	Std.	—	—
Engine Cooling	H.D.	—	—
Transmission Requirement	Select-Shift	—	—
Trans. Aux. Oil Cooler	Yes	—	—
Axle Ratio Recommended	3.00:1	—	—
Differential Type	Std.	—	—
Wheels Recommended	Std.	—	—
Tires	Std.	—	—
Brakes Recommended	Power	—	—
Front	Disc	—	—
Rear	Drum	—	—
Springs	Std.①	—	—
Shock Absorbers	Std.	—	—
Sway Bar	—	—	—
Steering Recommended	Power	—	—
Battery Recommended	Std.	—	—
Alternator	Std.	—	—
Turn Signal Flasher	Std.	—	—
Type Hitch Required	Frame	—	—

● It is not recommended that this car tow a Class II or III trailer.
① Air springs recommended if without Equalizer hitch.

1971 Trailer Towing Information

Continental, Mark III

Equipment	Class I	Class II	Class III
Trailer Type	Any	Any	Any
Tongue Load Limit (lbs)	200	500	700
Engine Requirement	460 cu in. V-8	460 cu in. V-8	460 cu in. V-8
Exhaust System	Std.	Std.	Std.
Engine Cooling	Std.	Std.	Std.
Transmission Requirement	Select-Shift	Select-Shift	Select-Shift
Trans. Aux. Oil Cooler	——	——	——
Axle Ratio Recommended	2.80:1	3.00:1	3.00:1
Differential Type	Std.	Std.	Std.
Wheels Recommended	Std.	Std.	Std.
Tires	Std.	Std.	Std.
Brakes Recommended	Power	Power	Power
Front	Disc	Disc	Disc
Rear	Drum	Drum	Drum
Springs	Std.	Std.	H.D.
Shock Absorbers	Std.	Std.	H.D.
Sway Bar	——	——	——
Steering Recommended	Power	Power	Power
Battery Recommended	Std.	Std.	Std.
Alternator	Std.	Std.	Std.
Turn Signal Flasher	Std.	Std.	Std.
Type Hitch Required	Frame	Equalizer	Equalizer

1970 Trailer Towing Information
Marquis, Marauder, Monterey

Equipment	Class I	Class II	Class III
Trailer Type	Any	Any	Any
Tongue Load Limit (lbs)	200	500	700
Engine Requirement	390 cu in. V-8	429 cu in. V-8	429 cu in. V-8
Exhaust System	Std.	Std.	Std.
Engine Cooling	Std.	H.D.	H.D.
Transmission Requirement	Select-Shift	Select-Shift	Select-Shift
Trans. Aux. Oil Cooler	—	—	—
Axle Ratio Recommended	2.75:1	3.25:1	3.25:1
Differential Type	Std.	Std.	Std.
Wheels Recommended	Std.	Std.	Std.
Tires	H78 x 15	H78 x 15	H78 x 15
Brakes Recommended	Power	Power	Power
Front	Disc	Disc	Disc
Rear	Drum	Drum	Drum
Springs	Std.	H.D.	H.D.
Shock Absorbers	Std.	H.D.	H.D.
Sway Bar	—	—	—
Steering Recommended	Power	Power	Power
Battery Recommended	Std.	H.D. 80 amp	H.D. 80 amp
Alternator	Std.	65 amp	65 amp
Turn Signal Flasher	Std.	Std.	Std.
Type Hitch Required	Frame	Equalizer	Equalizer

TOW VEHICLE

1970 Trailer Towing Information

Montego, Cyclone

Equipment	Class I	Class II	Class III
Trailer Type	Any	Any	②
Tongue Load Limit (lbs)	200	350	②
Engine Requirement	302 cu in. V-8	351 cu in. V-8	②
Exhaust System	Std.	Std.	②
Engine Cooling	Std.	H.D.	②
Transmission Requirement	Select-Shift	Select-Shift	②
Trans. Aux. Oil Cooler	——	——	②
Axle Ratio Recommended	3.00:1	3.25:1	②
Differential Type	Std.	Std.	②
Wheels Recommended	Std.	Std.	②
Tires	Std.	Std.	②
Brakes Recommended	Power	Power	②
Front	Disc	Disc	②
Rear	Drum	Drum	②
Springs	Std.①	H.D.	②
Shock Absorbers	Std.	H.D.	②
Sway Bar	——	——	②
Steering Recommended	Power	Power	②
Battery Recommended	Std.	70 amp	②
Alternator	Std.	55 amp	②
Turn Signal Flasher	Std.	Std.	②
Type Hitch Required	Frame	Equalizer	②

① Air springs recommended.
② It is not recommended that these cars tow Class III trailers.

Trailer Towing Information

1972 Oldsmobile (F-85, Cutlass, Cutlass S, Cutlass Supreme and Vista Cruiser)

Equipment	Class I	Class II	Class III
Trailer Type	Any	Any	Vista Cruiser only
Tongue Load Limit (lbs)	to 200 lbs	to 350 lbs	to 600 lbs
Engine Requirement	350 V-8	350 V-8	455 V-8
Exhaust System	Std.	Std.	Std.
Engine Cooling	H.D. System (Recommended)	H.D. System (Required)	H.D. System (Required)
Transmission Requirement	Turbo-Hydra-Matic 350	Turbo-Hydra-Matic 350	Turbo-Hydra-Matic 400
Trans. Aux. Oil Cooler	Available	Available	Recommended
Axle Ratio Recommended	3.08:1	3.08:1	3.23:1
Differential Type	Std.	Std.	Std.
Wheels Recommended	H.D. Required	H.D. Required	H.D. Required
Tires	Std.	Std.	Std.
Brakes Recommended	Std.	Std.	Std.
Front	Std.	Std.	Std.
Rear	Std.	Std.	Std.
Springs	*	*	*
Shock Absorbers	*	*	*
Sway Bar	*	*	*
Steering Recommended	Std.	Std.	Std.
Battery Recommended	Std.	Std.	Std.
Alternator	Std.	Std.	Std.
Turn Signal Flasher	**	**	**
Type Hitch Required	Frame	Equalizer	Equalizer

* H.D. Suspension is available. It is recommended for all Class II trailers and required for Class III.
** Trailer wiring harness is recommended.

Trailer Towing Information

1972 Oldsmobile (Delta 88, Custom Cruiser, Ninety-Eight, Toronado Custom)

Equipment	Class I	Class II	Class III
Trailer Type	Any	Any	Any
Tongue Load Limit (lbs)	to 200 lbs	to 350 lbs	to 600 lbs
Engine Requirement	Std.	455 V-8	455 V-8
Exhaust System	Std.	Dual	Dual
Engine Cooling	H.D. System Recommended	H.D. System Required	H.D. System Required
Transmission Requirement	Turbo-Hydra-Matic 400		
Trans. Aux. Oil Cooler	Available	Available	Recommended
Axle Ratio Recommended	Std.	2.93:1	3.23:1 for all except Toronado which uses a 3.07:1 Ratio
Differential Type	Std.	Std.	Std.
Wheels Recommended	Std.*	Std.*	Std.
Tires	Std.	Std.	Std.
Brakes Recommended	Std.	Std.	Std.
Front	Std.	Std.	Std.
Rear	Std.	Std.	Std.
Springs	**	**	**
Shock Absorbers	**	**	**
Sway Bar	**	**	**
Steering Recommended	Std.	Std.	Std.
Battery Recommended	Std.	Std.	Std.
Alternator	Std.	Std.	Std.
Turn Signal Flasher	***	***	***
Type Hitch Required	Frame	Equalizing	Equalizing

* Delta 88 and Ninety-Eight require the use of H.D. wheels.
** A suspension package is recommended.
*** Trailer wiring harness recommended.

Trailer Towing Information

1972 Oldsmobile (F-85, Cutlass, Cutlass S, Cutlass Supreme, 4-4-2, Vista Cruiser)

Equipment	Class I	Class II	Class III
Trailer Type	Any	Any	Only Vista Cruiser
Tongue Load Limit (lbs)	to 200 lbs	200 to 350 lbs	350 to 600 lbs
Engine Requirement	350 V-8	350 V-8	455 V-8
Exhaust System	Std.	Std.	Std.
Engine Cooling	H.D. System Recommended	H.D. System Required	H.D. System Required
Transmission Requirement	Turbo-Hydra-Matic 350 Recommended	Turbo-Hydra-Matic 350 Required	Turbo-Hydra-Matic 400 Required
Trans. Aux. Oil Cooler	—	—	—
Axle Ratio Recommended	3.08:1 Recommended	3.08:1 Required	3.08:1 Required
Differential Type	Anti-Spin Axle Available		
Wheels Recommended	Std.	Std.	Std.
Tires	Std.	Std.	Std.
Brakes Recommended	Std.	Std.	Std.
Front	Std.	Std.	Std.
Rear	Std.	Std.	Std.
Springs	H.D. System Available	H.D. System Required	H.D. System Required
Shock Absorbers	H.D. units Available		
Sway Bar	—	—	—
Steering Recommended	Std.	Std.	Std.
Battery Recommended	Std.	Std.	Std.
Alternator	Std.	Std.	Std.
Turn Signal Flasher	Std.	Std.	Std.
Type Hitch Required	Frame	Equalizing	Equalizing

Trailer Towing Information

1971 Oldsmobile (Delta 88 [Custom Royale], Custom Cruiser, Ninety Eight and Luxury Toronado)

Equipment	Class I	Class II	Class III
Trailer Type	Any	Any	Any
Tongue Load Limit (lbs)	to 200 lbs	200 to 350 lbs	350 to 600 lbs
Engine Requirement	Std.	455 V-8 Required	455 V-8 Required
Exhaust System	Std.	Dual	Dual
Engine Cooling	H.D. System Recommended	H.D. System Required	H.D. System Required
Transmission Requirement	Turbo-Hydra-Matic 350 Recommended	Turbo-Hydra-Matic 400 Required	Turbo-Hydra-Matic 400 Required
Trans. Aux. Oil Cooler	—	—	—
Axle Ratio Recommended	Std.	3.08:1 or 3.42:1 Required	3.42:1 Required
Differential Type	Std.	Std.	Std.
Wheels Recommended	H.D.	H.D. Recommended	H.D. Required
Tires	Std.	Std.	Std.
Brakes Recommended	Std.	Std.	Std.
Front	Std.	Std.	Std.
Rear	Std.	Std.	Std.
Springs	*	*	*
Shock Absorbers	H.D. units are Available		
Sway Bar	*	*	*
Steering Recommended	Std.	Std.	Std.
Battery Recommended	Std.	Std.	Std.
Alternator	Std.	Std.	Std.
Turn Signal Flasher	Std.	Std.	Std.
Type Hitch Required	Frame	Equalizer	Equalizer

* Heavy Duty Suspension is available.
Note: The trailer wiring harness is recommended.

Trailer Towing Information

1970 Oldsmobile (Vista Cruiser, 4-4-2, Cutlass Supreme, Cutlass S, Cutlass and F-85)

Equipment	Class I	Class II	Class III
Trailer Type	Any	Any	Vista Cruiser
Tongue Load Limit (lbs)	to 200 lbs	200 to 350 lbs	350 to 600 lbs
Engine Requirement	350 V-8	350 V-8	455 V-8
Exhaust System	Std.	Std.	Std.
Engine Cooling	H.D. System Recommended	H.D. System Required	H.D. System Required
Transmission Requirement	Turbo-Hydra-Matic 350 Recommended	Turbo-Hydra-Matic 350 Required	Turbo-Hydra-Matic 400 Required
Trans. Aux. Oil Cooler	Recommended	Required	Required
Axle Ratio Recommended	3.08:1 Recommended	3.08:1 Required	3.08:1 Required
Differential Type	Anti-Spin Available		
Wheels Recommended	Std.	Std.	Std.
Tires	Std.	Std.	Std.
Brakes Recommended	Power Front Disc (Recommended)		
Front	Disc	Disc	Disc
Rear	Drum	Drum	Drum
Springs	*	*	*
Shock Absorbers	H.D. units are Available		
Sway Bar	*	*	*
Steering Recommended	Vari-Ratio Steering Available		
Battery Recommended	Std.	Std.	Std.
Alternator	Std.	Std.	Std.
Turn Signal Flasher	**	**	**
Type Hitch Required	Frame	Equalizer	Equalizer

* H.D. Suspension is recommended for all units.
** Trailer wiring harness is recommended.

Trailer Towing Information
1970 Oldsmobile (Toronado, Ninety-Eight, Delta Series Cars)

Equipment	Class I	Class II	Class III
Trailer Type	Any	Any	Any
Tongue Load Limit (lbs)	to 200 lbs	200 to 350 lbs	350 to 600 lbs
Engine Requirement	350 V-8	455 V-8	455 V-8
Exhaust System	Std.	Std.	Std.
Engine Cooling	H.D. System Required		
Transmission Requirement	Std.	Std.	Std.
Trans. Aux. Oil Cooler	Recommended	Required	Required
Axle Ratio Recommended	Std.	2.93:1 Required on All 98 Series	2.93:1 Required in all Delta Series
Differential Type	Std.	Anti-Spin Available	Anti-Spin Available
Wheels Recommended	Std.	Std.	Std.
Tires	Std.	Std.	Std.
Brakes Recommended	Front Disc Std.	Front Disc Std.	Front Disc Std.
Front	Disc	Disc	Disc
Rear	Drum	Drum	Drum
Springs	*	*	*
Shock Absorbers	H.D. units available		
Sway Bar	*	*	*
Steering Recommended	Std.	Std.	Std.
Battery Recommended	Std.	Std.	Std.
Alternator	Std.	Std.	Std.
Turn Signal Flasher	**	**	**
Type Hitch Required	Frame	Equalizing	Equalizing

* H.D. Suspension is available for all models.
** Trailer wiring harness is available.

Trailer Towing Information
1969 Oldsmobile (Toronado, Ninety-Eight and Delta Series Cars)

Equipment	Class I	Class II	Class III
Trailer Type	Any	Any	All except Toronado
Tongue Load Limit (lbs)	to 200 lbs	200 to 350 lbs	350 to 600 lbs
Engine Requirement	350 V-8	455 V-8	455 V-8
Exhaust System	Std.	Std.	Std.
Engine Cooling	H.D. System Recommended	H.D. System Required	H.D. System Required
Transmission Requirement	Turbo-Hydra-Matic 400 Recommended	Turbo-Hydra-Matic 400 Required	Turbo-Hydra-Matic 400 Required
Trans. Aux. Oil Cooler	Recommended	Required	Required
Axle Ratio Recommended	Std.	2.93:1 Required Except Toronado 3.07:1	2.93:1 Required
Differential Type		Anti-Spin is Available	
Wheels Recommended	Std.	Std.	Std.
Tires	Fiberglass Belted units Available	Fiberglass Belted units Recommended	Fiberglass Belted Required
Brakes Recommended	Std.	Std.	Std.
Front	Std.	Std.	Std.
Rear	Std.	Std.	Std.
Springs	H.D. Not Required	H.D. Recommended	H.D. Required
Shock Absorbers	H.D. units Available	H.D. units Recommended	H.D. units Required
Sway Bar	—	—	—
Steering Recommended	Std.	Std.	Std.
Battery Recommended	Std.	Std.	Std.
Alternator	Std.	Std.	Std.
Turn Signal Flasher	✲	✲	✲
Type Hitch Required	Frame	Equalizer	Equalizer

✲ An electrical harness for all units is recommended.

Trailer Towing Information

1969 Oldsmobile (Vista Cruiser, 4-4-2, Cutlass Supreme, Cutlass Series Cars)

Equipment	Class I	Class II	Class III ▲
Trailer Type	Any	Any	—
Tongue Load Limit (lbs)	to 200 lbs	200 to 350 lbs	—
Engine Requirement	350 V-8 or 400 V-8	350 V-8 or 400 V-8	—
Exhaust System	Std.	Std.	—
Engine Cooling	H.D. System Recommended	H.D. System Required	—
Transmission Requirement	Turbo-Hydra-Matic 350 Required	Turbo-Hydra-Matic 400 Required	—
Trans. Aux. Oil Cooler	Recommended	Required	—
Axle Ratio Recommended	3.08:1 Required	3.08:1 Required	—
Differential Type	Anti-Spin Axle-Available	Anti-Spin Axle-Available	—
Wheels Recommended	Std.	Std.	—
Tires	Fiberglass Belted Available	Fiberglass Belted Required	—
Brakes Recommended	Std.	Std.	—
Front	Std.	Std.	—
Rear	Std.	Std.	—
Springs	H.D. units Recommended	H.D. units Required	—
Shock Absorbers	H.D. units Recommended	H.D. units Required	—
Sway Bar	—	—	—
Steering Recommended	Std.	Std.	—
Battery Recommended	Std.	Std.	—
Alternator	Std.	Std.	—
Turn Signal Flasher	✻	✻	—
Type Hitch Required	Frame	Equalizing	—

✻ A trailer electrical package is recommended.
▲ It is not recommended that these cars tow Class III trailers.

1972 Trailer Towing Information

Pontiac (Full Size)

Equipment	Class I ●	Class II	Class III
Trailer Type	Any	Any	Any
Tongue Load Limit (lbs)	200	350	600
Engine Requirement	Std.①	400 cu in. V-8①	400 cu in. V-8①
Exhaust System	Std.	Std.②	Std.②
Engine Cooling	H.D.	H.D.	H.D.
Transmission Requirement	Std.	H.D.	H.D.
Trans. Aux. Oil Cooler	——	Yes	Yes
Axle Ratio Recommended	Std.	3.08:1	3.21:1
Differential Type	Std.	Std.	Std.
Wheels Recommended	H.D. 15 x 6	H.D. 15 x 6	H.D. 15 x 6
Tires	Std.	H78 x 15D③	H78 x 15D③
Brakes Recommended	Std.	Std.	Std.
Front	Std.	Std.	Std.
Rear	Std.	Std.	Std.
Springs	Std.	H.D.	H.D.④
Shock Absorbers	Std.	H.D.	H.D.
Sway Bar	——	——	——
Steering Recommended	Std.	Std.	Std.
Battery Recommended	Std.	Std.	Std.
Alternator	Std.	Std.	Std.
Turn Signal Flasher	H.D.	H.D.	H.D.
Type Hitch Required	Frame	Equalizer	Equalizer

● Firebird and Ventura can not tow a trailer over 1,000 lbs or 100 lbs tongue weight.
① Special spark plugs.
② Dual exhaust on 455 cu in. V-8 and 400 cu in. V-8 with 4 bbl. except Safaris.
③ L78 x 15D on Safaris.
④ H.D. frame.

1972 Trailer Towing Information

Le Mans and GTO

Equipment	Class I	Class II	Class III
Trailer Type	Any	Any	③
Tongue Load Limit (lbs)	200	350	③
Engine Requirement	350 cu in. V-8	350 cu in. V-8	③
Exhaust System	Std.	Std.	③
Engine Cooling	H.D.	H.D.	③
Transmission Requirement	Turbo-Hydra-Matic	Turbo-Hydra-Matic	③
Trans. Aux. Oil Cooler	—	—	③
Axle Ratio Recommended	Std.	Std.	③
Differential Type	Std.	Std.	③
Wheels Recommended	Std.	Std.	③
Tires	G78 x 14D①	G78 x 14D①	③
Brakes Recommended	Power	Power	③
Front	Std.	Std.	③
Rear	Std.	Std.	③
Springs	H.D.②	H.D.②	③
Shock Absorbers	H.D.	H.D.	③
Sway Bar	—	—	③
Steering Recommended	Std.	Std.	③
Battery Recommended	Std.	Std.	③
Alternator	Std.	Std.	③
Turn Signal Flasher	H.D.	H.D.	③
Type Hitch Required	Frame	Equalizer	③

① H78 x 14B on Wagons.
② H.D. Frame.
③ Vehicle is not recommended to tow a Class III trailer.

1972 Trailer Towing Information

Grand Prix

Equipment	Class I	Class II	Class III
Trailer Type	Any	Any	①
Tongue Load Limit (lbs)	200	350	①
Engine Requirement	400 cu in. V-8	400 cu in. V-8	①
Exhaust System	Std.	Std.	①
Engine Cooling	H.D.	H.D.	①
Transmission Requirement	Std.	Std.	①
Trans. Aux. Oil Cooler	——	——	①
Axle Ratio Recommended	Std.	Std.	①
Differential Type	Std.	Std.	①
Wheels Recommended	Std.	Std.	①
Tires	G78 x 14D	G78 x 14D	①
Brakes Recommended	Std.	Std.	①
Front	Std.	Std.	①
Rear	Std.	Std.	①
Springs	H.D.	H.D.	①
Shock Absorbers	H.D.	H.D.	①
Sway Bar	——	——	①
Steering Recommended	Std.	Std.	①
Battery Recommended	Std.	Std.	①
Alternator	Std.	Std.	①
Turn Signal Flasher	H.D.	H.D.	①
Type Hitch Required	Frame	Equalizer	①

① It is not recommended that Grand Prix tow Class III trailers.

1971 Trailer Towing Information

Pontiac except Grand Prix and Le Mans

Equipment	Class I	Class II	Class III
Trailer Type	Any	Any	Any
Tongue Load Limit (lbs)	200	350	600
Engine Requirement	Std.②	Std.②	Std.②
Exhaust System	Std.	Std.①	Std.①
Engine Cooling	H.D.	H.D.	H.D.
Transmission Requirement		H.D. Turbo Hydro	
Trans. Aux. Oil Cooler	—	Yes	Yes
Axle Ratio Recommended	3.08:1	3.08:1	3.23:1
Differential Type	Std.	Std.	Std.
Wheels Recommended	H.D.	H.D.	H.D.
Tires	Std.	H78 x 15D③	H78 x 15D③
Brakes Recommended	Std.	Std.	Std.
Front	Std.	Std.	Std.
Rear	Std.	Std.	Std.
Springs	Std.	H.D.	H.D.
Shock Absorbers	Std.	H.D.	H.D.
Sway Bar	—	—	—
Steering Recommended	Std.	Std.	Std.
Battery Recommended	Std.	Std.	Std.
Alternator	Std.	Std.	Std.
Turn Signal Flasher	H.D.	H.D.	H.D.
Type Hitch Required	Frame	Equalizer	Equalizer

① Dual Exhaust with 455 cu in. and 400 cu in. 4 bbl.
② Special spark plugs.
③ L78 x 15D on wagons.

1971 Trailer Towing Information
Grand Prix

Equipment	Class I	Class II	Class III
Trailer Type	Any	Any	①
Tongue Load Limit (lbs)	200	350	①
Engine Requirement	Std.	Std.	①
Exhaust System	Std.	Std.	①
Engine Cooling	H.D.	H.D.	①
Transmission Requirement	Std.	Std.	①
Trans. Aux. Oil Cooler	——	——	①
Axle Ratio Recommended	3.23:1	3.23:1	①
Differential Type	Std.	Std.	①
Wheels Recommended	Std.	Std.	①
Tires	G78 x 14D	G78 x 14D	①
Brakes Recommended	Std.	Std.	①
Front	Std.	Std.	①
Rear	Std.	Std.	①
Springs	H.D.	H.D.	①
Shock Absorbers	H.D.	H.D.	①
Sway Bar	——	——	①
Steering Recommended	Std.	Std.	①
Battery Recommended	Std.	Std.	①
Alternator	Std.	Std.	①
Turn Signal Flasher	H.D.	H.D.	①
Type Hitch Required	Frame	Equalizer	①

① It is not recommended that Grand Prix tow Class III trailers.

1971 Trailer Towing Information

Le Mans, GTO

Equipment	Class I	Class II	Class III
Trailer Type	Any	Any	③
Tongue Load Limit (lbs)	200	350	③
Engine Requirement	Std.	Std.	③
Exhaust System	Std.	Std.	③
Engine Cooling	H.D.	H.D.	③
Transmission Requirement	Std.	Std.	③
Trans. Aux. Oil Cooler	—	—	③
Axle Ratio Recommended	3.55:1	3.55:1	③
Differential Type	Std.	Std.	③
Wheels Recommended	Std.	Std.	③
Tires	G78 x 14D①	G78 x 14D①	③
Brakes Recommended	Power	Power	③
Front	Std.	Std.	③
Rear	Std.	Std.	③
Springs	H.D.②	H.D.②	③
Shock Absorbers	H.D.	H.D.	③
Sway Bar	—	—	③
Steering Recommended	Std.	Std.	③
Battery Recommended	Std.	Std.	③
Alternator	Std.	Std.	③
Turn Signal Flasher	H.D.	H.D.	③
Type Hitch Required	Frame	Equalizer	③

① H78 x 14B on wagons.
② H.D. frame.
③ Vehicle is not recommended to tow Class III trailers.

Trailer Towing Information
1970 Pontiac (Tempest, Le Mans, Le Mans Sport, GTO)

Equipment	Class I	Class II	Class III ▲
Trailer Type	Any	Any	—
Tongue Load Limit (lbs)	up to 200 lbs	200 to 350 lbs	—
Engine Requirement	Std.	Std.	—
Exhaust System	Std.	Std.	—
Engine Cooling	H.D. System & Flex Fan	H.D. System & Flex Fan	—
Transmission Requirement	Man. or Auto.	Man. or Auto.	—
Trans. Aux. Oil Cooler	Not Required	Not Required	—
Axle Ratio Recommended	3.55:1 Auto. 3.55:1 Man.	3.55:1 Auto. 3.55:1 Man.	—
Differential Type	Std.	Std.	—
Wheels Recommended	Std.	Std.	—
Tires	G78-14 Range D H78-14 Range B (Station Wagons)	G78-14 Range D H-78-14 Range B (Station Wagons)	—
Brakes Recommended	Std.	Std.	—
Front	Std.	Std.	—
Rear	Std.	Std.	—
Springs	H.D.	H.D.	—
Shock Absorbers	H.D.	H.D.	—
Sway Bar	N.A.	N.A.	—
Steering Recommended	Std.	Std.	—
Battery Recommended	Std.	Std.	—
Alternator	Std.	Std.	—
Turn Signal Flasher	Std.	Std.	—
Type Hitch Required	Frame	Equalizer Type	—

H.D.—Heavy Duty
Man.—Manual
Auto.—Automatic

Note: A special trailer-hauling package is available for all classes. It includes:
1. A constant rate directional flasher.
2. A special wiring harness.
3. Special spark plugs and heavy-duty wheels.

▲ Towing Class III trailers not recommended.

Trailer Towing Information

1970 Pontiac (Grand Prix)

Equipment	Class I	Class II	Class III ▲
Trailer Type	Any	Any	—
Tongue Load Limit (lbs)	up to 200 lbs	200 to 350 lbs	—
Engine Requirement	Std.	Std.	—
Exhaust System	Std.	Std.	—
Engine Cooling	H.D. System w/ Flex-Fan	H.D. System w/ Flex-Fan	—
Transmission Requirement	Std.	Std.	—
Trans. Aux. Oil Cooler	Not Required	Not Required	—
Axle Ratio Recommended	3.23:1 Auto. 3.23:1 Manual	3.23:1 Auto. 3.23:1 Manual	—
Differential Type	Std.	Std.	—
Wheels Recommended	Std.	Std.	—
Tires	G78-14 Range D	G78-14 Range D	—
Brakes Recommended	Std.	Std.	—
Front	Std.	Std.	—
Rear	Std.	Std.	—
Springs	H.D.	H.D.	—
Shock Absorbers	H.D.	H.D.	—
Sway Bar	—	—	—
Steering Recommended	Std.	Std.	—
Battery Recommended	Std.	Std.	—
Alternator	Std.	Std.	—
Turn Signal Flasher	Std.	Std.	—
Type Hitch Required	Frame	Equalizer Type	—

H.D.—Heavy Duty.
Man.—Manual.
Auto.—Automatic.
Note: A special trailer-hauling package is available for all classes. It includes:
1. A constant rate directional flasher.
2. A special wiring harness.
3. Special spark plugs and heavy-duty wheels.
▲ Towing Class III trailers not recommended.

Trailer Towing Information
1970 Pontiac (Bonneville, Executive, Catalina)

Equipment	Class I	Class II	Class III
Trailer Type	Any	Any	Any
Tongue Load Limit (lbs)	up to 200 lbs	200 to 350 lbs	350 to 600 lbs
Engine Requirement	Std.	Std.	Std.
Exhaust System	Standard	Dual	Dual
Engine Cooling	H.D. System w/ Flex Fan		
Transmission Requirement	Man. or Auto.	Man. or Auto. H.D. Turbo Hydromatic	Man. or Auto. H.D. Turbo Hydromatic
Trans. Aux. Oil Cooler	Not Required	Required	Required
Axle Ratio Recommended	2.93:1 Auto. 3.42:1 Manual	2.93:1 Auto. 3.42:1 Manual	2.93:1 Auto. 3.42:1 Manual
Differential Type	Std.	Std.	Std.
Wheels Recommended	H.D.	H.D.	H.D.
Tires	Std.	H78-15 Load Range D L78-15 or 9.15-15 on Station Wagons	H78-15 Load Range D L78-15 or 9.15-15 on Station Wagons
Brakes Recommended	Std.	Std.	Std.
Front	Std.	Std.	Std.
Rear	Std.	Std.	Std.
Springs	Std.	H.D.	H.D.
Shock Absorbers	Std.	H.D.	H.D.
Sway Bar	N.A.	N.A.	N.A.
Steering Recommended	Std.	Std.	Std.
Battery Recommended	Std.	Std.	Std.
Alternator	Std.	Std.	Std.
Turn Signal Flasher	Constant Rate Flasher		
Type Hitch Required	Frame	Frame	H.D. Frame

H.D.—Heavy Duty.
Note: A special trailer-hauling package is available for all classes. It includes:
1. A constant rate directional flasher.
2. A special wiring harness.
3. Special spark plugs and heavy-duty wheels.

Trailer Towing Information
1969 Pontiac (Tempest, Custom S, Le Mans, Le Mans Safari, GTO)

Equipment	Class I	Class II	Class III
Trailer Type	Any	—	—
Tongue Load Limit (lbs)	up to 200 lbs	—	—
Engine Requirement	Std.	—	—
Exhaust System	Std.	—	—
Engine Cooling	H.D. System w/ Flex Fan	—	—
Transmission Requirement	Man. or Auto.	—	—
Trans. Aux. Oil Cooler	Not Required	—	—
Axle Ratio Recommended	3.55:1 OHC 6 3.36:1 350 V-8	—	—
Differential Type	Std.	—	—
Wheels Recommended	Std.	—	—
Tires	8.25-14	—	—
Brakes Recommended	Std.	—	—
Front	Std.	—	—
Rear	Std.	—	—
Springs	H.D.	—	—
Shock Absorbers	H.D.	—	—
Sway Bar	—	—	—
Steering Recommended	Std.	—	—
Battery Recommended	Std.	—	—
Alternator	Std.	—	—
Turn Signal Flasher	Constant Rate Flasher	—	—
Type Hitch Required	Frame	—	—

H.D.—Heavy Duty.
Note: A special trailer-hauling package is available for all classes. It includes:
1. A constant rate directional flasher.
2. A special wiring harness.
3. Special spark plugs and heavy-duty wheels.

Trailer Towing Information
1969 Pontiac (Grand Prix)

Equipment	Class I	Class II	Class III
Trailer Type	Any	——	——
Tongue Load Limit (lbs)	up to 200 lbs	——	——
Engine Requirement	400 cu in. V-8	——	——
Exhaust System	Std.	——	——
Engine Cooling	H.D. System w/ Flex Fan	——	——
Transmission Requirement	Turbo-Hydra-Matic	——	——
Trans. Aux. Oil Cooler	Not Required	——	——
Axle Ratio Recommended	Std.	——	——
Differential Type	Std.	——	——
Wheels Recommended	Std.	——	——
Tires	Std.	——	——
Brakes Recommended	Std.	——	——
Front	Std.	——	——
Rear	Std.	——	——
Springs	H.D.	——	——
Shock Absorbers	H.D.	——	——
Sway Bar	——	——	——
Steering Recommended	Std.	——	——
Battery Recommended	Std.	——	——
Alternator	Std.	——	——
Turn Signal Flasher	Contant Rate Flasher	——	——
Type Hitch Required	Frame	——	——

H.D.—Heavy Duty
Note: A special trailer-hauling package is available for all classes. It includes:
1. A constant rate directional flasher.
2. A special wiring harness.
3. Special spark plugs and heavy-duty wheels.

Trailer Towing Information
1969 Pontiac (Catalina, Executive, Bonneville)

Equipment	Class I	Class II	Class III
Trailer Type	Any	Any	Any
Tongue Load Limit (lbs)	up to 200 lbs	200 to 350 lbs	350 to 600 lbs
Engine Requirement	Std.	Std.	Std.
Exhaust System	Std.	Std.	Std.
Engine Cooling	H.D. System w/ Flex Fan		
Transmission Requirement	Man. or Auto.	Auto. (Turbo-Hydra-Matic)	Auto. (Turbo-Hydra-Matic)
Trans. Aux. Oil Cooler	Not Required	Required	Required
Axle Ratio Recommended	2.93:1 Catalina & Executive 3.08:1 Bonneville	3.08:1 All Models	3.23:1 All Models
Differential Type	Std.	Std.	Std.
Wheels Recommended	Std.	Std.	Std.
Tires	Std.	8.85-15	8.85-15
Brakes Recommended	Std.	Std.	Std.
Front	Std.	Std.	Std.
Rear	Std.	Std.	Std.
Springs	Std.	H.D.	H.D.
Shock Absorbers	Std.	H.D.	H.D.
Sway Bar	—	—	—
Steering Recommended	Std.	Std.	Std.
Battery Recommended	Std.	Std.	Std.
Alternator	Std.	Std.	Std.
Turn Signal Flasher	Constant Rate Flasher		
Type Hitch Required	Frame	Frame	H.D. Frame

H.D.—Heavy Duty
Note: A special trailer-hauling package is available for all classes. It includes:
1. A constant rate directional flasher.
2. A special wiring harness.
3. Special spark plugs and heavy-duty wheels.

Trailer Towing Information

1968 Pontiac (Tempest, Tempest Custom, Tempest Safari, Le Mans, GTO)

Equipment	Class I	Class II	Class III
Trailer Type	Any	—	—
Tongue Load Limit (lbs)	up to 200 lbs	—	—
Engine Requirement	Std.	—	—
Exhaust System	Std.	—	—
Engine Cooling	H.D. System w/ H.D. Fan	—	—
Transmission Requirement	Man. & Auto.	—	—
Trans. Aux. Oil Cooler	Not Required	—	—
Axle Ratio Recommended	3.55:1 w/ OHC 6 cyl. 3.36:1 w/ 350 V-8	—	—
Differential Type	Std.	—	—
Wheels Recommended	Std.	—	—
Tires	Std.	—	—
Brakes Recommended	Std.	—	—
Front	Std.	—	—
Rear	Std.	—	—
Springs	H.D.	—	—
Shock Absorbers	H.D.	—	—
Sway Bar	—	—	—
Steering Recommended	Std.	—	—
Battery Recommended	Std.	—	—
Alternator	Std.	—	—
Turn Signal Flasher	Constant Rate Flasher	—	—
Type Hitch Required	Frame	—	—

H.D.—Heavy Duty.
Note: A special trailer-hauling package is available for all classes. It includes:
1. A constant rate directional flasher.
2. A special wiring harness.
3. Special spark plugs and heavy-duty wheels.

Trailer Towing Information
1968 Pontiac (Catalina, Executive, Bonneville, Grand Prix)

Equipment	Class I	Class II	Class III
Trailer Type	Any	Any	Any
Tongue Load Limit (lbs)	up to 200 lbs	200 to 350 lbs	350 to 600 lbs
Engine Requirement	Std.	Std.	Std.
Exhaust System	Std.	Std.	Std.
Engine Cooling	H.D. w/ H.D. Fan		
Transmission Requirement	Man. or Auto. (Turbo-Hydra-Matic)		
Trans. Aux. Oil Cooler	Not Required	Required	Required
Axle Ratio Recommended	2.93:1 w/ Turbo-Hydra-Matic	3.08:1 w/ H.D. Turbo-Hydra-Matic	3.23:1 w/ H.D. Turbo-Hydra-Matic
Differential Type	Std.	Std.	Std.
Wheels Recommended	Std.	Std.	Std.
Tires	Std.	Std.	Std.
Brakes Recommended	Std.	Std.	Std.
Front	Std.	Std.	Std.
Rear	Std.	Std.	Std.
Springs	Std.	H.D.	H.D.
Shock Absorbers	Std.	H.D.	H.D.
Sway Bar	—	—	—
Steering Recommended	Std.	Std.	Std.
Battery Recommended	Std.	Std.	Std.
Alternator	Std.	Std.	Std.
Turn Signal Flasher	Constant Rate Flasher		
Type Hitch Required	Frame	Equalizer	Equalizer

H.D.—Heavy Duty
Note: A special trailer-hauling package is available for all classes. It includes:
1. A constant rate directional flasher.
2. A special wiring harness.
3. Special spark plugs and heavy-duty wheels.

3 · Water and Sewage

The Water System

The water system in the average travel trailer can vary from just a water tank, hand pump, and drain, to a fairly complicated plumbing system complete with a water tank, electric pump with a pressure-sensitive switch, hot and cold water faucets, showers heads, and all of the necessary drains which can either empty into the holding tank or out of the trailer by way of a sewer line.

You should become familiar with your trailer's water system. Refer to the owner's manual for the diagram of the system and find out where all of the components are located so if one goes bad you can replace it without having to hunt all around looking for the part that has to be replaced. Also there might be an access panel somewhere that will help you to get at the particular part without tearing everything apart.

THE WATER PUMP

There are several varieties of water pumping systems that are installed in travel trailers. Some rely on the city water pressure to supply the system with water. If such is the case, you must be careful about pressure. Be sure that your trailer's plumbing can handle the pressure of a city's water system. (Most cities' water pressure is about 40 to 60 psi.) While most trailers are able to cope with this pressure range, problems may arise with camp ground facilities. Campsite water pressure may reach as high as 250 psi for short periods of time which can damage the plumbing in a travel trailer.

There are devices available that reduce pressure to 35 psi, coming into the trailer. They are installed in the incoming line of the trailer before any components and some trailers come from the manufacturer with these regulators already fitted. It would be wise to have one of these installed if your trailer is not equipped with one.

A hand-operated pump is usually installed on the smaller travel trailers where space is at a premium. It is mounted at the sink and works on the muscle principle: the harder you pump, the more you get. The plunger in the cylinder of the pump creates a limited vacuum which sucks the water from the water tank and "blows" it out through the faucet.

Electric pumps are fastened in an inline connection between the water tank and the faucets. The switch to activate the pump is sometimes located in the handle of the faucet. When the faucet is turned on, the circuit is closed and the pump starts to operate. When the water is turned off, so is the switch and the pump stops

WATER AND SEWAGE

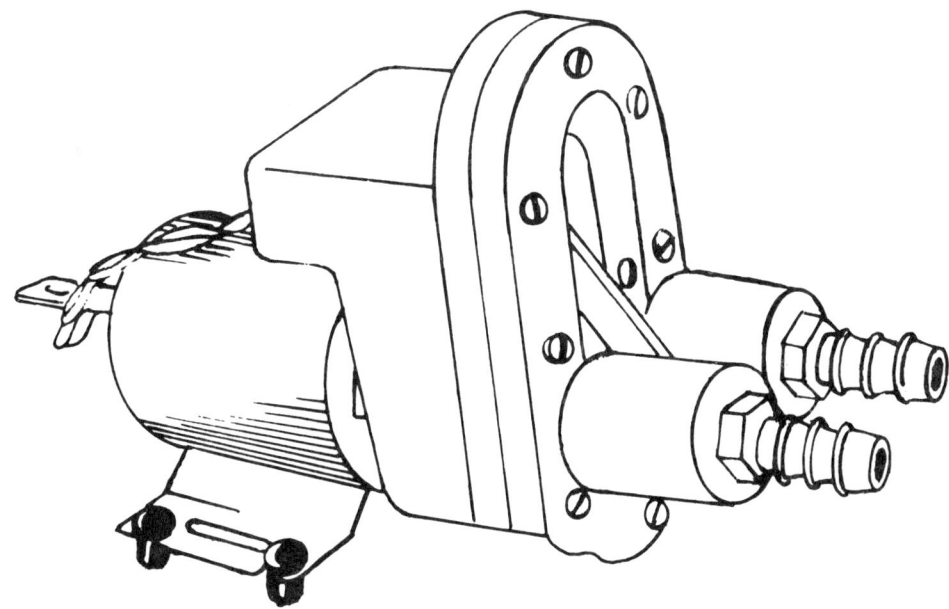

An electric pump.

pumping. This type of set-up is used only on systems with one faucet.

On trailers with more than one faucet, it is rather inconvenient to install several electrical circuits to operate the pump, so a pressure-sensitive switch is installed in the output line of the pump. When the pressure decreases due to the opening of a faucet, the pump goes on; when the faucet is shut, the pressure builds up and the switch turns off the pump.

There are also combinations of the three types of systems mentioned above. One in particular combines all three into one faucet fixture.

One other type of system uses an air pump to induce pressure into the system. An electric motor is activated by a pressure-sensitive switch when the air pressure in the water tank is lowered to a certain point by the removal of water from the tank. Air is then pumped into the remaining air space in the tank. On most of these systems it is possible to "charge" the system with an air pressure hose similar to those found in gas stations. There is a valve on the outside of the trailer that can receive the nozzle of a standard air hose so the system can be charged from outside the trailer. It is also possible to put air pressure into the tank by using a hand tire pump. This would be handy to have in case the electric driven pump should fail.

NOTE: *Always remember to turn off the main switch to the water pump when the pump is not being used; even for a matter of hours.*

A fuse should be installed in the power line to the water pump as close to the power source as possible. A filter should also be present in the line from the water source to the pump to prevent any harmful sand or grit from damaging the mechanism.

Water Pump Removal

To remove the water pump from the trailer, use the following procedure.

1. Turn off the water supply and the pump switch.
2. Remove the electrical input to the pump.
3. Remove the input and output hoses to the pump, being certain to tag them before removal.

An air pump.

100 WATER AND SEWAGE

Water Pump Troubleshooting Chart

Condition	Remedy
1. Pump runs but there is no pressure	1. Check the water level in the holding tank. 2. Make certain that the electrical power is sufficient. 3. See that all the required valves are open. 4. Check for leaks. 5. Check for suction at the pump. If there is none, the pump must be repaired or replaced.
2. Noise in the pump	1. Examine the pump mounting bolts for looseness. 2. Make certain that both inlet and outlet hoses are clear and properly installed. 3. If the faucet has an aerator, remove it and check for blockage.
3. Pump does not run	1. Check the electrical connections for contact. 2. Check the amount of current to the pump motor. 3. Examine the pump for defects.

4. Loosen and remove the pump attaching screws and remove the pump from the trailer.

5. Replacement is accomplished by reversing the above procedure.

OPERATION

To prime the system, perform the following steps.

1. Fill the fresh water holding tank, making sure all the drain valves are closed.
2. Energize the main current to the pump.
3. Keep all outlets open until water appears.
4. Close the outlet and de-energize the pump (if the pump is equipped with a manual energizer switch.)

NOTE: *Large iron and lime deposits are found in the water of some sections of the country. Because of this, it is a good idea to flush the water tank frequently by mixing a cleaning solution of bicarbonate of soda and water (¼ to ½ lbs of soda). This mixture is then poured into the water tank and left overnight. Rinse the tank clean and refill it with drinking water.*

WATER HEATER

Water heaters are usually not included, in smaller travel trailers. They are, however, offered as an option on most models. The heater serves as one more means of bringing the comforts of home with you away from home.

The two basic types of water heaters are gas and electric. The gas type heats the water by means of a flame encompassing the cold water coils while the electric

Water heater showing outside vent.

heats by transferring heat from the electric coils which surround the water jackets. Neither type, to work correctly, can allow any air in its water system. This condition is ensured by allowing water to run from all the hot water faucets until it runs smoothly.

Gas-operated heaters work on the same principle as gas-operated refrigerators. (See "Refrigerator.") They utilize a thermocouple. Use the same procedure for

WATER AND SEWAGE

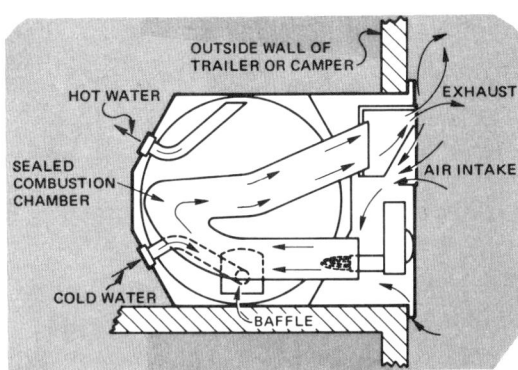

Diagram of a gas hot water heater showing the flow of air through the unit.

starting the pilot as was used to start the pilot on the refrigerator.

Since the heater's operating principles are similar to those of the gas-operated refrigerator, it will have approximately the same malfunctions. If the heater does not operate, check the obvious causes first. It is usually something simple such as having the gas run out or having the pilot blow out. Malfunctions in the electric system are few but the most frequent are shorted or loose wires. Any other problem with either gas or electric units should be serviced by qualified personnel only.

NOTE: *There have been some cases in which a low, off-colored flame has been produced by an obstruction in the air supply tube located just before the burner of the gas units. Compressed air is recommended to remove the obstruction.*

Whenever the unit is to be stored, especially during the winter season when the temperature drops below freezing, it is necessary to drain the water heater before storage. This is accomplished by opening the faucets in the camper and then opening the drain valve located on the outside of the trailer. Allow the system to drain completely before closing the drain valve and the faucets. See "Storage and Winterizing."

The Sewage System

The sewage system of the average travel trailer consists of the toilet assembly, the plumbing, and the holding tank assembly with various valves for draining and dumping the holding tank. There is also a large hose (usually 3-4 in. in diameter) that is used for dumping the holding tank.

Some travel trailers have just one holding tank that receives the waste from the toilet, while others receive the wastes from the toilet, and the wash basins and sinks. Still other trailers have two holding tanks, one for the toilet and one for the basins and the sinks.

Consult the trailer owner's manual for the location of the various components and the access panels that can be removed for servicing. Also follow the recommended maintenance procedures to minimize the possibility of component failure.

Be careful to note which chemicals can be added to your holding tank without fear of damage. Chemicals are added to deodorize and dissolve the waste matter in the tank. If you have a Thermasan® waste destruction unit, you must use special chemicals to treat waste materials.

TOILET ASSEMBLY

There are three basic types of toilets used in trailers: the fresh water type; recirculating type; and the portable type.

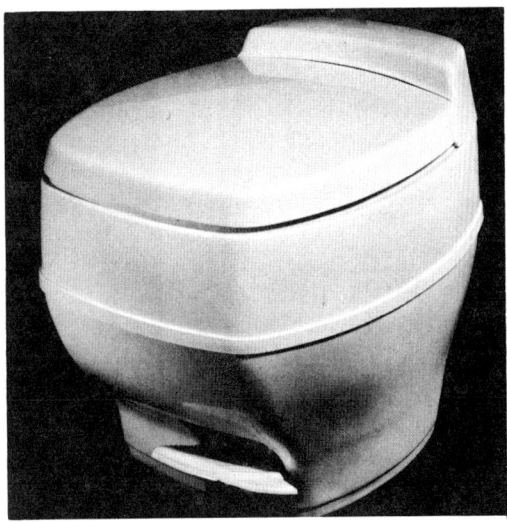

A fresh water type toilet.

The fresh water type works, as the name indicates, from the fresh water holding tank. Every time the unit is used, a new supply of water is circulated by the pump through the toilet and transferred with the waste to the holding tank.

The recirculating type toilet was adapted from aircraft use. It is a completely independent type, powered by an

WATER AND SEWAGE

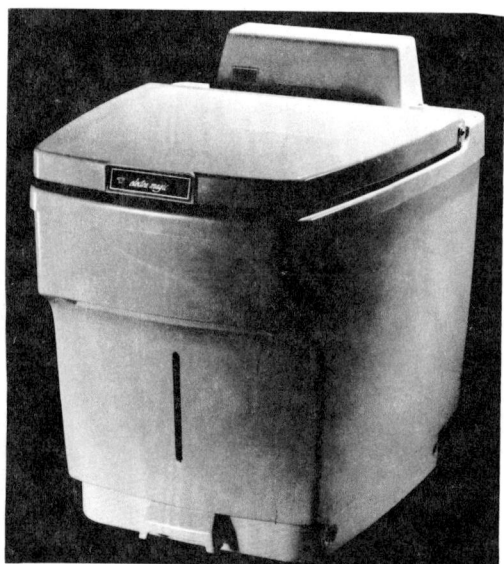

A recirculating type toilet.

electric motor. There is a storage facility for approximately eight gallons of fluid inside the tank. It is filled with four gallons of water and the added chemicals, and is good for about 80 to 100 uses. On trailers equipped with a holding tank, the toilet may be drained into the tank and refilled for continued usage.

The portable type toilets are most common on smaller travel trailers and consist of a unit which can be moved from one place to another. It is totally self-con-

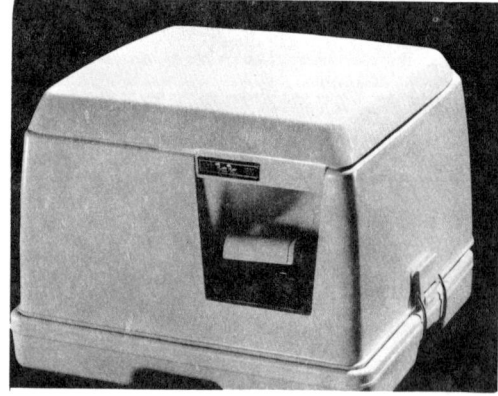

A portable type toilet.

tained, simply consisting of the toilet assembly and two separate tanks. One tank holds fresh water while the other acts as the holding tank into which the chemicals are added.

To use this type of unit, there are usually two foot controls: one lever to open the holding tank valve which will allow the entrance of the waste from the bowl to the holding tank, and the pump lever which will circulate the fresh water from the fresh water tank into the toilet bowl. Most of the units include a detachable waste tank which can be removed for disposal.

The portable types are truly movable with limited effort. Because of this and their ease of maintenance they are most popular in the smaller trailers when the owner does not truly want to rough it.

Installing a Toilet

Before you start cutting holes in your floor, decide whether or not it is practical to have a toilet in your trailer. Do you have the space to spare? Will you have to install a holding tank? Where will you put it? Just what type do you want? Would a portable toilet be sufficient or do you need something with a little more capacity and self-containment? You should talk over these questions with your local travel trailer dealer or RV center.

Once you have decided what type of toilet you want, try to find a place to put it. It is often hard to give up valuable storage space, but if you do a clever job, you might not lose that much. It might be possible to install it in an existing floor-length closet if you want it fully enclosed. Another approach is to locate it under a dinette seat or in an unused corner, covering it with a cabinet that can be used as a regular seat. The trick here is to use your imagination and engineering know-how.

Of course you will have to locate the toilet close to the holding tank, if your toilet requires one. Preferably, it will be mounted directly over the holding tank.

If you are adding a toilet to your rig, figure on a space 15–20 in. wide and 20 in. deep. Most models are 18–19 in. high but there are some as low as 12 in.

If you are replacing a toilet, your job is a bit easier. Be sure to check the dimensions so that the new one will fit in the old one's space. You might even be able to pick up some additional space if you use one of the compact designs that are now available. Always use a new seal under the toilet when you replace the old one.

Make sure that the holding tank in your trailer is designed to handle toilet wastes.

If not, you will have to install one that is so designed. If your trailer never had a holding tank, you will have to be careful where you put it. Invariably it has to go under the floor. Be sure it has enough road clearance for the tank to be safe from objects being thrown up by the tires or bottoming out when the trailer hits a hole. Install the holding tank so it is easily accesible for emptying and cleaning.

Drill the correct size hole in the floor over the spot you have picked out and install the floor flange. Secure the toilet over the hole with the proper hardware that should be supplied by the manufacturer. Do not tighten the nuts too tightly because of the danger of cracking the toilet bowl

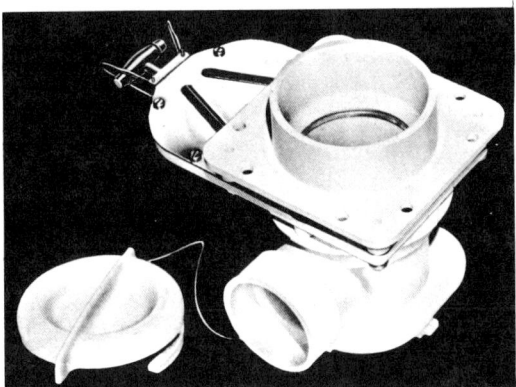

Waste valve.

or housing. Tap into the nearest water line and run it to the toilet. Of course, if you choose one of the self-contained types, you won't have to worry about this particular job.

NOTE: *Remember that the installation of a toilet will cause your present holding tank to fill more rapidly than before so it will require emptying more often. Maybe you should install a larger one if at all possible.*

Operation of a Recirculating Type Toilet

Generally these units are primed with a prescribed amount of water, usually 4–5 gallons. Check the operating instructions obtained with the unit. When the system is flushed, there is an apparent change in the noise level of the water on some units. This signals that the water has reached the water capacity.

Once the water is added, flush the toilet and add the necessary chemicals. The manufacturer of the system will state the type of chemicals to be used and the intervals at which they are to be added. Once the chemicals are added, flush through about five cycles to ensure thorough mixing of the chemicals and water. The unit is now ready for use.

The newly charged system is capable of about 80 usages or approximately five days. It is recommended that the system be cleaned after each trip. The unit is full when the fluid level becomes evident at the bottom of the bowl.

If the unit is used when the temperature drops below freezing, add antifreeze to the initial charge. Some manufacturers recommend that only ethylene glycol base antifreeze be used and not any alcohol products. Check the manufacturer's literature for the recommended antifreeze before experimenting.

Emptying the System

If the trailer is equipped with a holding tank, a direct line can be connected from the toilet to the holding tank to allow the toilet to be drained at will.

If there is no holding tank available, connect a hose to the drainage duct, at the base of the toilet assembly, and slowly open the discharge valve to release the waste. Discharge the waste at only a certified disposal station. Once the waste is discharged, fill the unit with approximately 4–6 gallons of water and ½ cup of toilet cleaner. Leave the mixture overnight for the best results, then drain and flush the unit with clean water before recharging.

Winterizing the System

Drain the input line to the toilet assembly and then, by pumping the foot pedal of the toilet, remove all the water from the system. It is important to remove *all* water since freezing temperatures will cause water expansion and subsequent damage to the plumbing system.

The waste holding tank should be cleaned, rinsed, and drained of all water, and then blown dry with compressed air if possible. Once the system is cleaned and drained, some chemicals should be added to the system to prevent rust and the other harmful effects of low temperatures. Consult your owner's manual for those chemicals the manufacturer recommends.

If the camper is to be used during the

WATER AND SEWAGE

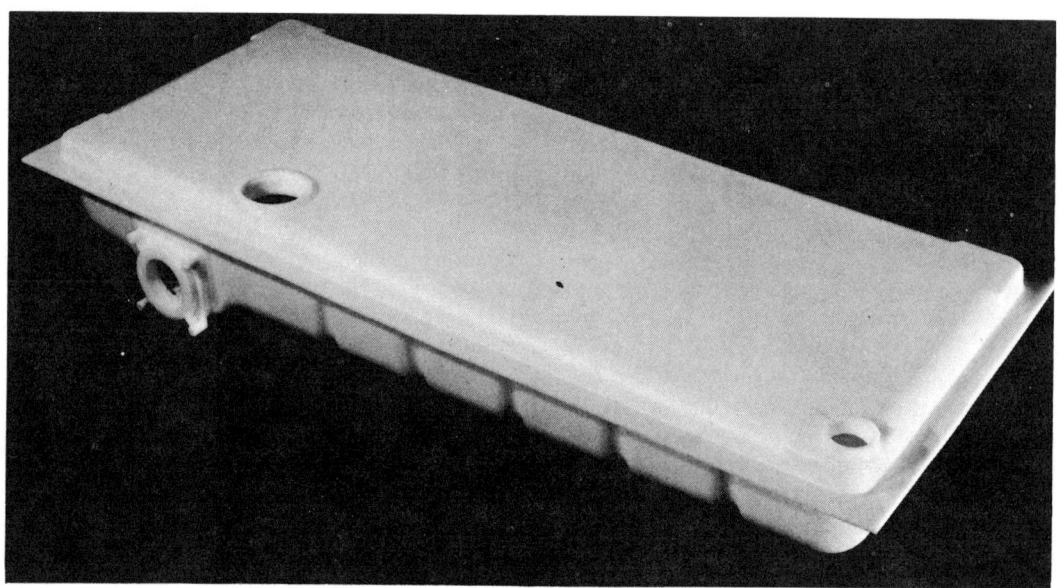

Holding Tank.

winter, the system must be protected from freezing. There are a great number of commercial antifreeze additives which are normally added but first consult your dealer for his recommendations.

WATER TANK REMOVAL

Because of the various locations of water tanks, the procedure listed below is a general removal procedure which can be adapted for each specific model.

To remove the water tank, perform the following:

1. Drain the water tank completely.
2. Remove the connections from the inlet and outlet hoses and also the vent hose.
3. Make sure all the connections to the tank are removed (including the electrical connections if they are present).
4. Remove the tank shielding from the underside of the tank (if so equipped).
5. Loosen and remove the tank supports while bracing the tank assembly from the bottom.
6. Remove the tank from the chassis.
7. Installation may be accomplished by reversing the removal procedure.

NOTE: *Any insulating material which is removed must be replaced when the tank is reinstalled.*

HOLDING TANK

Holding tank capacities usually vary from 15 to 25 gallons. The size depends on the type of system used in the trailer. Generally there are three types of drainage systems: single-tank; two-tank; and the by-pass holding tank systems.

The single-tank system is the type where all the drainage outlets empty into one holding tank. Of course this necessitates the use of a larger holding tank than the others. The two-tank system provides a separate tank which is directly connected to the toilet while another tank holds the waste from the shower and sink. The by-pass system consists of a holding tank for the toilet waste while all other waste is channeled from the camper, either through a sewer line or a catch receptacle.

Emptying the Holding Tank

NOTE: *It is of paramount importance that the holding tank of any trailer be emptied only at an approved disposal site. Most well-equipped campgrounds have dumping stations. There are severe penalties imposed by law enforcement agencies for violators.*

Drainage of the tank can be accomplished by fastening the discharge hose from the trailer to the fitting on the sewer opening. Make certain that both connections—at the trailer and the sewer—are made securely as there will be a fair amount of pressure flowing through the waste line and a leak may prove to be unpleasant. The tank should be washed out with clean water once it has been drained.

Also wash the inside of the drain hose. As a final measure, add the proper chemicals to the holding tank as recommended by the trailer manufacturer.

THERMASAN

The Thermasan is a waste disposal or, more appropriately, a waste destruction system. It utilizes the very high temperatures in the exhaust system of the tow vehicle to actually burn up the waste materials. The operating temperatures that must be reached inside the exhaust system are anywhere from 900 to 1000° F. It is absolutely impossible for any bacteria, small waste particles, or odors to survive these temperatures.

The greatest advantage of this system is that it eliminates the need to frequently empty the holding tank. This is not to say that it completely does away with having to find a dumping station once in a while. The Thermasan does not interfere in any way with the manual method of evacuating the holding tank. Since the Thermasan will only operate at speeds above 30 or 40 mph, there will be times that the unit will not operate, such as in stop-and-go traffic and on country roads where you can't reach and maintain the necessary speed for a sufficient amount of time. You will not be able to evacuate your holding tank completely every time you have it turned on.

The Thermasan system is broken down into two basic sections, the plumbing circuit and the electrical circuits. Basically, the plumbing portions of the system are mounted on the trailer and the electrical portions are mounted on the tow vehicle.

The components of the system are listed below. They are broken into the two divisions of plumbing and electrical components.

Plumbing

1. The evacuation probe in the holding tank.
2. The rubber tubing that runs from the holding tank to the tongue of the trailer.

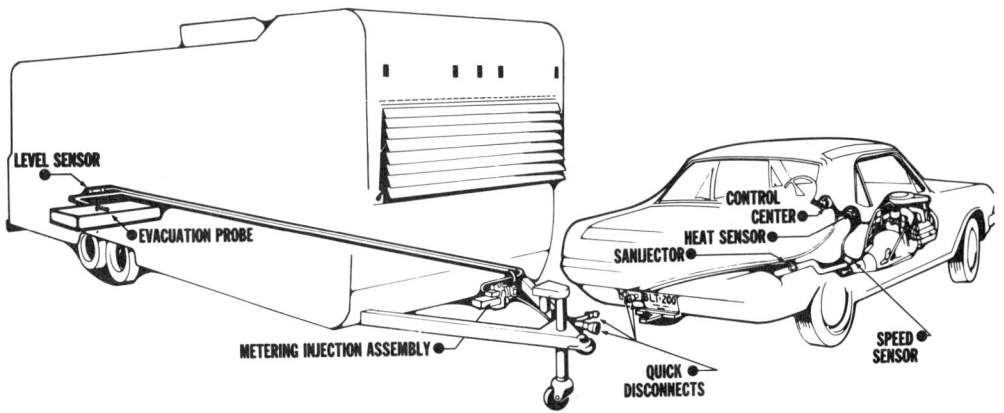

Location of all the components of the Thermasan on the two vehicles.

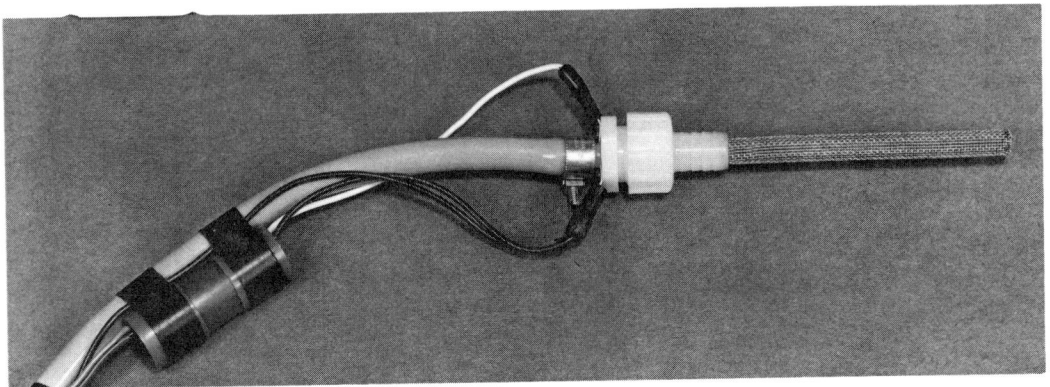

Evacuation probe with the level sensor attached.

106 WATER AND SEWAGE

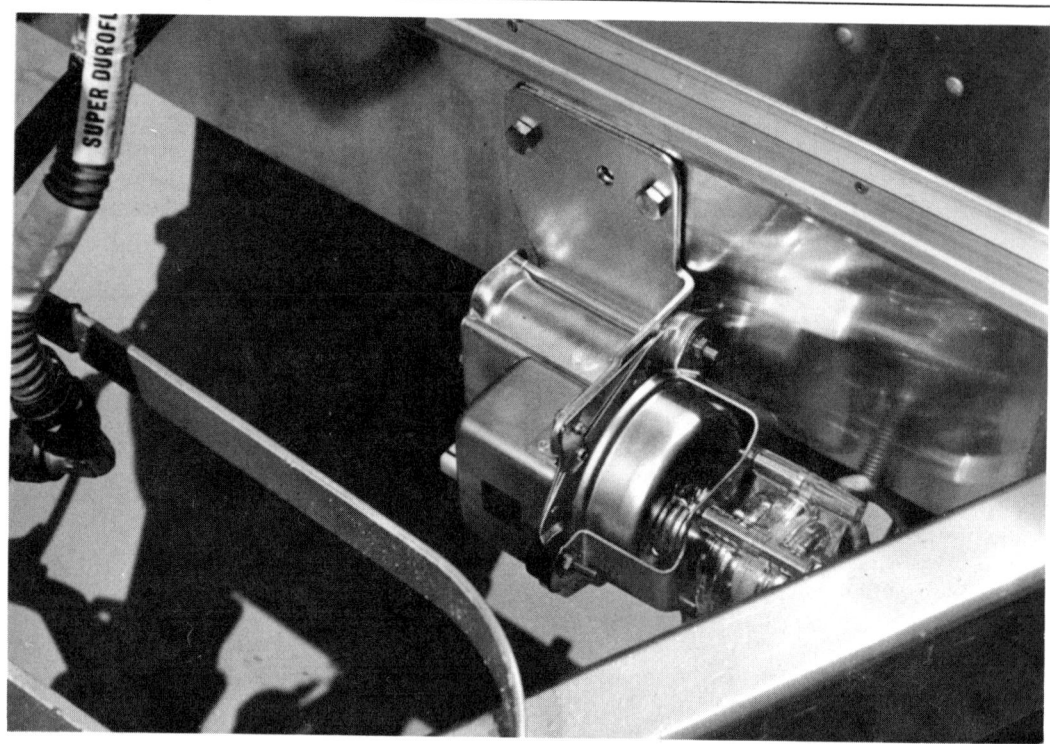

Metering injection assembly mounted on the trailer in the proper position.

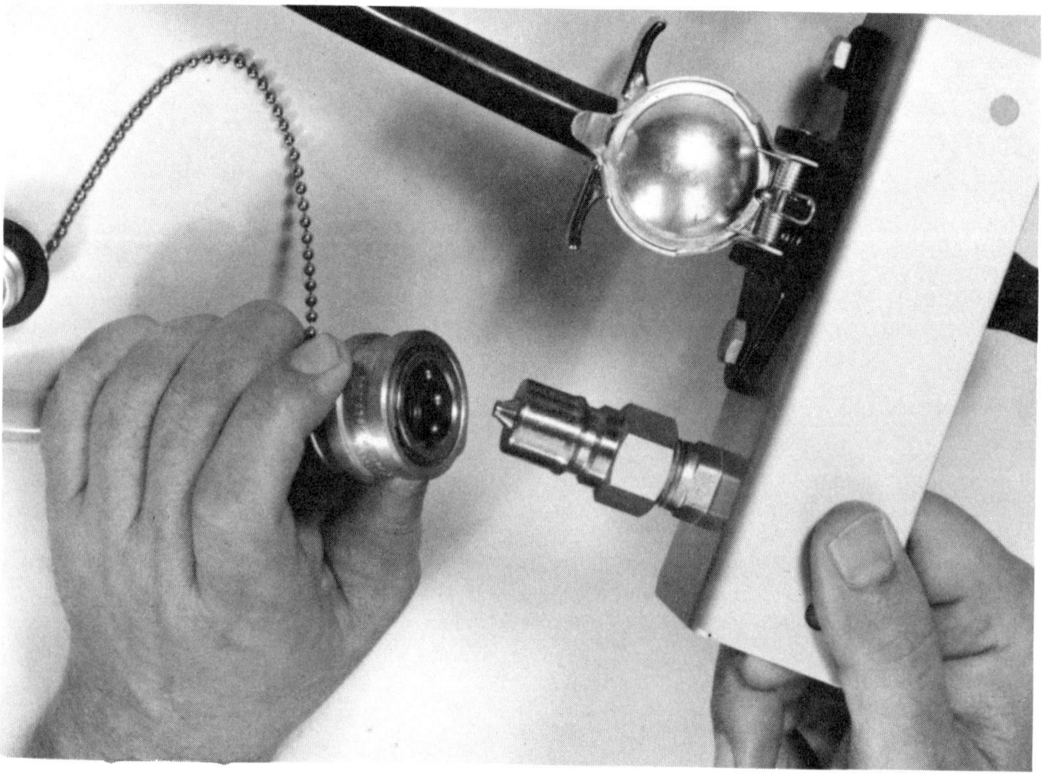

The liquid and electrical quick-disconnect assembly.

3. A metering injection assembly that regulates the flow of waste material into the tow vehicle's exhaust system. This component is mounted on the tongue of the trailer.

4. Liquid quick-disconnect coupler between the tow vehicle and the trailer.

5. Rubber tubing that runs from the rear of the car to the sanijector.

6. The sanijector, which is hooked into the tow vehicle's exhaust system. The sanijector's nozzle sprays the treated waste into the exhaust pipes.

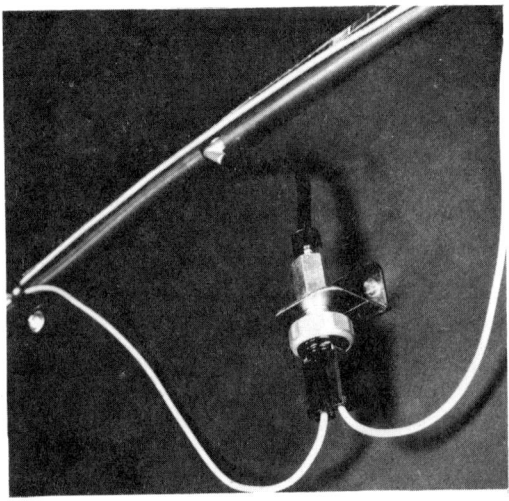

The heat sensor.

The sanijector installed on an exhaust pipe.

Also included in the plumbing component could be the chemicals that are placed in the holding tank to break down and deodorize the waste material.

Electrical

1. A level sensor that tells the system, when the holding tank is empty, to stop operating.

2. Electrical quick-disconnects between the tow vehicle and the trailer.

3. The speed sensor that tells the unit when the car is going fast enough for the system to operate.

4. A heat sensor that tells the unit when the exhaust gases are hot enough to burn the treated wastes.

5. The control center that is mounted under the tow vehicle's dash. The control unit monitors the speed and temperature of the car. If either the speed or the temperature of the tow vehicle drops below certain levels, the Thermasan stops pumping the treated wastes into the exhaust system. There are three lights on the control center's face that tell the driver whether or not the Thermasan is on, if it is burning the treated wastes, and if the holding tank is empty and he should turn off the unit. The on/off switch is also located on the control center's face.

Following is an explanation of how all of the components work and what happens when you turn that little button on the control panel.

Let's assume that you have already put the chemical solvent in the holding tank before you started driving. Now you are out on the road starting to cruise at about 50 mph and are expecting to maintain that speed for some time.

Turn on the on/off switch on the control center and a red light will come on to tell you that the Thermasan is on. The heat sensor tells the control center whether or not the engine is hot enough for the waste to burn. If it is, then it closes an electrical

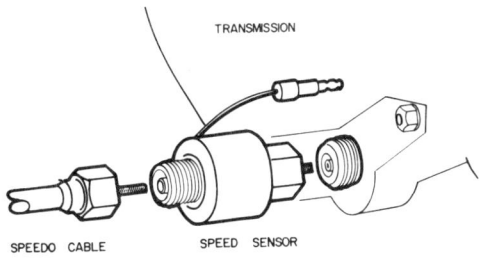

The speed sensor is mounted on the transmission before the speedometer cable.

WATER AND SEWAGE

The control center mounted under the dash of a tow vehicle.

circuit to the speed sensor. The speed sensor tells whether or not the car is traveling fast enough. If so, an electrical circuit is closed to the control center. When the circuit is closed, a green light comes on and the control center closes another electrical circuit to the metering injection assembly mounted on the trailer tongue. The metering injection assembly then begins to drain the holding tank through the evacuation probe. The waste material flows up toward the front of the trailer and into the metering injection assembly. The flow is regulated and pumped through the quick-disconnect coupler and up to the sanijector. The treated waste is injected into the exhaust pipe and completely destroyed. All wastes, bacteria, and gaseous by-products are destroyed and rendered odorless and harmless. When the tank is almost empty, a white light comes on at the control center to let you know that you should soon turn off the system. This is done by the level sensor in the holding tank. When the tank is empty, the green light goes out letting you know that the pump has stopped and the unit is to be turned off.

There are three types of Thermasan arrangements for travel trailers. One is for holding tanks that collect both toilet wastes and sink, basin, and shower wash water. Another type is only to be used to evacuate toilet wastes. The third type is for trailers with two holding tanks; one for toilet wastes only, and one for sink, basin, and shower wash water wastes. This type of unit draws from both tanks at the same rate.

If odors develop, don't immediately conclude that the system is malfunctioning. It may be a temporary lack of sufficient heat in the exhaust system. This can happen during a heavy rainstorm when water is splashing up on the exhaust pipes and cooling them enough to prevent the wastes from burning at a high enough temperature.

Take good care of the quick-disconnect couplers. Put the caps over them when they are not in use. Be very careful not to get dirt or any other foreign substance in the coupler.

Installation

The installation of the Thermasan is a fairly complicated procedure, requiring twenty-four separate operations. Unless

		Travel Trailers		
Model BT	200	●	Model 200	In this system, only toilet wastes are collected in the holding tank. Sink, shower and basin wash water bypass the holding tank.
	600	●	Model 600	Sink, shower and basin wash water and toilet wastes all collect in a single holding tank.
	2-500	●		
Model BLT	200	●	Model 2-500	The Vehicle has two holding tanks. One for toilet wastes and the other for waste water. Order this type when you want your Thermasan to draw wastes from both tanks at the same time.
	600	●		
	2-500	●	Note:	The BLT is the system with the level sensor. All systems for travel trailers are "BT" labeled.

The two models and three applications of the Thermasan.

you have a reasonable amount of mechanical ability, have your Thermasan installed by a dealer. If you do, however, decide to perform the installation yourself, follow the procedure carefully—especially noting those italicized subdivisions with separate heads.

When you receive your Thermasan kit, the carton should contain the following pieces:
1. Hardware package
2. Wiring harness assembly
3. Metering injection assembly
4. PVC hose
5. Tank sensor assembly
6. Probe assembly—evacuation
7. Level indicator (optional equipment).

The above items are installed on the trailer half of the system. The items listed below are installed on the tow vehicle half of the system.
1. Control center assembly
2. Speed sensor assembly
3. Heat sensor assembly
4. Sanijector assembly
5. Quick-disconnect assembly
6. Harness assembly
7. Hose silicone
8. Hardware package

MOUNTING OF THE CONTROL CENTER
MODULE TO THE DASH OF THE
TOW VEHICLE

Position the control center module where it is visible to the vehicle operator but not where it will obstruct movement or vision.

1. Drill $1/8$ in. diameter holes in the dash. Mount the base to the dash with two no. 6 screws, $1/2$ in. long.

2. The panel slides onto the base after the mount is connected to the dash. It snaps into place.

3. Drive a $1/2$ in. no. 6 black screw into the side of the base to ensure a secure mounting of the panel.

INSTALLATION OF THE
HEAT SENSOR UNIT

The heat sensor unit is, in effect, a vacuum-sensing unit. Since there is a direct relationship between vacuum condition in the intake manifold and the amount of heat that is expelled into the exhaust pipes of the tow vehicle, the heat sensor can be installed in any vacuum line that is directly connected to the intake manifold. Just make sure that there is a strong, constant vacuum present when the engine is at idle speed.

The mounting area must be clear of all moving parts and allow the hood to be closed.

If the hose to the heat sensor has to be shortened, it must be done at the engine side of the hose. An inline restrictor is at the other end.

4. Drill $9/64$ in. holes in the desired mounting position on the firewall of the tow vehicle. Mount the bracket with two no. 8 screws, $3/4$ in. long.

5. Cut into the crankcase ventilation hose and insert the "T" fitting provided with the hose or the larger one in the hardware package. No clamps are necessary. If the crankcase ventilation hose is not available, follow the directions given above.

INSTALLATION OF THE SPEED
SENSOR TO THE TRANSMISSION

Since there are various makes of transmissions, Thermasan provides a variety of adaptors so the speed sensor can be mounted on just about any type of American transmission. There is also a separate set of directions enclosed in the package with the adaptors to simplify the selection of the correct adaptor. If the transmission cable is too inconvenient to use, the connection may be made to a speed control device.

6. Once you have selected the correct adaptor for your particular tow vehicle, remove the speedometer cable at the transmission.

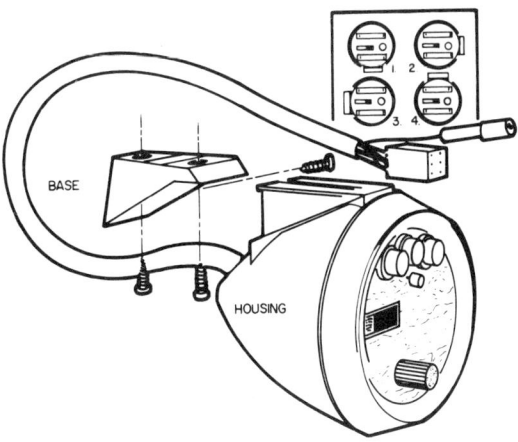

Installation of the control center.

110 WATER AND SEWAGE

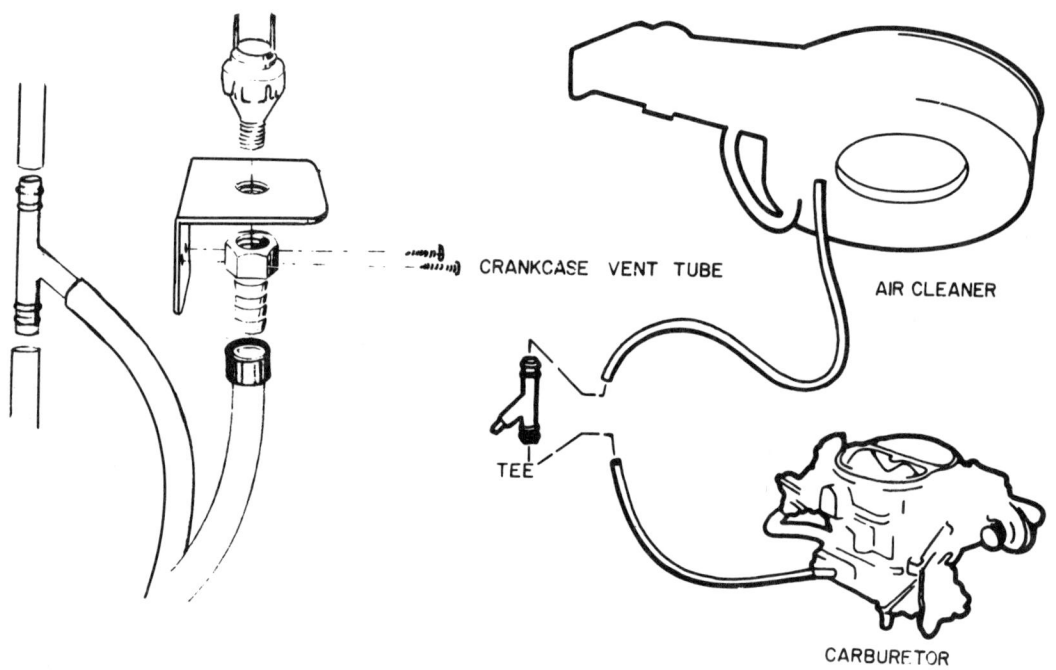

Installation of the heat sensor.

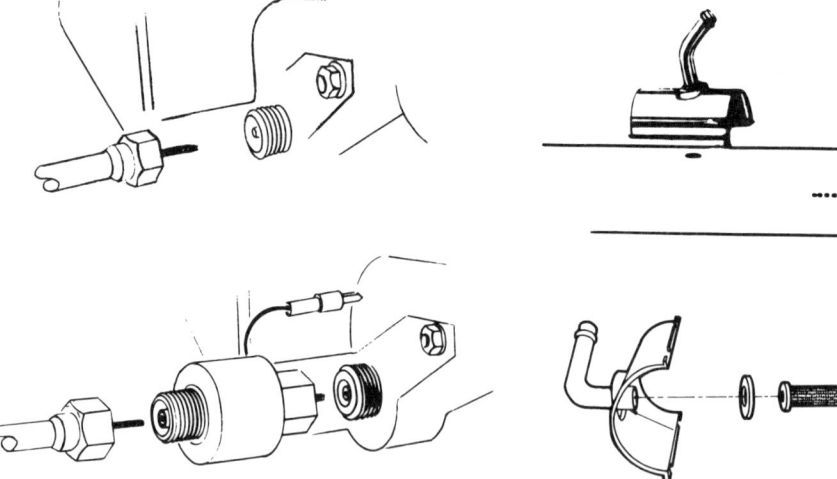

Installation of the speed sensor.

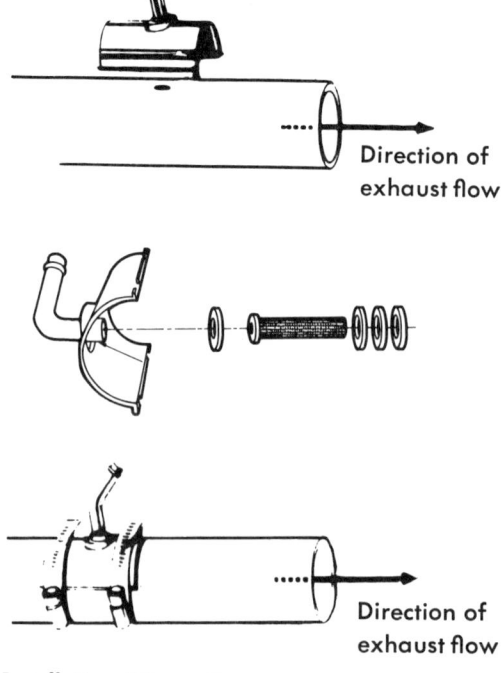

Installation of the sanijector.

7. Assemble the speed sensor to the transmission. Screw the sensor ¼ turn past finger-tightness but do not overtighten.

8. Replace the speedometer cable to the speed sensor, screwing it ¼ turn past finger-tightness but do not overtighten.

INSTALLATION OF THE SANIJECTOR

The rubber hose must be at least 2 in. from the exhaust pipes when the installation is complete. Allow sufficient clearance from all other obstructions.

9. Drill a ½ in. diameter hole in the exhaust pipe. Install it as close to the engine as possible, ahead of the mufflers, but behind any catalytic pollution control de-

WATER AND SEWAGE 111

vice. Install the unit at the point where the two exhaust pipes come together on vehicles with V8 engines and a single exhaust pipe.

10. Set the screen end of the sanijector into the hole.

11. Install the clamps and tighten them into place. The gaskets will compress to make a seal, preventing an exhaust leak.

Installation of the Tank Evacuation Probe

The evacuation probe must be installed a few inches above the bottom of the tank. This allows the solids to break up and the toilet paper to separate through chemical additive activity. Failure to mount the probe off the bottom of the tank will result in the clogging of the probe. This means that the Thermasan is not capable of emptying the holding tank 100 per cent. The probe should not be installed near the dump valve outlet. If difficulty is encountered, soap may be used as a lubricant to aid in installation.

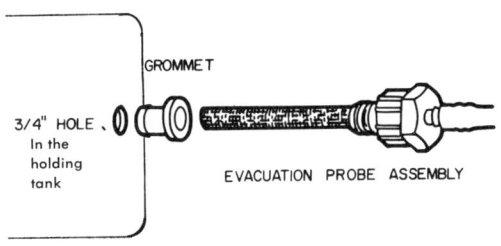

Installation of the evacuation probe.

12. Cut a ¾ in. hole in the side of the holding tank with a hole saw.

13. Insert the grommet into the hole.

14. Insert the tank access probe into the grommet.

Installation of the Metering Injection Assembly

The metering injection assembly must be mounted as close as possible to the tongue-frame junction on the trailer's left side.

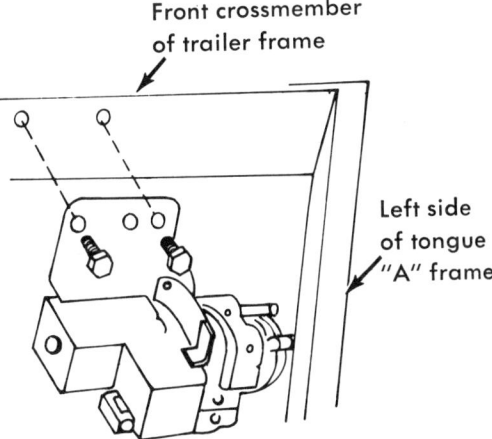

Installation of the metering injection assembly.

15. Drill two ⁷⁄₁₆ in. holes through the frame and mount the metering injection assembly with ⅜ x 1 in. bolts.

Installation of the Quick-Disconnect Assembly to the Tow Vehicle

The quick-disconnect assembly should be mounted as close to the hitch as possi-

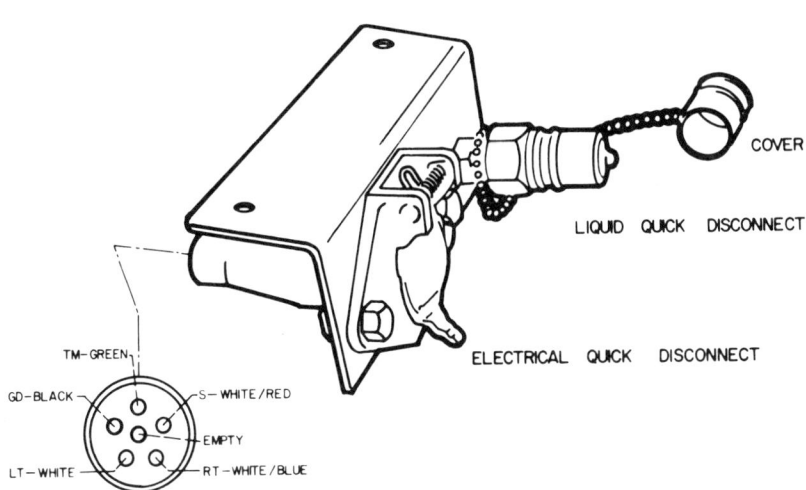

Installation of the quick-disconnect assembly.

ble. *The outlets should be facing out and straight back when the installation is completed.*

16. Drill two 5/16 in. holes in the bumper of the tow vehicle. Mount the quick-disconnect bracket using the two 1/4 x 1/2 in. hex-head screws, and the nuts and lockwashers provided with the hardware package.

Installation of the Hoses on the Tow Vehicle

The milky colored hose can withstand extreme temperatures. No other hose can be substituted.

17. Cut the 16 ft length of hose to the desired length and connect it to the liquid quick-disconnect on the tow vehicle bumper.
18. Using the tie wraps, string the wiring harness and the hoses to the bottom of the tow vehicle, carefully clearing all hot areas and abrasive surfaces.

Installation of Hoses on the Trailer Side of the Unit

The shaft of the pump rotates in a counterclockwise direction. The shorter of the two gray hoses inserts on the left-side hose mender as you face the pump. Secure the hose with the hose clamp provided in the hardware package.

20. Secure the 6 ft gray hose to the trailer tongue and insert the open end on the hose mender at the metering injection assembly.
21. The longer gray hose must be strung from the holding tank evacuation probe to the remaining hose mender on the metering injection assembly. Depending on the available route, either below or through the trailer frame, secure this piece of hose with the cable ties provided in the hardware package. Cut the hose to length and, with the clamps provided, secure the ends to the hose mender and tank evacuation probe respectively.

Installation of the Level Indicator Module

Make sure that there is no current in the electric lines before installing the level indicator. When installing the clamp to the hose on the evacuation probe, be careful not to touch the screws or the terminals.

22. Install the evacuation probe in the manner described in steps 12–14. The two screws in the probe must be at a 45 degree angle with the yellow lead on top.
23. Plug the black and yellow leads into either of the two terminals on the evacuation probe.
24. The plug can then be inserted into its counterpart in the harness. Firmly affix the module to the evacuation probe hose, using either black electrical tape or the tie wraps, but do not pinch the hose. See the section on "Thermasan Plumbing."

Installation of the Wiring Harness

Assemble the wiring harness as shown in the diagram. Do not tie it in place until the hoses are installed because you may wish to route them together and save the work of double fastening.

The installation of the Thermasan is now complete. Perform the following test procedures to confirm that everything is working properly.

Stationary Check (with vehicle ignition off)

1. Turn the Thermasan control center switch to the "on" position.
   a. The green light will come on unless the system is wired to the ignition.
   b. The white light will come on if the holding tank is empty.
   c. The red light will not come on.
2. Remove the wire from the terminal on the heat sensor that connects the heat sensor to the speed sensor.
3. Ground the heat sensor to the terminal. The red light will come on and the pump will run.
4. Start the engine of the tow vehicle and rev it slightly. The red light will go

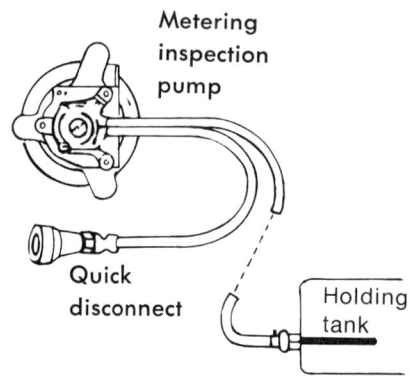

Hose installation.

WATER AND SEWAGE 113

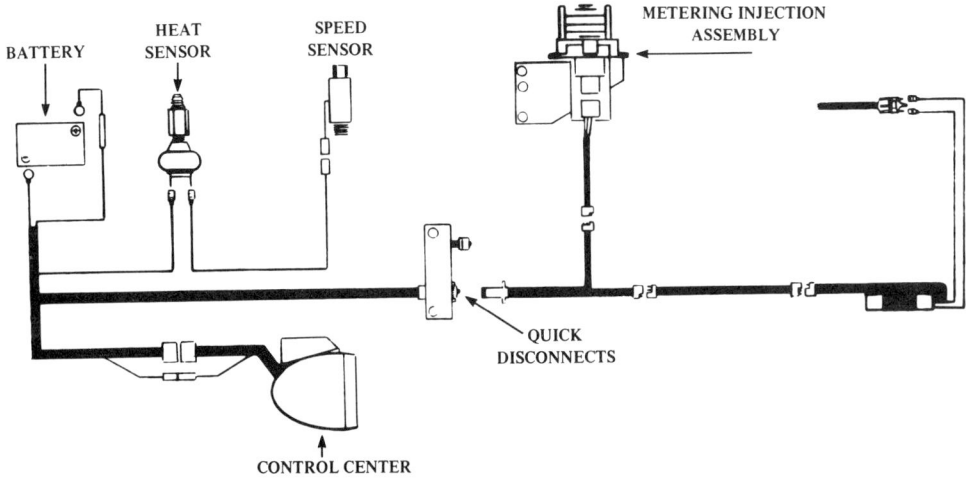

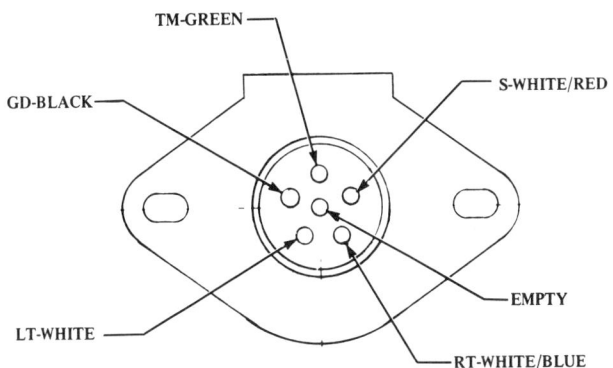

Wiring diagram of the Thermasan.

out and the pump will stop. Fifteen seconds should be allowed for the light to go out.

5. Put the wire back on the heat sensor.
6. Add water to the holding tank until the white light goes out.

NOTE: *The white light will remain lit when the tow vehicle is disconnected from the trailer.*

Road Check (with the Thermasan control switch turned on)

1. Accelerate to 45 mph. The red light will come on between 25 and 35 mph.
2. Remove your foot from the accelerator. The red light will go out in 2–6 seconds.
3. Accelerate again to 45 mph. The red light will come on in 2–6 seconds.
4. Remove your foot from the accelerator. The red light will go out in 2–6 seconds.
5. Drive the vehicle on a relatively flat highway at 45 mph for ½ mile. The red light will stay on until deceleration.
6. Press the black button on the control center when the red light is lit. The red and green lights will flash on and off together.

NOTE: *The white light will come on occasionally indicating that the water level is nearing the bottom.*

Troubleshooting Guide

The Thermasan troubleshooting guide is designed to give fast and easy solutions to service problems. To use the guide, simply select the particular symptoms observed and match them with the "Problem Index" below. The sequence of steps for locating the cause of the problem has been carefully designed to save time. Skipping steps will cost time and make finding an answer more difficult if not impossible. After replacing a part, recheck the system. Take a test drive to be sure everything is operating properly.

WATER AND SEWAGE

Problem Index

Problems Indicated by the Control Center

1. Neither ready nor reaction light glows when the system is turned on.
2. The ready light works but there is no reaction light.
3. The reaction light works but there is no ready light.
4. Both lights work but the unit does not seem to pump waste.
5. The reaction light stays on even when decelerating.
6. Both ready and reaction lights are flickering on and off.
7. The ready light flickers on and off.
8. The reaction light flickers on and off.
9. Both ready and reaction lights operate but do not pulse when the press-to-test button is pushed.
10. The empty light does not come on.
11. The empty light does not go off.

Odor Problems

12. Odors are noticeable inside the vehicle while driving.
13. Odors are noticeable outside the vehicle after operating the Thermasan.
14. Residual odors at the tailpipe.

Problems

1. Neither ready nor reaction light glows when system is turned on.
   a. Inspect the connection at the battery for possible corrosion or loose connections. If the terminals are found to be corroded, clean them with a fine sandpaper and return the *red* lead to the positive (+) terminal and the *black* lead to the negative (−) terminal. Tighten all connections.
   b. Remove and inspect the inline fuse on the red lead near the battery connection. If the fuse has "blown," this is symptomatic of a "short" in the electrical system; the entire harness and its connections should be inspected for possible frayed or burned wires or loose connections allowing a "short" to ground. *Do not replace* the 5 amp fuse until the harness has been inspected and *under no circumstances should a larger amp fuse be used.*
   c. Check the connector between the harness and the control center module for proper connections. The male and fe-

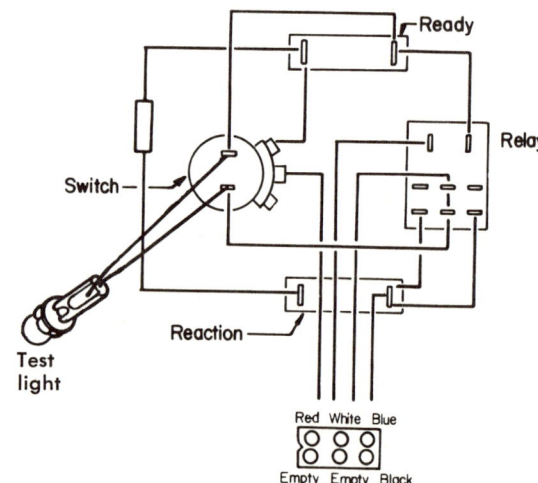

Wiring diagram for the control center on Model "BT."

male pins housed within the connector body should be straight and of equal height. They should be firmly attached to their respective wires. Compare the numbered holes at the rear of the connector and the color of the wire inserted in that hole with the appropriate diagram provided. When the inspection is completed, carefully mate the connector bodies and press firmly until the snap tabs are locked into place.
   d. Test the switch and its connections for defects. Remove the setscrew from the side of the base on the control center module. Slide the control center off its base by exerting a firm forward pull. Remove the screw from the back of the control center and separate the housing from the bezel. Using a test lamp for locating shorts, check the switch. By reversing the steps above, reinstall the control center module.

2. The ready light works, but there is no reaction light after 35 mph.
   a. Check the reaction light for a burned-out bulb and/or loose connections. Remove the setscrew from the side of the base on the control center module. Slide the control center off its base by exerting a firm forward pull. Remove the screw from the back of the control center and separate the housing from the bezel. Using a test lamp for locating shorts, test the reaction light for a burned-out bulb. Inspect connections and reinstall by reversing the above steps.
   b. Inspect the connector between the

WATER AND SEWAGE

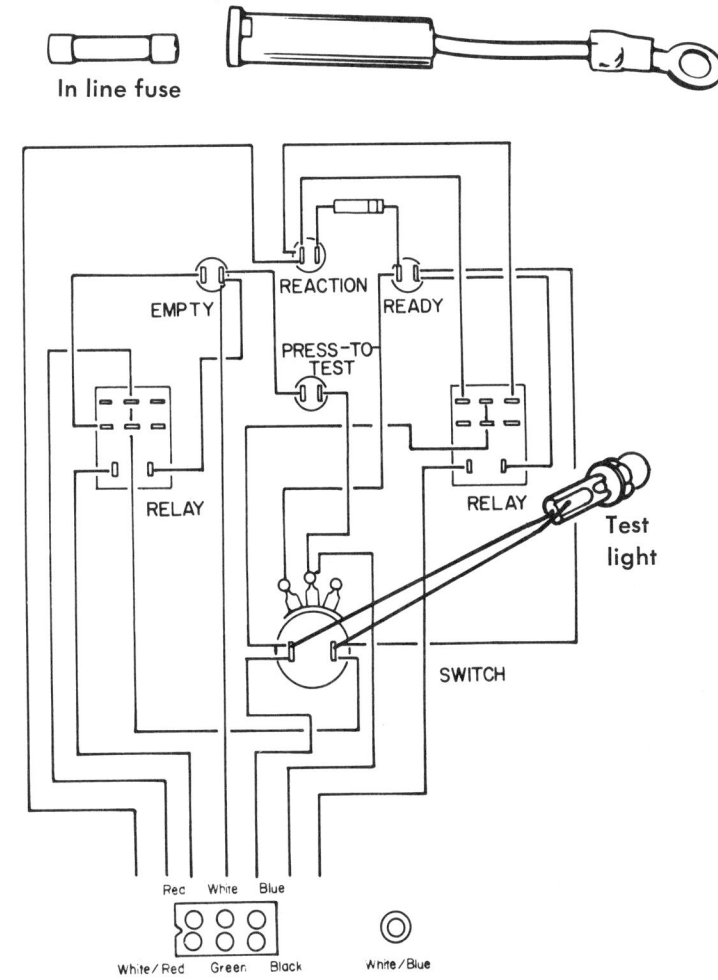

Wiring diagram for the control center on Model "BLT."

harness and control center module for proper connections. The male and female pins housed within the connector body should be straight and of equal height. They should be firmly attached to their respective wires. Compare the numbered holes, at the rear of the connector, and the color of the wire inserted in that hose with the appropriate diagram provided. When the inspection is completed, carefully mate the connector bodies and press firmly until the snap tabs are locked firmly into place.

c. Check the heat sensor leads for loose connections at the terminals.

d. Test for a possible faulty relay. Remove the blue lead traveling from the harness to the heat sensor. With the system turned on, ground the lead to any clean, unpainted part of the frame. If the ready light does not come on, the relay is faulty. Replace the control center module. See "Installation Instructions" for more details.

e. Test for a faulty heat sensor. With the system turned on, but the engine not running, ground the blue lead from the heat sensor to the speed sensor. If the system does not operate, the heat sensor is at fault. Remove the terminals and hose from the heat sensor. Remove the heat sensor from the vehicle by extracting the two screws in the bracket. Replace by reversing this procedure.

f. If, after testing for the above, the system does not operate at 35 mph, the problem lies with the speed sensor and it must be replaced. Remove the speedometer cable from the speed sensor and disconnect its electrical fitting. Unscrew

116 WATER AND SEWAGE

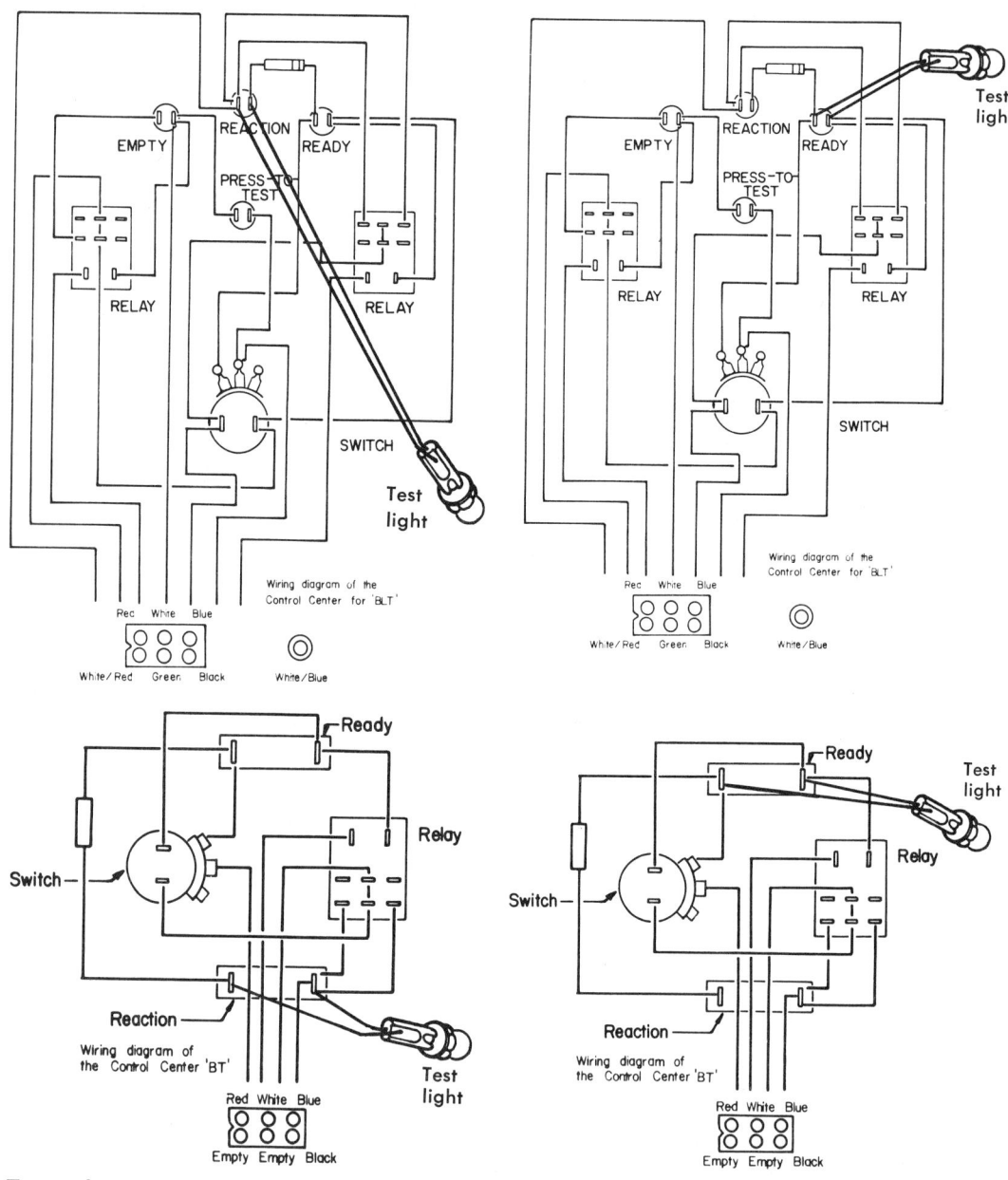

Testing the reaction light.

Testing the ready light.

the speed sensor and replace it with a new part by reversing this procedure.
3. The reaction light works, but there is no ready light.
  a. Check the ready light for a burned-out bulb and/or loose connections. Remove the setscrew from the side of the base on the control center module. Slide the control center off its base by exerting a strong forward pull. Remove the screw from the back of the control center and separate the housing from the bezel. Using a test lamp for lo-

cating shorts, test the ready light for a burned-out bulb. Inspect the connections and reinstall by reversing the above steps.
4. Both lights work, but unit does not seem to pump waste.
  a. The pump's motor leads may be disconnected. Remove the two pan head screws holding the terminal dust cover in place. Check the terminals and their leads for a faulty connection. Also inspect the connections in the plastic pin housing that plugs into the dust cover.

Return it to position and replace the screws.

b. Inspect all waste lines for possible kinks. Manually straighten any kinks and secure the hoses.

c. The waste lines or the hose menders within those lines may be plugged. Remove the blue wire from the harness side of the heat sensor and short that lead to the vehicle body. With the system turned on, watch the metering injection pump hoses for movement of waste. If waste does move, go directly to step "e" for solutions. If no waste is moving at this point, drain the contents of the holding tank. If the hose on the inlet side of the pump has collapsed, the plug should be found in the hose mender at the pump, the gray waste hose, or at the evacuation probe. (The evacuation probe plug is covered under letter "d.") Remove the gray hose at the hose mender near the pump. Operate the system again, as above. If the inlet hose to the pump collapses, the blockage is in the hose mender and can be cleaned with a steel rod. If the hose does not collapse with the gray line disconnected, the blockage is within the gray line or the evacuation probe. The gray line can be cleaned with compressed air or a steel rod. If, after cleaning the line and returning the hose to position, the pump still does not pump waste, the evacuation probe has become plugged. Continue to "d" for instructions.

NOTE: *In some rare instances, a blockage may occur in the hose mender on the outlet side of the pump causing a ballooning of that hose and a subsequent rupture of that line at the pump.*

In this case the hose within the pump must be replaced. Remove the two 5/16 in. nuts from the thumbscrews holding the front of the pump in place. Pull the front off the pump and remove the old hose from the rollers. Depress the springs on the hose menders and hold them in position. Slide the hose into position on the rollers and replace the front of the pump.

CAUTION: *Make sure the two halves of the pump assembly are not pinching the hose.*

Replace the two thumbscrews, tightening the nuts until the lockwashers flatten. Do not overtighten. Insert the tabs on the springs into the holes in the pump. Reclamp the waste lines to the inlet and outlet hose menders.

REMINDER: *The pump shaft rotates counterclockwise. The gray waste line has to be attached to the inlet side.*

d. Remove the holding tank evacuation probe and inspect it for a possible clog. Remove the evacuation probe screen by unscrewing the plastic nut on the outside of the holding tank. If your system includes a level control, remove the terminals first and note the alignment of the terminal screws. After separating the nut, remove the rubber washer and draw out the screen. Flush the screen to remove the plug. Insert the screen and press the rubber washer back into place. Screw the nut back into its fitting. If your system has the level indicator, orient the two terminal screws as before and plug the terminal wires back into place.

NOTE: *Either lead can be placed on the right or left terminals.*

e. Inspect the clamps on the gray waste line. Loose clamps can allow air to be pumped through the system instead of waste. Tighten all clamps.

f. Press the evacuation probe more firmly into the rubber grommet. Here too, an air leak may occur and not allow the full potential to be drawn from the holding tank.

g. Inspect the hose to the sanijector for possible burning. The burning of this hose is usually accompanied by an odor problem and is caused by an air leak between the metering injection assembly and the sanijector. The hose must be replaced with the same high-temperature hose and the air leak prevented by tightening the clamps sufficiently.

CAUTION: *Do not substitute any other hose.*

If the Thermasan has been installed on an auto for travel trailer use, the liquid quick-disconnect should be inspected for possible leakage and replaced if necessary.

h. Check the type of system in the vehicle. Type 200 systems are for use in vehicles where toilet wastes *only* are collected in the holding tank. Sink, shower, and basin water bypass the holding tank.

Type 600 systems are for use where sink, shower, and basin water, and toilet waste are collected in the same tank. If a Type 600 is needed, remove the dust cover from the back of the metering injection assembly. Remove the jumper wire and install the terminals as shown in the diagram and refit the dust cover.

5. The reaction light stays on even when decelerating.

a. In this case the heat sensor is defective and should be replaced. To test for a faulty heat sensor, turn on the system with the engine not running and ground the blue lead from the heat sensor to the speed sensor. If the system does not operate, the heat sensor is at fault and must be replaced. Remove the mounting bracket and heat sensor by removing the two screws from the bracket. Pull the hose from the hose barb fitting. Reinstall by reversing the above procedure.

6. Both the ready and reaction lights flicker on and off.

a. If the lights are flickering on and off at a constant rate, the problem stems from the press-to-test feature. Remove the setscrew from the side of the base on the control center module. Slide the control center off its base by exerting a firm forward pull. Remove the screw from the back of the control center housing and separate the housing from the bezel. Using a test lamp for locating shorts, check the press-to-test button. Inspect the leads for a broken solder joint. If the press-to-test is at fault, replace the control center module. See "Installation Instructions" for details.

b. If the ground to the battery is not connected, the ready and reaction lights may flicker at a constant rate. Inspect the contact of the black wire at the battery. Clean the terminal and tighten in place.

c. If the lights flicker intermittently, the red line from the battery or fuse block should be checked over its entire length. In addition, inspect the connection at the plastic connector near the control center and the connections at the on/off switch in the control center. Begin by inspecting the red lead for possible frayed spots or bare areas. Inspect the six-pin plastic connector for bent pins or loose connections at the pins. Remove the control center module by removing the setscrew from the side of the base. Slide the control center off the base by exerting a strong forward pull. Remove the screw from the back of the control center housing and separate it from the bezel. Inspect the switch for broken solder joints. Replace by reversing the above instructions. If the problem still exists, a new control center must be installed. See "Installation Instructions" for details.

7. The green light flickers on and off.

a. A lead is loose at the light, on/off switch, or at the battery or fuse block. Begin the inspection at the battery or fuse block. Make sure all connections are secure and not corroded.

b. To check the switch and the light, remove the setscrew in the base of the control center module. Slide the control center from the base by exerting a strong forward pull. Remove the screw from the back of the control center housing and separate it from the bezel. Check the switch for broken solder joints. Inspect the terminals at the light for loose contacts and reassemble the module by reversing the above procedure. If the problem still exists, a new control center must be installed. See "Installation Instructions" for details.

8. The reaction light flickers on and off.

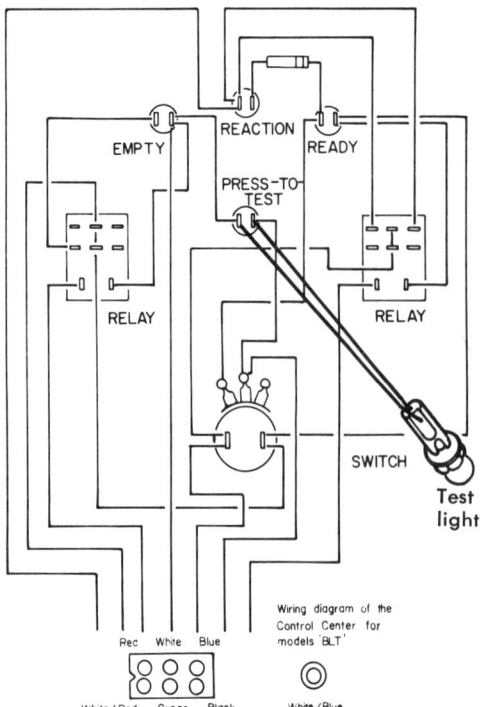

Testing the press-to-test button.

a. If the flicker is constant, then the speed sensor is faulty and must be replaced. Using an adjustable wrench, remove the speedometer cable from the speed switch. Disconnect the electrical supply to the speed sensor. Using the adjustable wrench, remove the speed sensor from the transmission. Reinstall the replacement part by reversing the above procedure.

CAUTION: *When tightening the speed sensor to the transmission, one quarter turn past finger-tightness is sufficient. Do not overtighten.*

b. If the flicker is intermittent, a loose connection is at fault. Beginning at the connection with the battery or fuse block, inspect all terminals and connections. Inspect the blue wire to the heat sensor and speed sensor for a possible short or incomplete connection. Disconnect the six-pin plastic connector near the control center module and inspect the pins to be certain that they are seated properly and making a good connection. Carefully mate the connector bodies again and press firmly together until the snap fitting lock is heard to connect. If the problem still exists, a new control center must be installed. See "Installation Instructions" for details.

9. Both the ready and reaction light operate but do not pulse when the press-to-test button is pushed.

a. Check the one-pin connector near the control center module. Inspect the pin and socket for a loose connection. Mate the plastic housings until the snap connector is heard.

b. Inspect the connection of the blue/white wire at the pump. Remove the two screws from the terminal duct cover on the motor. Check the blue/white wire for a broken solder joint or poor connection with its terminal. Replace the terminal cover and screws.

c. Remove the control center and inspect the press-to-test switch for broken solder joints. Remove the setscrew from the side of the base of the control center assembly. Exert a strong forward pull on the housing to separate it from the base. Remove the screw from the back of the housing to separate the bezel from the housing. Inspect the press-to-test switch for broken leads. Using a test lamp for locating shorts, test for a faulty press-to-test switch. If the switch is faulty, replace the control center assembly. See "Installation Instructions" for details. See figure "w".

10. The empty light does not come on.
NOTE: *This may simply indicate that the holding tank level is not low enough to trigger the light. If the holding tank has been dumped and the light does not come on, begin your investigation at the evacuation probe.*

a. Visually inspect the clamp holding the hose on the evacuation probe. Make sure that the clamp is not in contact with the two screws or terminals on the evacuation probe. Move the clamp enough to clear the terminals and retighten it.

b. Inspect the evacuation probe for a possible faulty installation. The screw heads should be 45° to the pavement with the yellow wire at the top. If a faulty installation is discovered, simply turn the evacuation probe, by hand, to the proper position, making certain that the probe is still firmly planted in its rubber grommet.

c. Inspect the yellow lead from the evacuation probe to the level control module for a possible short to ground.

Remove the yellow lead from the terminal. The empty light should come on. If it doesn't, the level control module must be replaced. See "Installation Instructions" for details.

d. Drain the holding tank. Separate the nut from its mating part on the evacuation probe with an adjustable wrench. Inspect the two screws inside the probe fitting for anything that might be touching them both. Reassemble and return to its proper installation orientation. See "b" above.

e. Inspect the control center module for a loose connection at the light or a burned-out bulb. Remove the setscrew from the side of the base of the control center module. Pull the control center off the base with a firm forward pressure. Separate the housing from the bezel by removing the screw at the back of the housing. Using a test lamp for locating shorts, check the light for a burned-out bulb. Inspect the terminals for a good connection.

WATER AND SEWAGE

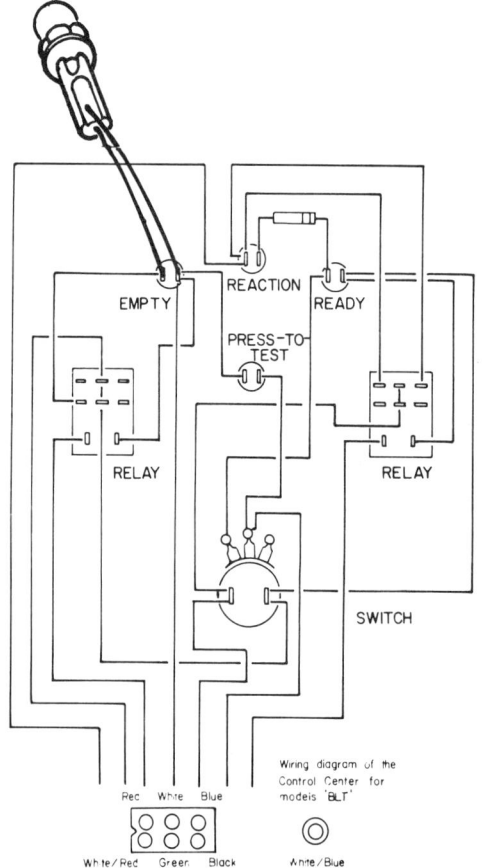

Testing the empty light.

f. If after checking all of the above, one cannot get an empty light, the switch or relay must be at fault and a new control center must be installed. See "Installation Instructions."

11. The empty light does not go off.

a. This is the normal operating condition of the system when the level of the holding tank is below the probe. This simply indicates to you that no more waste is available for pumping and your system should be turned off. Your tank is never pumped dry. If the light is on and visual inspection of the tank indicates it is full, then: (a) Inspect the black and yellow connections to the evacuation probe. (b) Test for a possible defective level indicator module. Remove the yellow lead to the evacuation probe. Insert a terminal or wire and touch it to the screw head of the black wire. If the light remains on, replace the level indicator module. See "Installation Instructions" for replacement information.

12. Odors are noticeable inside the coach while driving.

a. Investigate for dry traps in sink or bathroom. Use Aqua-Kem or another suitable chemical odor control as instructed. This does not indicate a malfunction of your Thermasan.

13. Odors are noticeable outside the vehicle after operating the Thermasan.

a. Visually inspect the exhaust pipe at the point of waste injection for waste dripping on the exhaust pipe. If the leak is at the hose and sanijector junction, reclamp the hose at that point. If the leak is at the sanijector, remove the sanijector by loosening the two large clamps. Replace the asbestos gaskets as shown in the diagram and reclamp in place.

14. Residual odors at the tailpipe.

a. Inspect the metering injection assembly for your model number. Type 600 systems are for use where sink, shower, wash water, as well as toilet wastes are all collected in a single holding tank. Type 200 systems are for units where toilet waste only is collected in the holding tank. If the wrong metering injection assembly has been installed, remove the dust cover from the back of the motor by removing the two screws that hold it in position. Place terminal receptacles on the desired terminals and replace dust cover. See the diagrams.

b. If the proper metering injection assembly has been installed, use Aqua-San for exhaust emission odor control.

4 · Fuel and Heating

The Liquid Petroleum Gas System

The liquid petroleum gas (LPG) system is used in most travel trailers for heating, cooking, lighting, and refrigeration. This system affords the mobility of bottled gas with its convenience.

The gas is usually stored in pressure containers which are mounted on the tongue assembly, from where they feed into the trailer chassis. The gas lines are usually ½ in. copper tubing with brass connectors—or possibly sweat fittings on older models. Gas feeds the different appliances in the trailer through these lines.

TYPES OF FUEL USED

Butane and propane are the two basic fuels for all trailers. They produce a clean, even flame which is ideal for cooking and heating the trailer.

Both gases can be stored in a closed container and converted by pressure from liquid to gas, which is a valuable asset. The gas remains at the top of the container while the liquid gas is on the bottom. As the gas at the top is used, the reduction in pressure inside the cylinder causes the liquid in the bottom to vaporize, converting it to gas. The container is empty when all the liquid gas has vaporized and all the upper gas has been used.

It has been proven that, per gallon of fuel, butane produces more BTUs (British Thermal Units) of heat than propane. However butane has a higher "boiling" point than propane. This means that the vaporization quality by which it turns from a liquid to a gas is stopped and it remains a liquid.

Butane cannot, consequently, be used in an area where the temperature is below 32° F. Propane, since it does have a lower

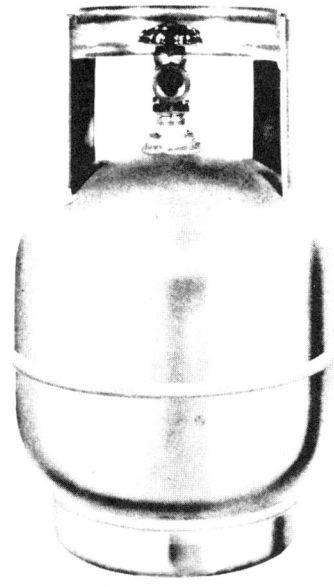

An exterior view of a 20 lb gas bottle.

122 FUEL AND HEATING

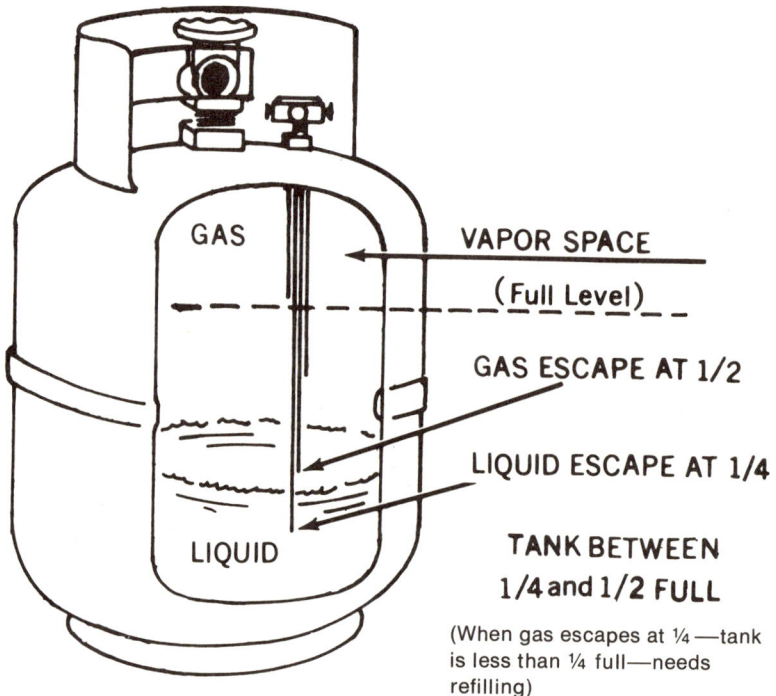

Internal view of a gas bottle.

boiling point, is sometimes mixed with butane to lower the overall boiling point. Propane can also be used alone—especially where the climate is extremely cold.

The size of the bottled-gas tank and the degree of vehicle heating which is done with the gas will regulate the life of the gas tank. Do not allow the tank to become empty as air will enter the gas lines causing them to be bled before the system can be reused.

On some units it is possible to fit the tank with a gauge which will make it possible to tell exactly how much gas the cylinder contains. The weight of the tank compared to a full cylinder is the easiest, commonest way of measuring the contents. It is also possible to tell by making a note of the condensation marks on the outside of the container which will mark the upper level of the gas.

TRAILER GAS FLOOR PLAN

Road vibration in the trailer may cause some of the connections for the gas line to become loose and cause a gas leak. It is, therefore, necessary to know the floor plan of the system and the location of the fittings and connections so that they can be easily accessible for a check.

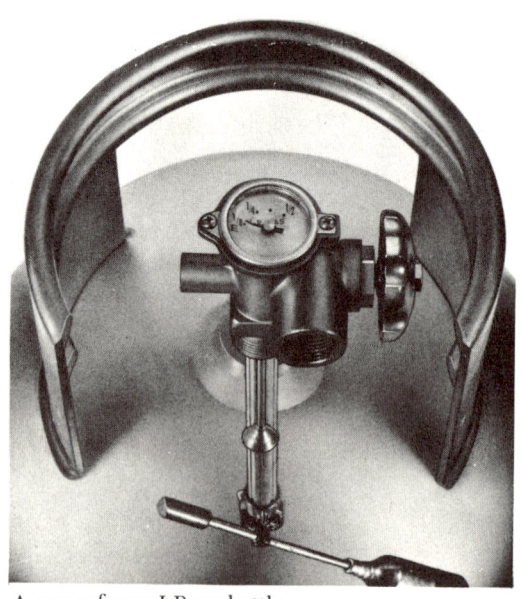

A gauge for an LP gas bottle.

The floor plan of the LPG system should be shown in the owner's manual for the trailer. If it is not, the service manual which your local dealer has should include the information you need. If your trailer was bought second-hand, see the local dealer for that particular brand of trailer to see if you can obtain the needed infor-

FUEL AND HEATING 123

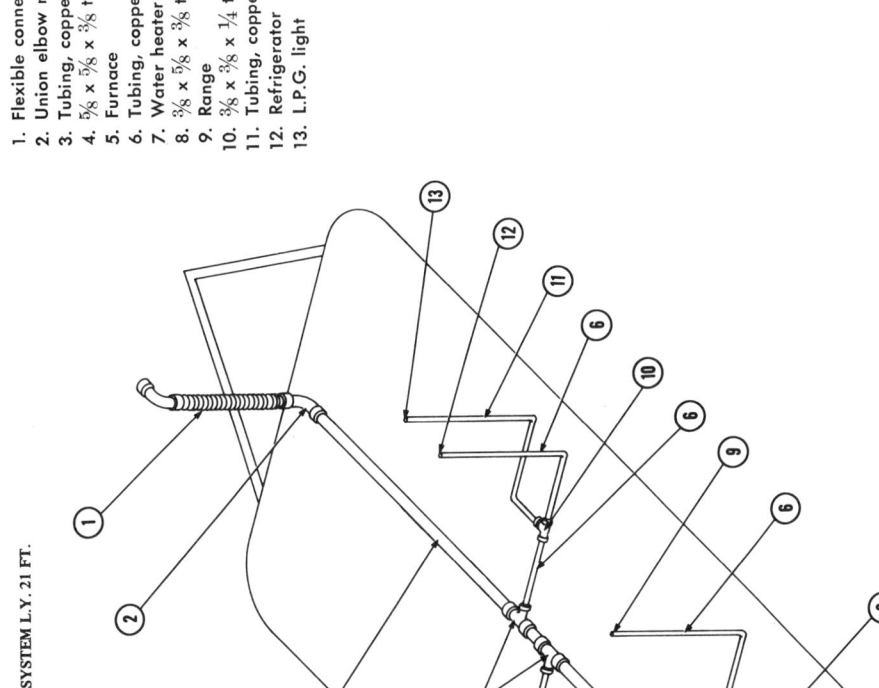

GAS DISTRIBUTION SYSTEM L.Y. 21 FT.

1. Flexible connector
2. Union elbow no. 55
3. Tubing, copper 5/8" O.D.
4. 5/8 x 5/8 x 3/8 tee
5. Furnace
6. Tubing, copper 3/8" O.D.
7. Water heater
8. 3/8 x 5/8 x 3/8 tee
9. Range
10. 3/8 x 3/8 x 1/4 tee
11. Tubing, copper 1/4" O.D.
12. Refrigerator
13. L.P.G. light

An example of a trailer gas floor plan (© Airstream Corp.)

mation. The only other means of gaining an idea of the layout of the LPG system is to find out for yourself. Trace the lines through the trailer to the various appliances. This is possibly a hard and time-consuming job but it is necessary in order to avoid leaks which may cause explosions.

GAS RACK ASSEMBLY

The bottled gas rack assembly is a welded or bolted unit which is attached to the tongue of the trailer and houses and supports the bottled gas tanks and the regulator mechanism. The rack is usually composed of a level plate which stretches across the two tongue beams. On double-tank models, there is also a stationary center bar which extends up from the middle of the rack plate.

4. The replacement procedure is the reverse of removal.

LPG REGULATOR

The regulator on the bottled gas containers is an important addition to the fuel system. The valve governs the amount of pressure that the gas appliances receive from the bottled gas container. Bottled gas appliances are under very high pressure. Gas appliances cannot operate with this amount of pressure, thus the need for a regulator to reduce pressure. Once the regulator is adjusted at the factory, it should not be touched again. If the regulator is found to be faulty, a new unit should be installed and adjusted by a qualified person.

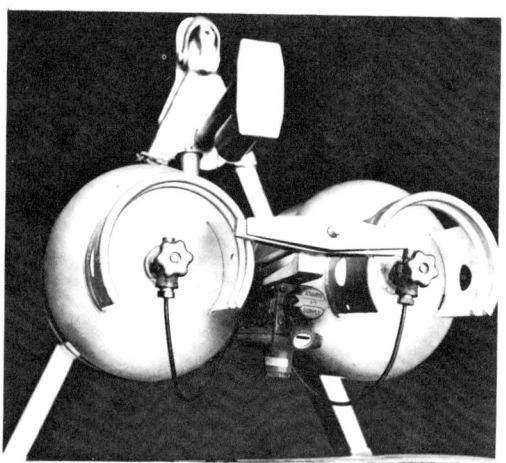

A gas rack assembly.

An LP gas regulator.

The LPG gas tank(s) are inserted into the bottom plate of the rack. The bottom plate usually has a rim around the edge to keep the gas container from slipping off the side of the plate. Once the tank is centered in position, it is securely fastened from the top so the container will not move when the unit is under tow.

LPG TANK REMOVAL AND REPLACEMENT

1. Remove the regulator assembly from the tank(s).
2. Loosen and remove the upper support brace.
3. Remove the tank from the bottom holder.

The regulator may be removed from the tank system by first closing the open-close valves on the tank(s). Remove the connecting lines with the regulator attached. The regulator may be removed from the attachment line(s) by releasing the coupling.

Some systems use an automatic gas regulator which is attached to both tanks. While the on-off valves on both tanks are open all the time, the regulator draws from only one tank at at time. One tank is used until it is empty and then the regulator automatically switches to the full tank. This system enables the empty tank to be disconnected and refilled while using the other tank. The empty tank's valve is shut off and the tank is removed and recharged. It can be reinstalled by connecting the output line from the regulator to the tank. Then just open the valve.

TESTING THE LPG SYSTEM FOR LEAKS

If there is evidence of a leak (sound or smell), testing procedures should begin immediately since this is a very dangerous situation. The probability of fire or explosion is great. In fact, frequent checks of the connections, fittings, and outlet valves should be made to lessen the possibility of a leak.

Since LP gas is clear and odorless after it is refined, federal law requires that it be combined with a substance called Mercaptan which has a distinctive odor. If there is any type of leak in the gas system of the trailer, the smell of the Mercaptan should be evident and the degree of the odor will give evidence as to the seriousness of the leak. If there is a great amount of odor, the gas should be turned off at the tanks, all windows and doors of the trailer should be opened, and the trailer should be evacuated until the smell subsides. Mix a combination of soap and water in solution. This will be the leak finder. NEVER USE A MATCH OR FLAME TO FIND GAS LEAKS. Once it is safe to enter the trailer, coat the fittings suspected of leaking with the solution, have an assistant turn on the gas, and watch for air bubbles at the fitting. Use this procedure at all the fittings suspected of leaking.

The average gas line is $3/4$ in. tubing with flared fitting endings. Usually the problem lies with fittings which have become loose because of road vibration. Tightening the fitting should cure the leak. Do not overtighten the fitting; the flared end could be damaged beyond repair. All that is necessary is a snug fit. NEVER use any type of sealing compound on a flared fitting as this will only clog the line and distort the seating surface of the connector.

The procedure listed above, through the use of the soap solution, is the best means of locating leaks, but it is not necessary to close off the gas entirely at the tank for small leaks. Finding the leak is easier if there can be some gas in the line.

If the lines are secure and not bent, but you still can't find the leak after testing all the connections along the gas line, turn off the gas, take the unit to a service center, and let trained servicemen locate the leak.

Heating System

OPERATION

Usually, travel trailer heaters are small and compact, and are constructed as an integral part of the lower cabinet assembly. With the popularity of year-round trailering in colder climates, the use of some type of heater is a necessity.

An external view of a gas heater used in a travel trailer.

The procedure by which the heater produces heat varies only slightly from model to model. The basic operation of a gas-operated heater is such that the air which is to be combined with the gas is drawn from the outside of the camper into the sealer burner chamber. The air is then combined with the gas at the venturi port where combustion takes place. The heat from the main and pilot burners is vented to the outside through the combustion vent. Most units, as explained, have a sealed combustion system which does not allow any of the products of combustion to enter the living area.

To be effective, the heat produced by combustion must be distributed throughout the camper by the air circulation system. An internal fan moves cooler air from the interior of the camper across the surfaces of the heat exchanger which warms the air. This air is then channeled out of the heating ducts and into the trailer. There is usually a filtering device at the air intake to remove dust and dirt particles.

THE PILOT

Most heaters work by means of a thermocouple. To light the unit it is usually necessary to depress a button (red) and light the pilot with an extension wick while keeping the button depressed until the unit will stay lit when the button is released.

Internal components of a heater.

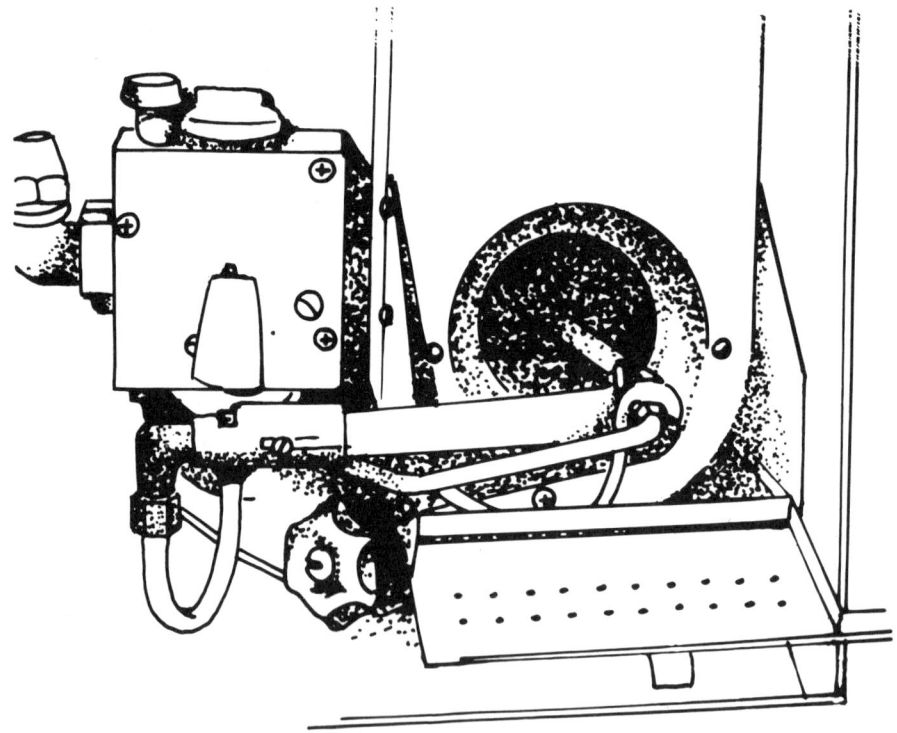

Heater pilot assembly.

GAS BURNER ADJUSTMENT

In order to adjust the main burner, it is necessary to gain access to the burner. This is usually located behind a lower access panel. It may be slightly harder to locate on some of the newer models. If the pilot is out, light it and note the color and intensity of the flame. The flame should be basically blue with a small yellow tip. An air screw offers the only possible adjustment. Generally, turning the screw clockwise increases the air which leans the flame; turning the screw counterclockwise lowers the air supply and enrichens the flame. If there is too much air, there will be a howling noise when the burner is working; a rich flame situation is evidenced by a large amount of sooting in the vent and a yellow burner flame.

FUEL AND HEATING

BLOWER ASSEMBLY

The blower assembly, which is situated inside the heating unit, circulates the inside trailer air over the heated coils to produce trailer heat. This is a completely closed system. There is no mixture of the burner gases which serve to heat the heating coils and the air which is moved by the blower around these coils to produce trailer heat.

When the thermostat indicates that heat is needed, the blower motor is engaged immediately. As the blower motor is in motion, the microswitch is tripped and the gas is channeled to the main burner where it is lit by the pilot. There is a tendency, on some units which have run for a period of time, to keep the blower motor running even though the burner is in the "off" position. This is done to remove the remaining air which may be trapped in the heat exchanger and to cool the heat exchanger.

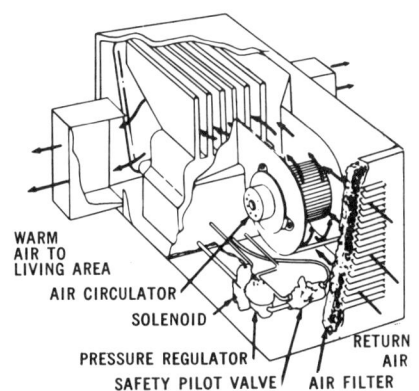

Heater blower assembly.

HEATER MAINTENANCE

If the burner is adjusted properly, there should generally be no need for maintenance to the heater assembly. A deposit of soot, however, frequently forms on the inside of the combustion chamber and it must be removed or it will cause blockage.

The best means of cleaning the combustion chamber is to lay either wet pieces of cloth or paper towels below the chamber to catch the soot as it falls. Use a soft brush or cloth to wipe the chamber clean. Some manufacturers recommend the use of a vacuum cleaner to suck the soot out but this may ruin the internal components of the vacuum. Make some provision for catching the soot or else a coating of soot will fill the trailer.

Heater Troubleshooting Chart

Symptom	Remedy
1. No heat	1. Check to see if there is gas in the cylinder and also make certain that the supply valve is in the "on" position. 2. Check to see that the pilot has not been blown out. 3. Examine the electrical connections to the blower for a short or loose connections. 4. Inspect the microswitch to see if it is functioning correctly. Clean all dirt deposits from the actuator pin. 5. Examine the blower for a burned-out motor.
2. Pilot will not stay lit	1. Check the thermocouple and replace it as necessary. 2. Check for air leakage into the combustion chamber. 3. Examine the pilot for lack of air (flame will be excessively high). 4. Check the gas supply and the pilot valve. 5. Examine the vent assembly filter for clogging.

Heater Troubleshooting Chart (cont.)

Symptom	Remedy
3. Excessive motor noise	1. If a screeching or howling is present, the air/gas mixture is too lean. (See "Pilot Adjustment.") 2. Check for blower motor imbalance or a motor hum. In either case, the motor must be replaced or serviced.
4. Insufficient heat	1. Check the heat transfer coils to see if they are clean. If not, clean them as recommended in the text. 2. The blower motor is not turning fast enough to circulate the heat efficiently. Check for a voltage shortage or a defective motor. 3. The flame is not burning at its most efficient temperature and should be adjusted as recommended in the text. 4. The gas bottle is low on fuel.

5 · Electrical, Refrigeration, and Air Conditioning

The Electrical System

Electrical systems vary according to the age of the trailer. Early models contained two separate systems; a 110 V AC system and a 12 V DC system. Most of the interior components had internal converters that could be switched from 110 V to 12 V when either was available. Light fixtures for this type of system usually contain two light bulbs per fixture—one for 12 V DC, the other for 110 V AC.

The new system is known as the "univolt system." It changes 110 V AC current to 12 V DC current by means of rectifiers and a transformer. This type of system allows only 12 V appliances to be used in trailers. Some units, however, supply 110 V AC current to wall sockets so that, when it is available, 110 V current can be used to power appliances that will not accept 12 V current.

SYSTEM CONTROL PANEL

It is important to know the location of the control panel or the fuse box. Consult your owner's manual for its exact location and to learn which fuse or circuit breaker controls which trailer component. It is a good idea to place a small tag near the circuit breaker to label it.

The newer trailers use switch type cir-

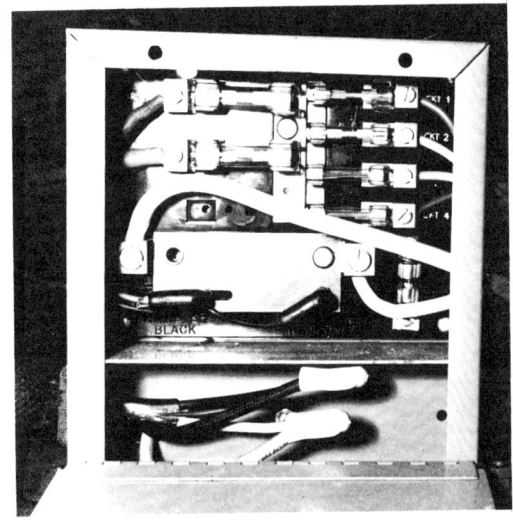

Fuse box. (© Airstream Corp.)

cuit breakers which, when the circuit is overloaded, will trip, moving to the "off" position. The switch can be energized once more by moving the switch to the "on" position. Older trailers use the conventional fuse circuit breaker which must be replaced when it is blown.

TRAILER ELECTRICAL CONNECTION

A trailer park can usually supply your travel trailer with electricity for a small charge. Most trailers have electrical connections built into their side which will

ELECTRICAL, REFRIGERATION, AND AIR CONDITIONING

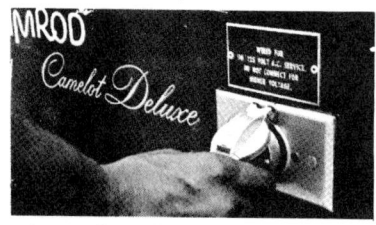

Trailer electrical inlet.

accept the three-prong electrical plug common at trailer parks. This plug is important since it contains an internal ground wire which is necessary for the trailer. Do not use any connections which do not have this wire.

WIRING DIAGRAMS

Most of the owners' manuals for the newer travel trailers contain a detailed wiring diagram showing the color coding of the wires and the location of the connectors. It is a good idea to have a copy of this diagram in the trailer at all times because it makes tracing a particular wire much easier.

Travel trailers have been engineered so that all the electrical connections are accessible. There are no connections within the trailer's walls. However, if structural damage to the trailer is present, electrical lines through the trailer skin should be checked.

Refrigerator

The refrigerating unit in travel trailers is one of four types: an ice chest; a gas-fired absorption type; an electrically heated absorption type; or an electric compressor type that operates in the same manner as an air conditioner.

The ice chest type is composed of an insulated compartment that is built into the cabinet structure of the kitchen section. It is sealed with rubber and the inside surface is lined with plastic. The insulation is located between the outer and inner shells. Ice is placed in the unit along with the items to be chilled and the rubber sealing of the door protects the inside from warm-air leaks.

The main drawbacks of this system are obvious. The ice melts in time and must be replenished. The water created by the melting ice has to be drained off often unless there is an automatic drain tube. And it is impossible to freeze food or keep it frozen in an ice chest.

The gas-fired absorption type of refrigerator is the most popular type for travel trailers. It operates off the propane gas system that also operates the gas lights, stove, oven, and gas hot-water heater. It is compact, clean, and quiet, and works very efficiently. The system uses gravity to op-

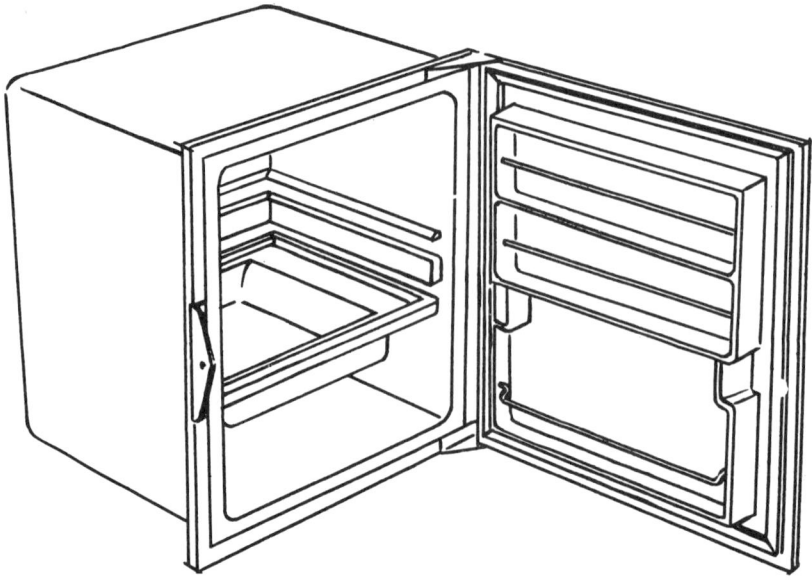

An external view of a typical travel trailer refrigerator.

ELECTRICAL, REFRIGERATION, AND AIR CONDITIONING

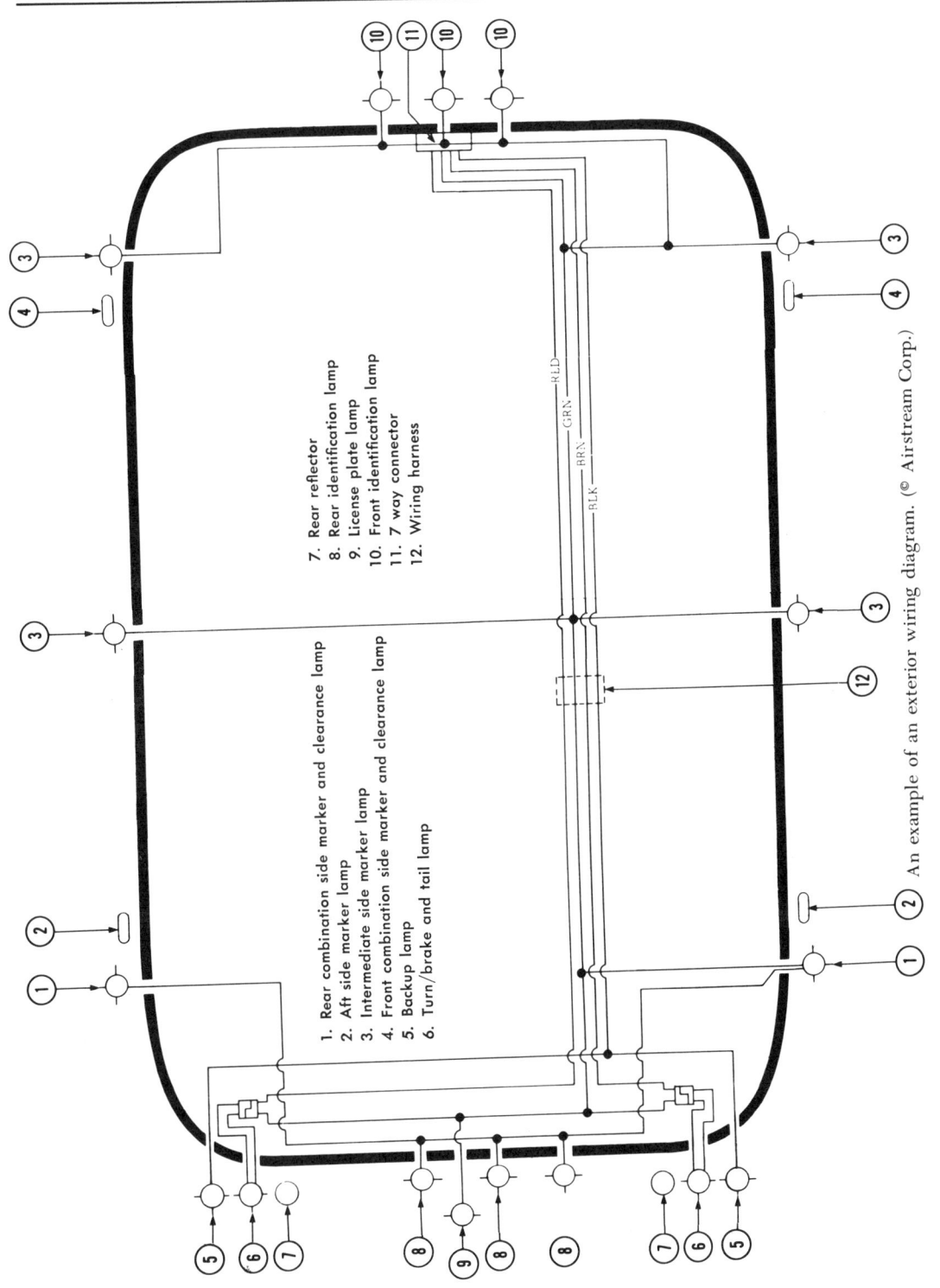

An example of an exterior wiring diagram. (© Airstream Corp.)

1. Rear combination side marker and clearance lamp
2. Aft side marker lamp
3. Intermediate side marker lamp
4. Front combination side marker and clearance lamp
5. Backup lamp
6. Turn/brake and tail lamp
7. Rear reflector
8. Rear identification lamp
9. License plate lamp
10. Front identification lamp
11. 7 way connector
12. Wiring harness

ELECTRICAL, REFRIGERATION, AND AIR CONDITIONING

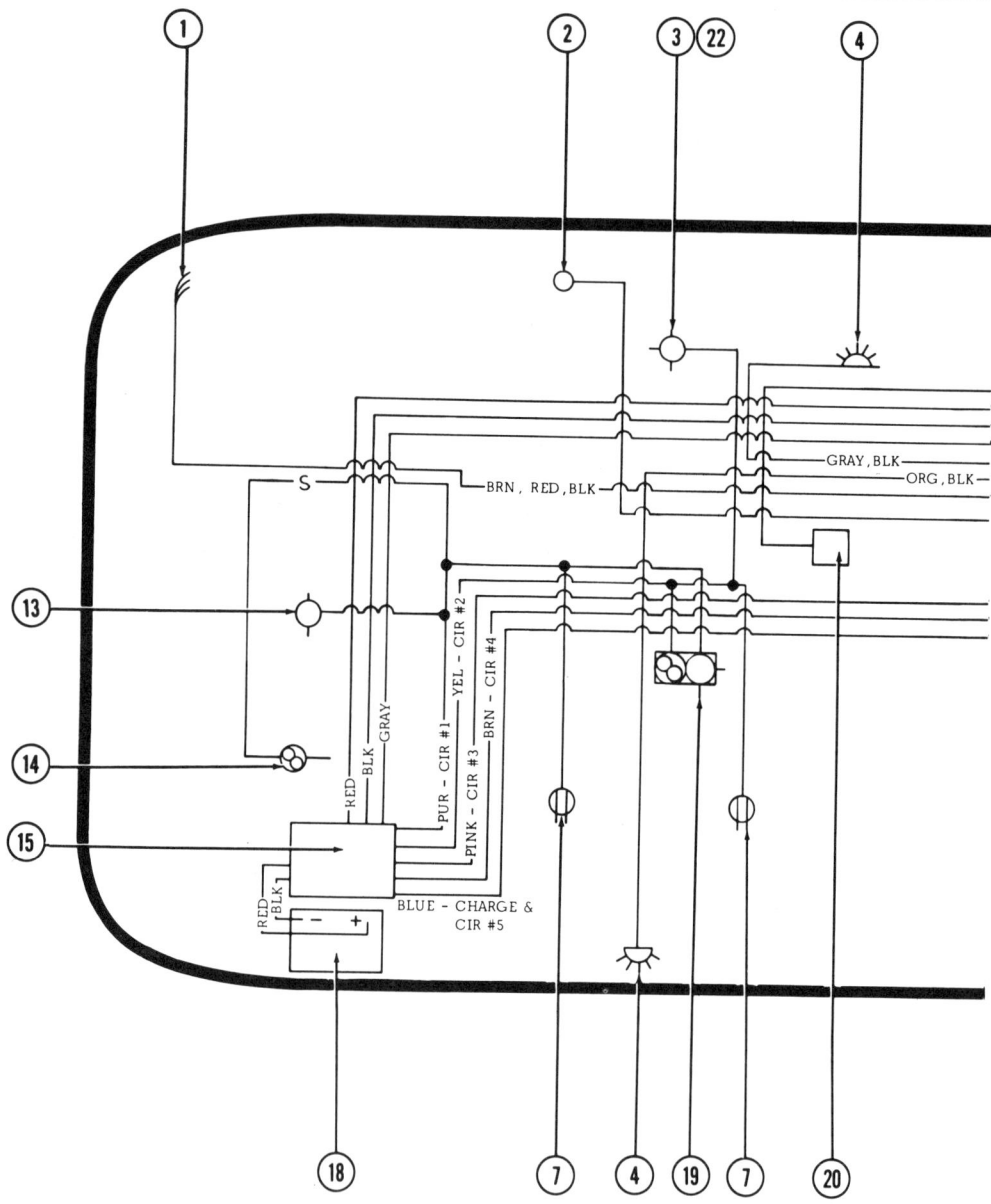

An example of an interior wiring diagram. (© Airstream Corp.)

1. Waste tank probes
2. Furnace control
3. Bed shelf light or vanity light
4. Speaker
5. Furnace
6. Furnace thermostat relay
7. 12 volt outlet
8. Air conditioner control
9. Water tank probes
10. Water pump
11. Ammeter
12. Roof locker
13. Bathroom light
14. Bathroom exhaust fan
15. Univolt
16. Radio—Stereo
17. Tow vehicle connector
18. Battery
19. Ceiling fan and light
20. Air conditioner
21. Range exhaust fan
22. Gally roof locker light
23. Step light
24. Flood light
25. Control panel
26. Wiring harness

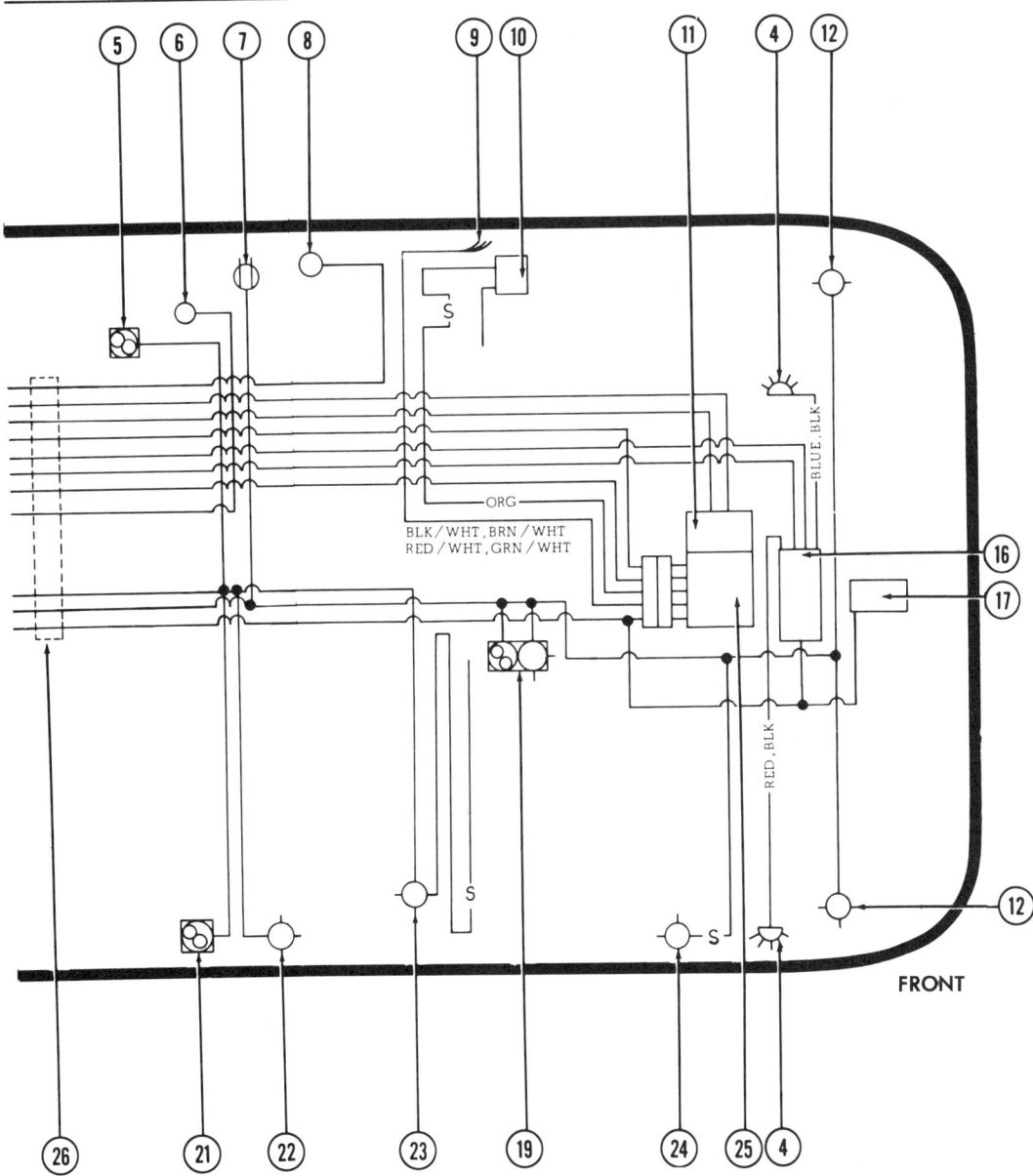

erate (eliminating the need for any compressors, expansion valves, or capillary tubes) which means that it is essential for the refrigerator to be level. The flow of refrigerant will otherwise be restricted and the unit will not cool.

In an absorption refrigerator, the refrigerant (ammonia), boils in the evaporator and condenses in the condensor, just as in the mechanical cycle of an air conditioner. However, pressure is not the only factor that changes its boiling point. During the evaporation process, the ammonia is exposed to hydrogen gas, which lowers its boiling point. It thus evaporates, removing heat from the compartment. The mixture of hydrogen and ammonia gases then drops into an "absorber" chamber containing water which has a very strong affinity for the ammonia, but does not attract the hydrogen. The attraction is sufficient for the water to attract all of the ammonia in liquid form, thus condensing it and permitting it to be separated from the hydrogen.

The hydrogen gas, being much lighter than the water-ammonia mixture, then returns to the evaporator. Now, the ammonia must be separated from the water if it is to be recovered and reused in the evaporator. The solution of water and ammonia flows into a boiler, known as the generator. A gas flame heats the solution in the generator until the tendency of the ammonia to evaporate becomes greater than the water's affinity for it, and it is boiled off. Because of the boiling action, the ammonia, and some water that boils off with it, now proceeds through a tube similar to that found in a percolator, to a separator. This separator is known as a rectifier. Here, the water, which is the heavier liquid, is allowed to separate and drain back to the absorber. On the way, it passes through its own section of the condensor and is cooled so that it will more readily absorb the ammonia when it gets there. The ammonia gas, being lighter, leaves the rectifier

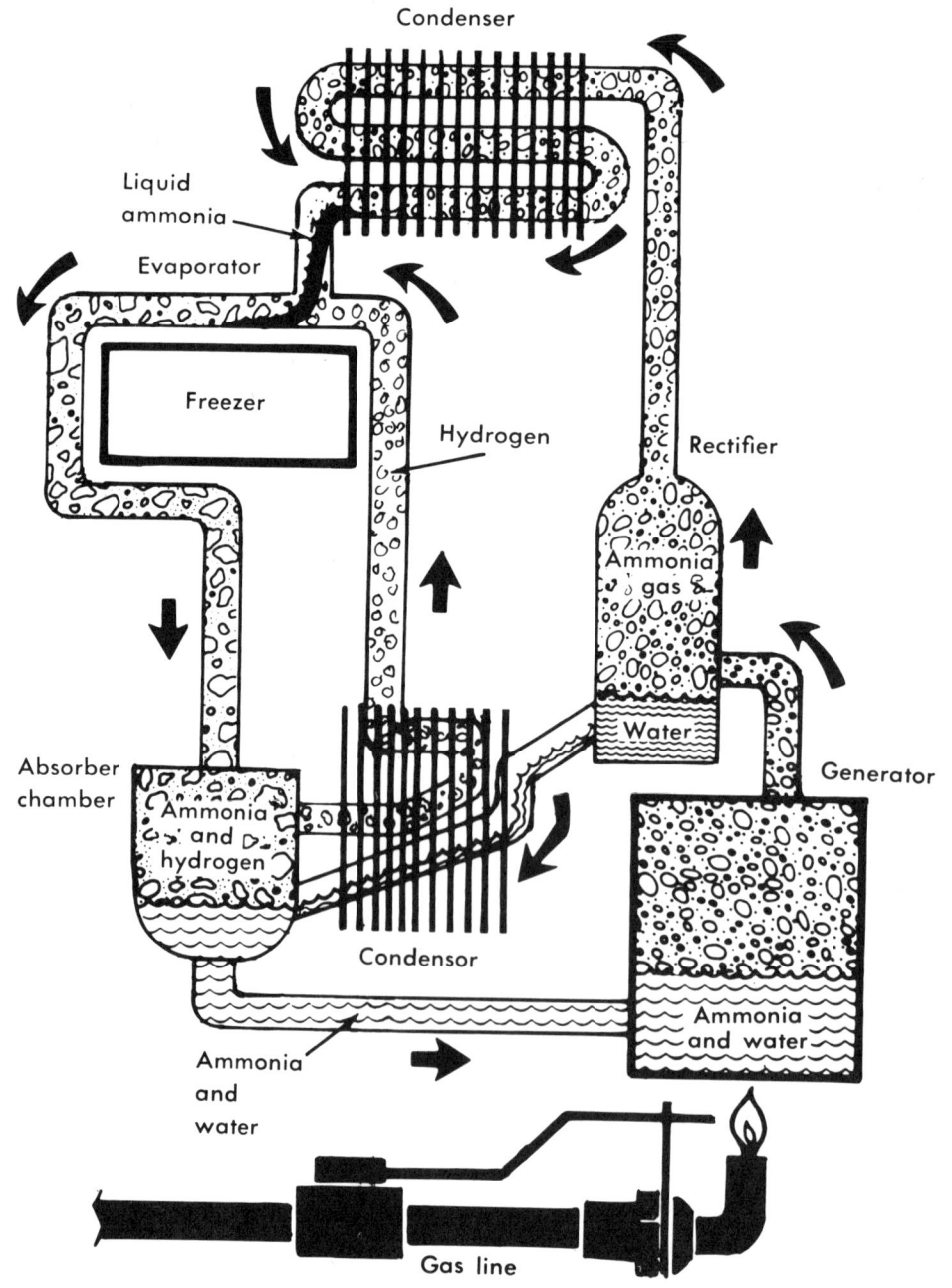

Diagram of an absorption type refrigerator.

ELECTRICAL, REFRIGERATION, AND AIR CONDITIONING

through a pipe leading from the top. It passes through the condensor, where the heat picked up in the generator is removed, and condenses on its way back to the evaporator.

Thus, it is the exposure to hydrogen in the evaporator and the exposure to the water in the absorber that changes the conditions and permits the ammonia to boil inside and later be condensed. The flame, by heating the ammonia-water solution, provides the energy required to separate the ammonia from the water and make the refrigerant reusable.

If you have an electric absorption type refrigerator, the only difference between the one you have and the one described above is that the heating element is electric; not gas flame. These are known to be more trouble-free than gas-heated refrigerators because of the fewer operating parts but the gas refrigerators are more self-sufficient since they do not require your trailer to be connected to electricity.

Refrigeration Troubleshooting Chart

Condition	Remedy
The pilot will not light.	Check the LP tank to see if it is empty. Look for damaged or blocked gas line.
The pilot goes out when the button is released.	Check the thermocouple; it is most likely defective. Make sure that the heat sensor is positioned in the flame properly.
The pilot lights, but the flame is low.	The LP gas tank is nearly empty. The refrigerator thermostat is defective and has to be replaced. The burner jets are dirty or clogged and need to be cleaned.
The refrigerator does not cool satisfactorily.	There is a restricted vent. Remove any restriction. The refrigerator is not level. The gas bottle is used up. The thermocouple is not being heated properly by the flame. Adjust it or replace it. The burner jet or the burner gauze is clogged. Clean the jet as described in the text. Clean the gauze with a brush. If your unit is designed to have a flue baffle in the exhaust flue, the problem might lie here. The baffle is designed to distribute heat and cause proper air flow. It may be missing altogether or be installed at the wrong height inside the flue. The gas pressure at the burner is wrong. The burner assembly may not be secured properly and is moving around when the trailer is being towed. The thermostat may be at the wrong setting. Turn it to a higher number. The refrigerating unit may have failed. It is possible that the gases in the unit have become separated and formed a type of "vapor lock." If possible, take the unit out of the cabinet and turn it upside down several times so that the liquid in the boiler can be mixed with the liquid in the absorber vessel. This procedure will restore the liquid balance in the unit.
The refrigerator is too cold.	The thermostat is set improperly. Turn the dial to a lower number. There is dirt in the valve of the thermostat. Clean the valve and the valve seat in the thermostat.

The electric compressor type of refrigerator operates exactly the same way that an air conditioner works. The only difference is the absence of a fan or blower circulating air over the evaporator.

The most frequent trouble with gas refrigerators is the pilot light blowing out. Since the system has a thermocouple, the entire gas supply to the refrigerator is turned off when the pilot goes out. When the pilot fails to supply sufficient heat to the thermocouple, it closes a valve by means of a thermo-element which expands and contracts with the application of heat and a magnetic safety valve. If this happens, try to light the pilot again by pushing down on the button (usually red) and lighting the pilot flame with a match. Keep the button depressed for about a minute, allowing the thermocouple sufficient time to heat up and open the gas valve. The pilot should remain lit when the button is released. If it does not, the thermocouple is defective and should either be replaced or repaired. Before replacing the thermocouple, check to see if the heat sensor is in the proper position. It should be right in the middle of the flame. If it is not, adjust it so that the end of the sensor is positioned in the center of the flame.

The flame should be blue with a yellow tip. If it is all yellow and is giving off soot and an odor, the flame is not burning properly and needs an adjustment.

Check to see if you have the right type of burner tip. Some tips are designed for burning butane and you might be burning propane. Adjust the air flow valves and check the tip of the burner for cleanliness. The holes in the tip are particularly small and could very easily become clogged. DO NOT clean the tip with a piece of wire or any other metal device. It will undoubtedly damage the holes in the tip of the burner jet. Clean the jet in alcohol and blow it dry with compressed air. Lighter fluid is a good substitute for alcohol.

Make sure that the burner is positioned so that it is pointing directly at the flue or chimney and in such a way that the proper amount of air can circulate for complete combustion.

The unit should be cleaned once every year. It is a relatively simple job but should not be neglected. First turn off gas, then remove the baffle plate or louver door. Remove the flame blowout guard and disconnect the gas pipeline from the pipe nipple. Be careful not to damage the nut. Remove the pipe nipple which holds the jet as a unit. Clean the unit in the alcohol or lighter fluid and blow it dry with compressed air. Remember that no metal object is to be inserted in the holes of the jet. Clean the burner tube (generator), paying close attention to the gauze. Use a brush or a cloth and blow out any dirt with air. It is not necessary to remove the burner tube for cleaning. Just make sure that you cover the burner jet with a clean cloth so that debris from the burner tube does not fall on the jet. When you replace the parts that have been serviced, be sure to check for leaks. Use the soapy water solution on all of the joints and check for the formation of bubbles.

Many trailer owners want their refrigerators to operate while they are on the road. This is not a recommended practice, but in theory most units should operate when the trailer is being towed. The motion of the trailer is much the same as a ship that is rolling in high seas. It passes from side to side and is out of level "equally" in all directions. Also, it must pass through the level stage every so often, thus allowing the refrigeration gases and liquids to circulate even at a restricted rate. The only problem that could possibly arise and usually does is that of keeping the pilot light lit.

If it becomes apparent that the refrigeration system itself needs to be repaired, take the unit to a qualified refrigeration mechanic. The refrigerant is corrosive and the hydrogen is very explosive. The whole system is under very high pressure. Chances are that if the sealed system goes bad, the whole thing will have to be replaced anyway so there is really nothing that can be done in the way of repairs.

Air Conditioning

Air conditioner assemblies are usually mounted on the roofs of travel trailers because there is no safe and convenient alternative location. The hazards of air conditioners hanging from windows or protruding from the bodies of trailers is immediately apparent. They could easily

ELECTRICAL, REFRIGERATION, AND AIR CONDITIONING 137

be damaged by tree branches sticking out over roads, car doors swinging open, or even by manuevering in close quarters. This precarious extension could also detract from the otherwise sleek appearance of your trailer and add to the already pressing problem of wind resistance. It is also possible that by mounting an air conditioner to the side of your trailer you could alter the weight distribution and balance enough to drastically change its towing characteristics.

Mounting the air conditioner in the center of the roof allows the cooling capacity to be fully realized. The cool air flow can be directed to the front and back of the inside of the trailer without too much restriction in the form of cabinets and fixtures. In general, a roof-mounted air conditioner is able to more efficiently cool

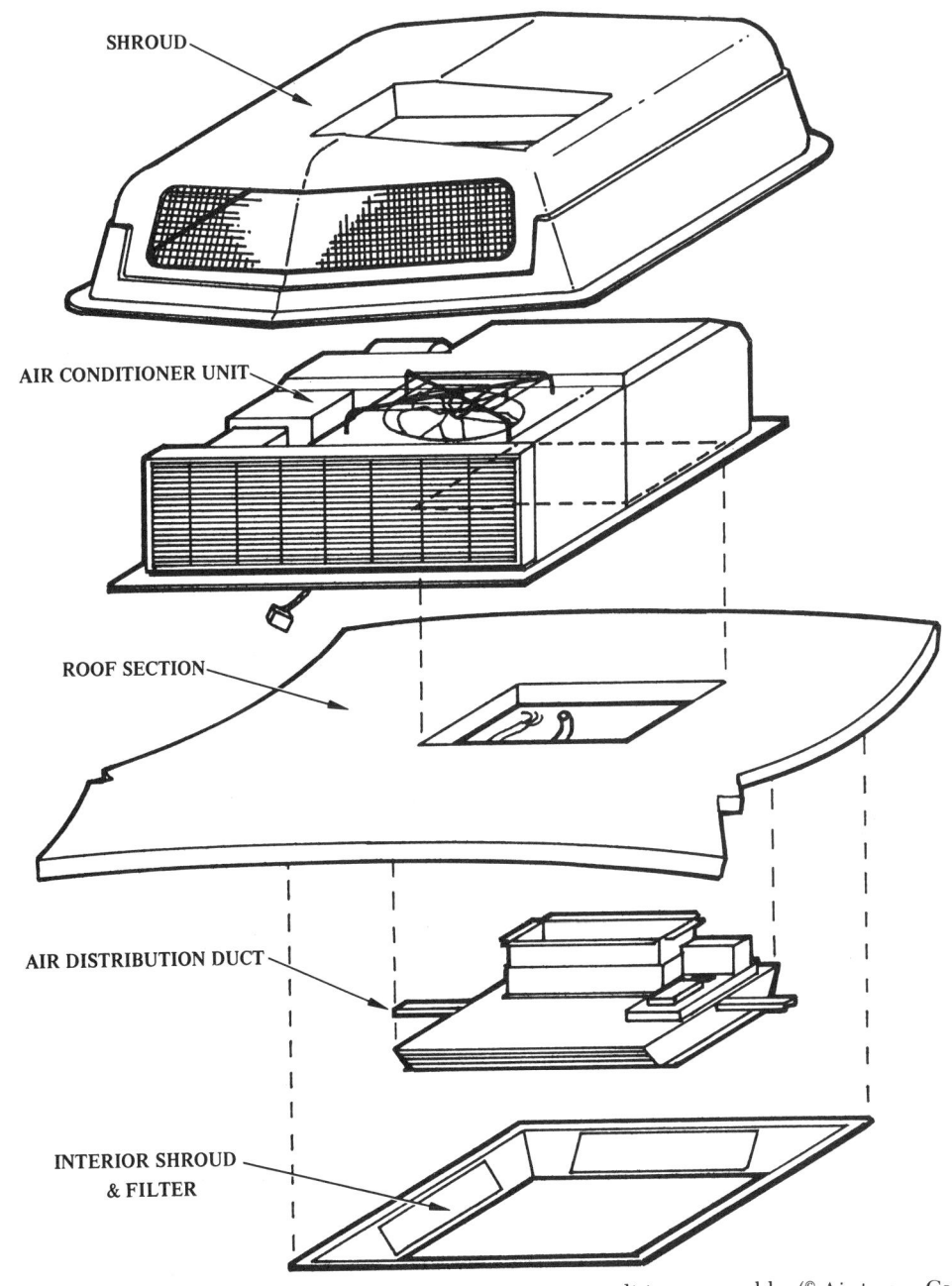

An exploded view of a typical roof-mounted travel trailer air conditioner assembly. (© Airstream Corp.)

ELECTRICAL, REFRIGERATION, AND AIR CONDITIONING

the inside of the trailer without adversely affecting its tow characteristics.

To fit an air conditioner on the roof of your travel trailer, cut a hole in the roof to facilitate the installation of ducts, wiring, and possibly a condensation drain tube. Make sure that the hole does not interfere with any of the structural framing or ribbing of the trailer's body.

There are intake and exhaust vents on the inside of the trailer. The intake vents should incorporate some type of air filter before the unit itself to protect it from dust and grit. These filters should be cleaned with warm water and soap often enough that the flow of air is never greatly restricted. The exhaust vents are usually adjustable to direct the flow of air throughout the trailer.

Most units also have a thermostat similar to the type hooked up to the heater or furnace. This thermostat is set up so that it reacts to the change in temperature of the air coming into the unit and turns off the air conditioner when the air inside the trailer is cooled to a predetermined temperature.

Aside from the recommended manufacturer's procedures, there is not much maintenance work the average owner can do to his travel trailer's air conditioner. Special tools and knowledge are needed to replace most parts. Most relatively small air conditioning units are hermetically sealed. There are no fittings that can be loosened or tightened with a wrench. All the joints are sweated together.

All that will be done here is to explain how an air conditioner works and give an abbreviated troubleshooting chart so you can have at least a general idea of what might be wrong if your air conditioner doesn't work properly.

Heat is absorbed when a liquid is changed to a vapor. A drop of alcohol on the back of your hand will demonstrate this principle.

Because the alcohol is highly unstable, it will evaporate quickly from a liquid to a vapor and absorb heat from your hand. This elementary evaporator process is the simplest form of refrigeration and, therefore, alcohol might be called a simple type of refrigerant.

An example of a travel trailer air conditioner. Notice the compactness and low profile of the unit. (© Airstream Corp.)

1. Compressor
2. Mounting hardware
3. Condenser coil
4. Evaporator blower motor assembly
5. Mounting hardware
6. Blower and evaporator coil cover panel assembly
7. End plate
8. The run capacitor for the compressor and fan motors
9. Rubber boot protector for the capacitors' terminals
10. Junction box
11. Plug and wiring harness assembly for the condenser fan and motor assembly

ELECTRICAL, REFRIGERATION, AND AIR CONDITIONING

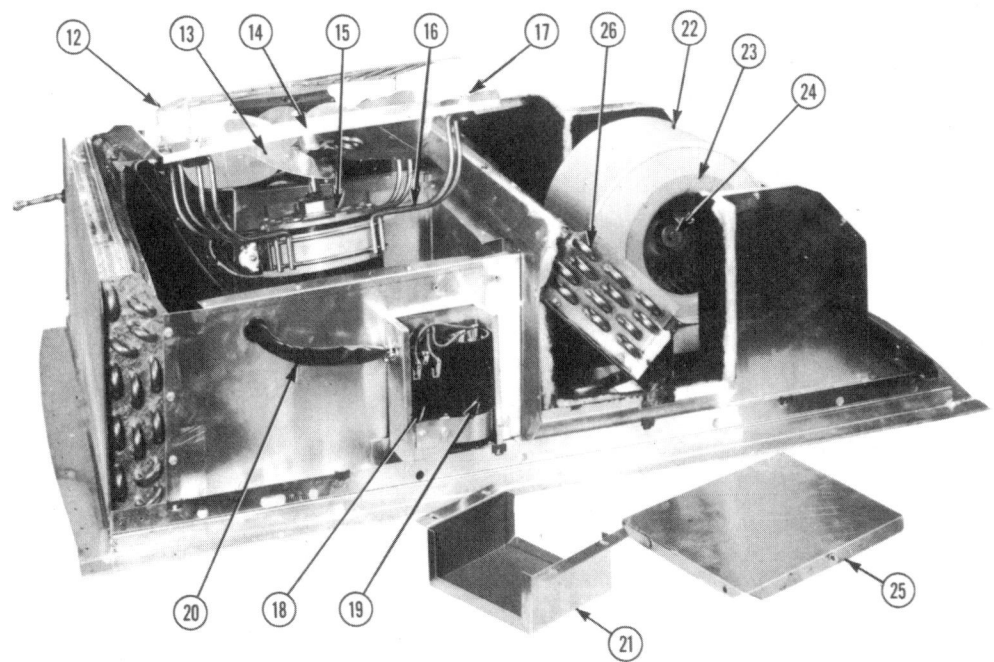

An example of a travel trailer air conditioner, back view. (© Airstream Corp.)

12. Fan guard
13. Fan blade
14. Venturi panel
15. Condenser coil fan motor
16. Motor support bracket assembly
17. Mounting hardware
18. Run capacitor
19. Start capacitor

20. Wiring harness assembly
21. Control box cover
22. Evaporator blower housing
23. Evaporator blower inlet rings
24. Blower wheel
25. End plate
26. Evaporator coil

If we had an unlimited supply of refrigerant and cost were no factor, we could continuously boil it off and continue to absorb heat by using the refrigerant only once.

To practically apply this system (i.e., recycle the refrigerant), we would need an evaporator, or coil, and a means of metering the refrigerant into one end of the coil. Air passing over the outside of the coils would be cooled as its heat was absorbed by the refrigerant evaporating inside. The gaseous refrigerant would then exhaust to the atmosphere through the open end of the coil.

This is the purpose of all the additional parts and components of the mechanical refrigeration system.

The basic components of a refrigeration system are as follows:

1. An evaporator cooling coil;
2. A suction line;
3. The compressor;
4. The condensing coil;
5. The liquid line;
6. A metering device.

Keep in mind these three basic assumptions:

1. Heat will flow only from a relatively warm substance to a relatively cool substance.

2. A refrigerant exists as both a gas and a liquid at the same temperature, if it is at its "boiling point." A refrigerant at its boiling point will boil and absorb heat from its surrounding air, if the air is warmer than the refrigerant. A refrigerant at its boiling point will condense and become liquid, losing heat to its surrounding air, if it is cooler than the refrigerant.

3. The boiling point of the refrigerant depends upon the pressure of the refrigerant rising as the pressure rises, and falling as the pressure falls.

The following is a description of a basic refrigeration cycle and the state of the refrigerant as it passes through each basic component.

140 ELECTRICAL, REFRIGERATION, AND AIR CONDITIONING

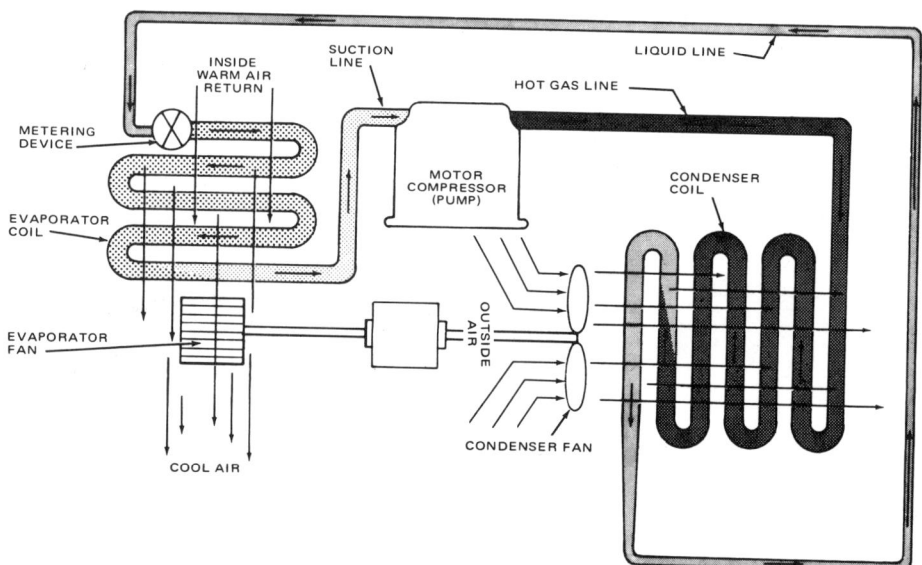

Diagram of the internal parts of a travel trailer air conditioner.

1. The compressor compresses the refrigerant vapor, increasing its temperature and pressure, and forces it along to the condensing coil.

2. At the condensing coil, air, which is cooler than the refrigerant, passes across the outside of the coil and absorbs some of the refrigerant's heat. The refrigerant temperature will decrease until cooled to its saturation point. In this state, the vapor will condense to a liquid.

3. The liquid, which is still under high pressure from the compressor, flows through the small liquid line to a metering device. The metering device can be either a valve or a capillary tube.

4. The high-pressure liquid refrigerant is forced through the metering device, is reduced in pressure, and then expands into the larger area of the evaporator. Under this low-pressure condition, the liquid begins to boil until it is in a vapor state.

5. During this change from a liquid to a vapor, the refrigerant absorbs heat from the air flowing across the outside of the coil. The air, losing its heat, becomes very cool, cooling the room.

6. The evaporated and heat-laden refrigerant at low pressure is then drawn into the compressor through the suction line. The whole cycle is then repeated.

The half of the system under high pressure is called the "high side." The other half of the system, which is under low pressure, is called the "low side."

In order to keep your air conditioner operating at peak efficiency, follow these normal maintenance procedures.

1. Clean the air filters regularly. These are usually made of fiberglass or foam rubber and can be washed in soap and warm water. The air conditioner should never be operated without the filters in place.

2. Keep the evaporator coil clean. If the passageways between the fins are plugged, carefully brush down the inner surface with a soft brush or cloth to remove surface lint. Be careful not to flatten or damage the fins. If the coil is clogged to any depth, it may have to be steam cleaned.

3. If your air conditioner is equipped with an evaporator drain tube, check it regularly. If it seems to be clogged by an overflow of condensation, blow through the tube to make sure it is open. If this doesn't work, run a wire (with the end protected) through the drain tube to open it. Check to see if the tube is kinked or bowed; make sure it is sloping toward the drain outlet.

4. Keep the condenser coils clean. (See step no. 2.)

5. Keep the louvers or screening on the outside cover free from leaves, paper, and the like; the flow of air to the unit could be restricted.

ELECTRICAL, REFRIGERATION, AND AIR CONDITIONING

Air Conditioning Troubleshooting Chart

Compressor Does Not Start; No Hum

Causes	Remedies
1. Open switch	1. Close switch
2. Fuse blown	2. Replace fuse
3. Broken connection	3. Check circuit and repair
4. Overload stuck	4. Wait for reset; check current
5. Frozen compressor or motor bearings	5. Replace compressor
6. Open circuit in compressor stator	6. Replace compressor

Compressor Starts; Motor Will Not Get Off Starting Windings; High Amperage and Rattle in the Compressor

Causes	Remedies
1. Improperly wired	1. Check wiring against diagram
2. Low line voltage	2. Check line voltage and correct
3. Relay defective	3. Replace relay if defective
4. Run capacitor defective	4. Replace capacitor
5. Compressor motor starting and running windings shorted	5. Replace compressor
6. Starting capacitor weak	6. Check capacitor; replace if necessary
7. Tight compressor	7. Check oil level or replace compressor

Compressor Will Not Start—Hums and Trips on Overload

Causes	Remedies
1. Improperly wired	1. Check wiring against diagram
2. Low line voltage	2. Check line voltage and correct
3. Starting capacitor defective	3. Replace capacitor
4. Relay contacts not closing	4. Check why the contact points are not closing; replace if defective
5. Compressor motor is grounded or has open winding	5. Replace compressor
6. Tight compressor	6. Check oil level or replace compressor

Compressor Starts and Runs but Short Cycles

Causes	Remedies
1. Low line voltage	1. Check line voltage and correct
2. Additional current passing through overload protector	2. Check for wiring diagram. Check the fan motors for connection to the wrong side of protector
3. Run capacitor defective	3. Check capacitance and replace
4. Compressor too hot; inadequate motor cooling	4. Check refrigerant charge; add if necessary
5. Compressor motor windings are shorted	5. Replace compressor

Air Conditioning Troubleshooting Chart (cont.)

Compressor Starts and Runs but Short Cycles

Causes	Remedies
6. Overload protector defective	6. Check current, give reset time; if it does not come back, replace compressor
7. Compressor tight	7. Check oil level, or replace compressor
8. Discharge valve defective	8. Replace compressor

Compressor Short Cycling

Causes	Remedies
1. Dirty air filter	1. Replace
2. Refrigerant charge low	2. Recharge system with correct charge
3. Restricted capillary tube	3. Replace
4. Dry condenser	4. Clean condenser
5. Compressor valve leaks	5. Replace compressor
6. Overload protector cutting out	6. Check current; give reset time; if it does not come back, replace compressor

Unit Operates Long or Continuously

Causes	Remedies
1. Shortage of refrigerant	1. Fix leak and recharge
2. Control contacts frozen or stuck closed	2. Clean points or replace
3. Insufficient air or dirty condenser	3. Find out and correct
4. Air-conditioned space is poorly insulated or excess load in home	4. Replace with larger unit
5. Compressor valves are defective	5. Replace compressor
6. Restriction in refrigerant system	6. Find out and correct
7. Filter dirty	7. Clean or replace
8. Air is by-passing the coil or service load	8. Check return air and keep doors closed

Space Temperature Too High

Causes	Remedies
1. Refrigerant charge low	1. Check for leaks and recharge
2. Control set too high	2. Reset control
3. Cap tube plugged	3. Repair or replace
4. Iced or dirty coils	4. Defrost or clean
5. Unit too small	5. Replace with larger unit
6. Insufficient air circulation	6. Correct air circulation
7. Cap tube does not allow enough refrigerant	7. Replace cap tube
8. High and low pressures approaching each other—compressor valves are defective	8. Replace compressor
9. Low line voltage	9. Decrease load on line or increase wire size

ELECTRICAL, REFRIGERATION, AND AIR CONDITIONING

Air Conditioning Troubleshooting Chart (cont.)

Space Temperature Too High

Causes	Remedies
10. Dirty air filter	10. Replace
11. Dirty condenser	11. Clean condenser

Starting Capacitor Open, Shorted, or Burned Out

Causes	Remedies
1. Relay contacts not operating properly	1. Clean contacts or replace
2. Improper capacitor	2. Check for proper MFD rating and voltage
3. Low voltage	3. Find the reason and correct
4. Improper relay	4. Check parts list and replace
5. Short cycling	5. See the section under the compressor starts and runs, but short cycles

Running Capacitor Open, Shorted, or Burned Out

Causes	Remedies
1. Improper capacitor	1. Check for proper MFD rating and voltage
2. Excessive high line voltage	2. Line voltage must be in range; not more than 10 per cent above rated motor voltage. Correct

Relay Shorted or Burned Out

Causes	Remedies
1. Line voltage is too low or too high	1. Find the reason and correct
2. Incorrect running capacitor	2. Replace with correct MFD capacitor
3. Relay loose	3. Tighten the relay
4. Short cycling	4. See, compressor starts and runs, but short cycles

Condenser Pressure Too High

Causes	Remedies
1. Air in system	1. Purge system
2. Dirty condenser	2. Clean condenser
3. Unit overcharged	3. Discharge some refrigerant
4. Condenser air is off	4. Check condenser motor connections for burn-out

Condenser Pressure Too Low

Causes	Remedies
1. Refrigerant charge too low	1. Fix leak and recharge the correct amount of refrigerant
2. Compressor discharge or suction valves defective	2. Replace compressor

Air Conditioning Troubleshooting Chart (cont.)

Condenser Pressure Too Low

Causes	Remedies
3. Entering temperature to evaporator is low	3. Raise temperature

Frosted or Sweating Suction Line

Causes	Remedies
1. Capillary tube passes excess refrigerant	1. Check the size and bore of capillary tube
2. Evaporator fan not running	2. Repair or replace
3. Overcharge of refrigerant	3. Correct to the right charge

Hot Liquid Line

Causes	Remedies
1. Low refrigerant charge	1. Fix leak and recharge

Frost on Capillary Tube

Causes	Remedies
1. Ice plugging capillary tube	1. Apply hot wet cloth to capillary tube. If suction pressure increases, it is indication of moisture

Noisy Unit

Causes	Remedies
1. Tubing rattle	1. Fix so it is free of contact
2. Fan blade causing vibration	2. Check for a bend, and if necessary, replace
3. Refrigerant overcharged. Liquid refrigerant in the compressor or oil is too high	3. Check for right refrigerant charge and maintain oil level. If necessary, replace capillary tube
4. Loose parts or mountings	4. Fix and tighten
5. Motor bearings worn	5. Replace motor
6. Leak of oil in the compressor	6. Add required oil

Generators

BASIC THEORY

Generators depend on the movement of an electrical conductor through the lines of force of a magnetic field to cause current to flow. The direction of flow is dependent upon the direction of the mechanical movement and the polarity of the magnets.

All generators that are discussed here generate alternating current (AC) only. However, for discussion purposes, one type will be referred to as an "alternator" and the other type will be called a "generator." The primary mechanical difference between the two, in this discussion, is the physical placement of the magnetic field.

In a generator, the magnetic field is stationary and the AC is taken from the revolving armature. In an alternator, the magnetic field revolves and the AC is gen-

ELECTRICAL, REFRIGERATION, AND AIR CONDITIONING 145

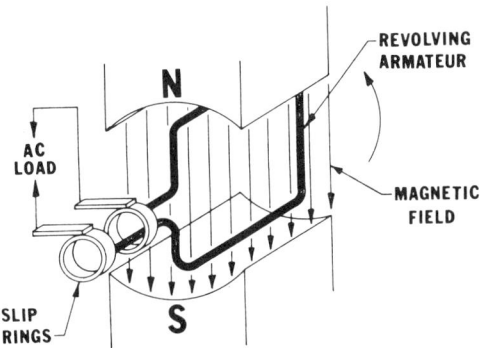

A "generator" with the stationary magnetic field.

erated in the fixed stator. This (alternator) is the type that is installed in cars. The AC is transformed into DC by diodes. The type of alternator that is used in trailers supplies AC only, therefore, there is no need for diodes and all output is AC.

The relationship between current flow and magnetism is the basic principle by which all electric motors, alternators, generators, and transformers operate. Any conductor that has current flowing through it has a magnetic field at right angles to

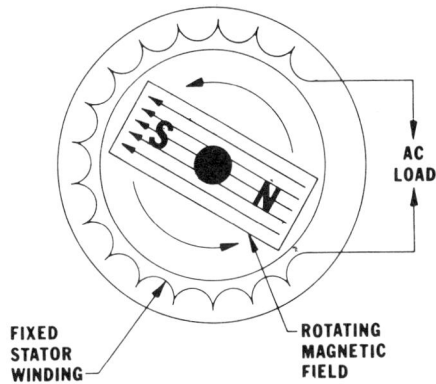

An alternator with the rotating magnetic field.

the direction of the flow. If a laminated core of iron is wrapped with a coil of wire and current is put through the wire, a magnetic field will be created. The end of the core where the current enters the coil will become the North end of the field and the end from which the current leaves the coil will become the South end of the magnetic field. This is true of a plain bar magnet as well as a horseshoe magnet.

The larger the amount of current flow, the greater the magnetic field.

As previously stated, a current flowing through a conductor creates a magnetic field. Conversely, the lines of force of the

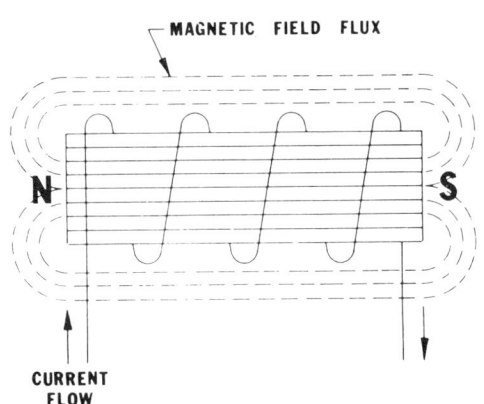

A laminated core of iron wrapped with a coil of wire with current flowing through it becomes a magnet with a magnetic field around it.

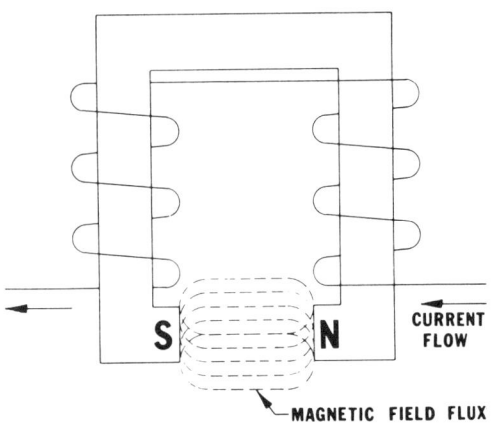

A horseshoe magnet with its magnetic field.

magnetic field passing through a conductor cause current to flow in that conductor. The current flowing in the primary, which is called the exciting current, must vary in amplitude to produce an expanding and collapsing magnetic field in the secondary where the current leaves the mechanism.

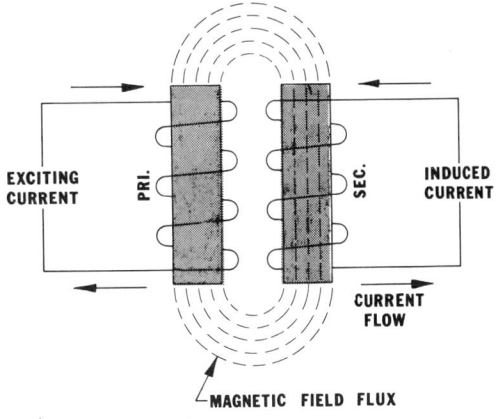

Diagram of a transformer.

ELECTRICAL, REFRIGERATION, AND AIR CONDITIONING

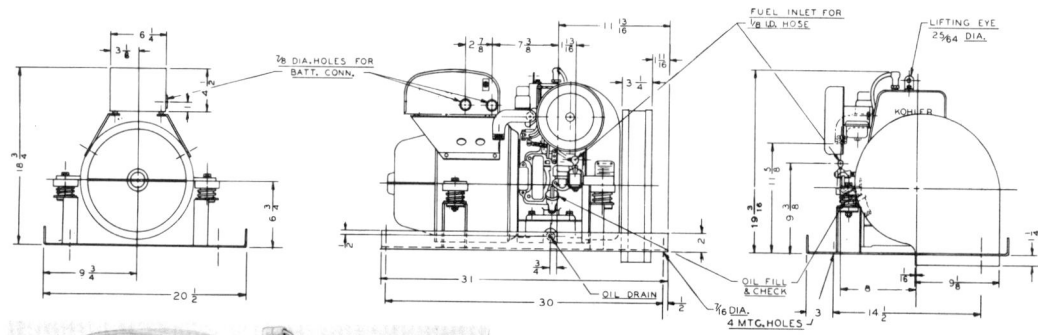

An example of the type of generator that can be installed in a travel trailer.

The current on the secondary is called induced current. Once again, a current is produced by either moving a conductor through magnetic lines of force or moving the magnetic lines of force through a conductor. The movement can be either physical, such as a rotor, or electrical, such as a transformer.

These are the basic principles by which all alternators of generators work. The explanation here is a much simplified and condensed version of what can be and often is a very complex process. Therefore, unless you are very skilled in electronics, do not attempt any major electrical repairs on your generator.

A generator installed in the rear of a travel trailer.

MAINTENANCE

In the following paragraphs some routine maintenance procedures are mentioned. These can be performed by almost anyone with a basic knowledge of mechanics and a limited supply of tools.

Any generator installed in a travel trailer requires a strict and complete maintenance schedule. Remember that an hour running time on a generator is equivalent to 42–82 miles on a car engine. The need for regular checks is obvious.

This particular model slides out on a track for easier servicing. It is completely enclosed for fire prevention and has an automatically actuated fire extinguisher inside the housing.

A great many generators are sold without engine hour meters. These register the amount of time the engine has run, and are very similar to clocks, but operate only when the engine is running. If your unit is not equipped with such a meter, you should get one and install it on your generator. Engine hour meters are relatively cheap, and since they could prevent major repair bills by keeping track of running hours and scheduled maintenance, the purchase of one could pay for itself in a very short time.

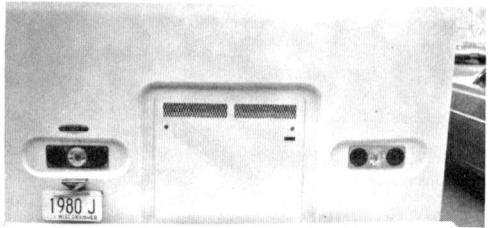

The generator in place with the cover on and ready for travel.

ELECTRICAL, REFRIGERATION, AND AIR CONDITIONING

Virtually all generators come with an owner's manual which should be followed very closely for operating and maintenance instructions. There is probably a maintenance log in the back of the manual where you should log all the maintenance checks you perform to keep track of what has, and what has not, been done.

The following maintenance procedures should be carried out to ensure trouble-free operation.

After every eight hours of running time, inspect the generator and its compartment housing. If dust has accumulated from off-the-road use, clean it with the compressed air hose at your local service station. Check the fuel supply and the oil level in the crankcase. Add to the reservoirs if they are below a safe level.

At the end of every 50 hours of running time, perform the eight-hour operation, service the air cleaner, and clean the governor linkage.

After 100 hours, perform the 50-hour operation, and clean and gap the spark plugs, change the oil, and clean out the crankcase breather.

As the running time begins to add up, so do the number of required maintenance checks. After 200 hours, there is the equivalent of at least 8400 miles on your generator. At this point, perform the normal 100-hour check-up, but also check the ignition points and replace them if they are badly worn, pitted, or burned. Clean the fuel filter and the top of the battery with water. If you operate your generator in warmer climates, check the battery more often. Pull off the covering or casing from the generator armature. Check and clean the collector ring where the brushes make contact with the armature and check the brushes for wear. Replace collector ring brushes if they are worn to $5/16$ in. or less. If you don't know that much about electrical mechanisms and aren't too sure what the brushes are, take the generator to a qualified electrical mechanic.

At 500 hours your generator has run an equivalent of 21,000 miles. The average generator runs at about 3600 rpm to generate a current of 60 cycles and 110 V. This is a relatively slow speed and the combustion chambers do get dirtied with combustion deposits. Have the combustion chambers cleaned and the valve clearances set to the correct gap.

For faster-turning units, the periodic maintenance should be performed more often than what has been recommended here. Be sure to check the owner's manual for the correct settings, specifications, and frequency of the various maintenance operations.

Some manufacturers offer emergency parts kits containing components that might go bad while you are out on the road. Such things as a point set, spark plugs, condenser, air cleaner, carburetor repair kits, fuel pump repair kits, choke element, and a selection of various gaskets should be included in such emergency repair kits.

If your generator is to be stored and not used over the winter months, protective measures should be taken. Gasoline should not be allowed to rest in the engine for any length of time. It will turn into a gummy substance and damage or clog the fuel pump, all the lines, and the carburetor. Before putting the generator away for the season, disconnect the fuel line from the carburetor and run the engine until it stops from a lack of gas. This drains all of the gas from the carburetor. Drain the gas lines and the gas tank. For added protection, remove the spark plug and squirt about an ounce of SAE 30 oil into the cylinder, turn the engine over a couple of times to distribute the oil, and replace the spark plug.

HOW TO CHOOSE THE RIGHT SIZE OF ALTERNATOR

In order to determine the right size of alternator, add the total watts of all the appliances, lights, and equipment to be connected to the unit. With lights, heaters, and appliances, simply add the nameplate ratings. For equipment and power tools, check the hp rating and the type of motor.

Electric motors require more current to start than to run. The starting current varies greatly depending on the type of motor. To start repulsion induction motors require two and one-half times the amount of current it takes to run. Split-phase motors require as much as five times the running current for starting. Universal motors such as the type used in portable power tools and appliances do not require extra starting current—only the running watts are figured.

To compute the number of watts required, if only the amps and volts are given, use the following formula:
Amps × Volts = Watts

Follow these three steps to determine the amount of power you will need.

1. List the wattage of the lights, heater, appliances, and so forth. (Obtain figures from the nameplate data when possible.)

2. Analyze the motor loads and check for starting watts.

3. Determine which of the loads can be staggered for emergency use. In most cases it is impractical to have an alternator that is large enough to handle the total connected load.

Small Appliance Current Requirements

Appliance and Equipment

Appliance	Watts	Equipment	Watts
Electric Iron	900	Hand Saw 8 in.	1500
TV Set	200–550	Electric Drill ½ in.	750
Toaster	1000	Electric Drill ¼ in.	250
Skillet	1250		
Coffee Maker	1000		
Radio	40–100		
Refrigerator	1200		
Electric Stove	3000–10000		
Electric Water Heater	1000–5000		

Motor Starting Requirements
Approximate Starting Watts Required

Motor Rating (hp)	Approx Running Watts	Universal Motors	Repulsion Induction Motors	Capacitor Motors	Split Phase Motors
⅙	275	400	600	850	1200
¼	400	500	850	1050	1700
⅓	450	600	975	1350	1950
½	600	750	1300	1800	2600
¾	850	1000	1900	2600	°
1	1000	1250	2300	3000	°
1½	1600	°	3200	4200	°
2	2000	°	3900	5100	°
3	3000	°	5200	6800	°
5	4800	°	7500	9800	°

° Motors of higher horsepower shown in this classification are not generally used.

Alternator Capability for Electric Motor Starting

TYPE OF MOTOR AND HP RATING

Alternator Rating In Watts	Universal	Repulsion Heavy Start Load	Induction Light Start Load	Capacitor Heavy Start Load	Capacitor Light Start Load	Split Phase Heavy Start Load	Split Phase Light Start Load
1000	½	—	—	—	—	—	—
1250	1	½	—	¼	—	¼	—
1750	1	½	¾	¼	½	⅓	—
2650	1½	1	1½	½	1	½	¾
3500	°	2	2½	1½	2	°	°
5000	°	2½	3	2	°	°	°
7500	°	4	5	2½	°	°	°
1500	1	½	½	¼	¼	¼	°
3000	2	1½	2	¾	1	¾	¾
5000	°	2½	3	2½	3	°	°

° Motors of higher horsepower rating than shown in this classification are not generally used.

6 · Running Gear Assembly

Most travel trailers have an underslung spring arrangement. The ends of the springs are pointed upward and attached to the chassis while the axle assembly is attached to the underside or top of the spring by U-bolts and a flat plate. This arrangement is common for both single-axle and tandem-axle trailers.

Another popular type of suspension is that using torsional springs. This type consists of a square torsion bar mounted inside a metal casing with rubber cords, known as elastomers, on each of the four sides of the torsion bar and the inside of the casing. When the bar twists in the casing it compresses the rubber cords which

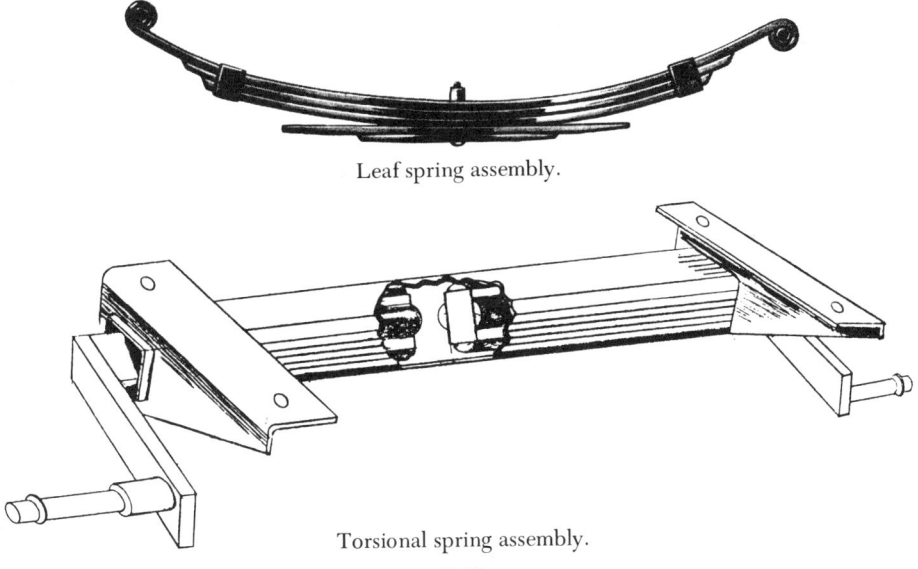

Leaf spring assembly.

Torsional spring assembly.

allow the torsion bar to turn only a limited distance. In effect, the trailer is mounted on rubber springs. Since there is no contact of any metal parts between the wheel and the chassis of the trailer, this system provides a smoother and quieter spring ac-

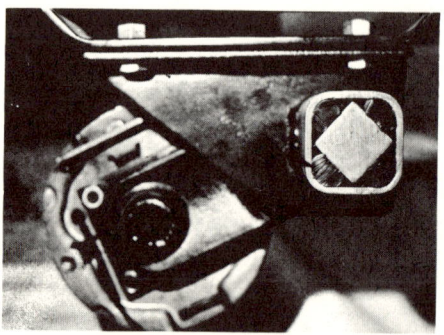

A cutaway view of a torsional spring axle. Note the rubber elastomers indicated by the arrow.

No load position. Note the rubber cords are compressed and still centered in the housing corners. Friction between the rubber and inner and outer metal parts prevents the torsion bar from slipping horizontally.

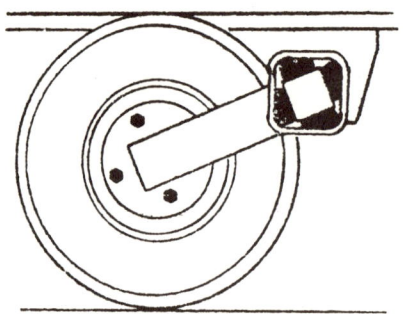

Normal load position. Note the rubber cords are deflected off center. They are further compressed and rolled from their original position.

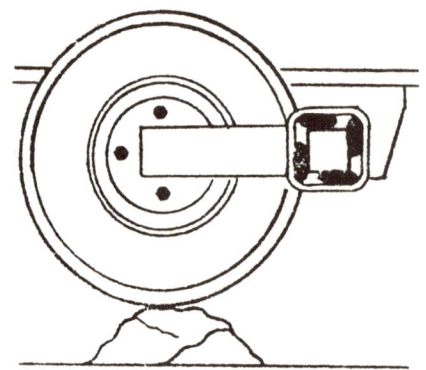

Nearly maximum of extreme shock load position. Note the rubber cords have been still further compressed and rolled almost to the off center limit. This condition occurs very rarely even over the roughest and bumpiest road surfaces. (Coleman)

tion. Since each wheel acts independently of the other, trailer sway is diminished considerably. This type of suspension system was first used on lighter trailers, such as boat trailers. It has since been perfected and adapted to use on heavier trailers.

Axle Removal

UNDERSLUNG SPRING TYPE SUSPENSION

1. Jack the trailer up so that all the wheels are raised off the ground at least one inch. Put two stand jacks under the tongue at the front end and at a suitable location at the rear of the trailer. It is important to consult each individual owner's manual for proper jacking instructions and locations.
2. Remove the wheel and tire assembly.
3. Disconnect all electric brake wires and hydraulic brake lines.
4. Remove the upper attachments of the shock absorbers and any axle locating arms.
5. Support the axle at the center with a floor jack.
6. Remove the nuts and washers from the U-bolts at both ends of the axle.
7. Lower the axle with the floor jack or slide the axle off the spring on one side, then down and out from beneath the trailer.
8. Check the axle for cracks and other visible damage. Check the shock absorbers for leakage and other visible damage.
9. To replace, reverse the above procedure.

TORSIONAL SPRING TYPE SUSPENSION

The procedure for removing the axle from trailers with torsional spring type suspensions is exactly the same as for underslung spring types except for step 6. Instead of removing the nuts and washers from the U-bolts holding the axle up to the springs, the nuts, bolts, and washers holding the axle mounting plate to the chassis of the trailer will be removed.

NOTE: *It is not recommended that the tongue jack be used alone for supporting the front end of the trailer. Two jackstands should be placed under the tongue on each side where the two members are separated the widest, just before they join the actual frame of the trailer and go under the body or outside shell. Also, after removal and replacement of the axles on trailers with hydraulic brakes, be sure to bleed the brakes at the wheel cylinder. See the "Brake" section for bleeding procedures.*

Axle Alignment

The most convenient method of checking to see if the wheels or axles are properly aligned is to check the tire for irregular wear patterns. To better understand trailer axle alignment it is necessary to study tire wear patterns and the causes.

Underinflation is probably the greatest cause of excessive tire wear. When the tire is underinflated it will wear on the outer edges only. This is due to the high profile of the trailer which will rock from side to side on soft tires. Tires on the curb side will usually wear faster than the tires on the road side since road surfaces usually slant down from the center out. This causes the trailer to lean toward the curb side and force the outer edge of the tire to roll under.

Improper toe-in is the second most common cause of abnormal tire wear. A tire that has too much toe-in or toe-out will side-slip on the road surface. Such misalignment will cause the tread of the tire to wear with a sharp edge on one side and a round edge on the other. A tire with an excessive amount of toe-out will wear the inside edge of the tire and the sharp edge of the tread will be pointing toward the outside. A tire with too much toe-in will wear the outside of the tread, much the same way that an underinflated tire would, but the grooves of the tread will have the sharp edges on the inside of the tread surface.

Camber is probably the least likely cause of alignment problems. The camber adjustment has to be extremely out of tolerance before any noticeable tire wear is observed. A tire or wheel with too much positive camber will wear the outer half of the tire; a tire with too much negative camber will wear the inner half of the tire. In both cases the tread will wear evenly around the tire, not in spots as with improper toe-in adjustment. (See the illustrations in the wheels and tires section.)

Alignment of the axles calls for special tools and equipment. This job should not be attempted by the back yard mechanic. Only persons experienced in this type of maintenance and the use of the special tools involved should attempt this operation.

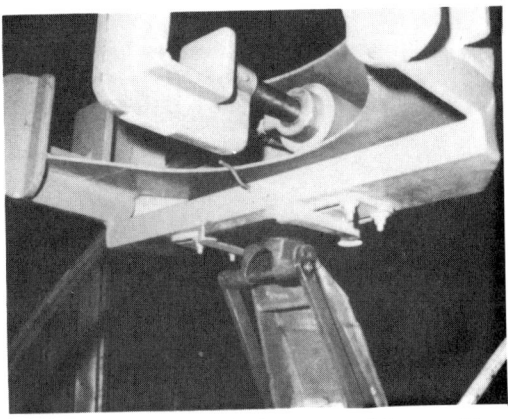

A hydraulic axle bender being raised into position via a floor jack. (© Airstream Corp.)

Most alignments are made by bending the axles either horizontally or vertically, depending on which adjustment (toe-in or camber) is being made. Bending the axle either forward or backward adjusts toe-in and toe-out. Bending the axle either up or down adjusts the camber. Very powerful hydraulic benders are clamped to the axle and pressure is applied very gradually so as not to damage the axle. The axle is bent to each trailer manufacturer's specifications. Never have the axle heated to have it bent because heating destroys the temper or hardness of the axle. Also, the rub-

RUNNING GEAR ASSEMBLY

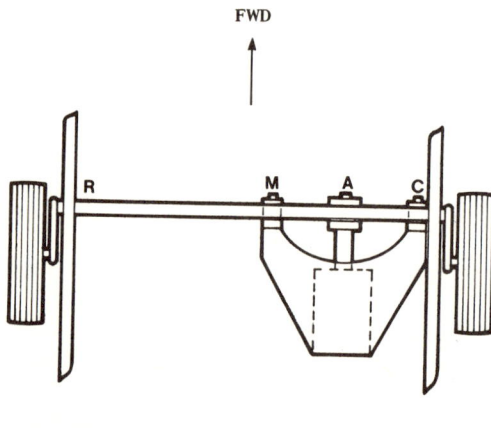

The positioning of an axle bender on a travel trailer axle. (© Airstream Corp.)

A. Cylinder jaw
C. Place the cylinder jaw at this position to correct the curbside wheel.
R. Place the cylinder jaw at this position to correct the roadside wheel.
M. Place the cylinder jaw at this position when both wheels need to be bent equal amounts in the same direction.
   The cylinder jaw is moved toward the front of the trailer to decrease the amount of toe-in.
   The cylinder jaw is moved toward the rear of the trailer to increase the amount of toe-in.
   To correct camber, remove the straightener from the jack and swing it into a vertical position (i.e., hanging from the axle tube). Use it in the same manner as for toe-in except that moving the cylinder jaw up increases the camber and moving it down decreases camber. This operation may require the underbelly to be cuffed for clearance of the bender.

ber elastomers of torsional spring axles would be destroyed by heat.

Trailer Tires and Wheels

Selecting tires for your trailer is not as complicated as it is for the tow vehicle simply because the trailer tires don't have to perform as many functions as do the tow vehicle's tires. Trailer tires don't have to steer; they don't have to drive or supply traction. The most important thing to know before you buy tires for your trailer is the total weight of your fully laden rig. Go to a commercial weighing station, determine the total weight of your trailer, then refer to the tire rating chart to find the best tire for your needs. If your trailer tips the scales right on the border line of the next higher-rated tire, use the higher-rated tire. Remember also that trailer tires are built to carry much higher pressures than car tires. Many service stations don't have tire gauges that are capable of measuring such high pressures. Once again, remember to have your own tire gauge; one that is capable of handling the pressure in your trailer's tires.

Wide oval and radial tires have lately been found satisfactory for use on trailers. Both designs have given greater stability and longer mileage than the conventional tires, and there are specially designed tires, of both types, for trailers. A tire dealer experienced in putting tires on trailers should be consulted about these relatively new developments.

WHEEL AND TIRE MAINTENANCE

Pressure is the most important item in tire maintenance. If the proper tire pressure is maintained, maximum tire life can be expected. Check tire pressures only when the tires are cool since pressure increases at running temperatures. Tires should not be bled when hot. Tire pressure gauges can be bought at a reasonable price and it would be a good idea to purchase one, store it in the trailer, and use it often.

Tires should be rotated after about 5000 miles. Consult the owner's manual for the proper tire rotating pattern.

Proper balancing of the wheel is very important because extreme vibration caused by an out-of-balance wheel can eventually cause structural damage to the trailer and its interior components. The wheel and tire should be balanced every time they are rotated or repaired.

It is important to consult the owner's manual of the trailer for proper jacking instructions and locations when changing a tire. On some tandem-axle trailers it is possible to change a tire without a jack. Simply pull the trailer up on a ramp until the wheel that is to be removed spins freely.

After the tire-wheel assembly is replaced on the hub, tighten the lug nuts—diametrically—to about 110 ft lbs. If a torque wrench is not available, tighten the lug nuts with a regular lug wrench to a reasonable tightness, being careful not to stretch the lug or break it off.

Wheel/Tire Assembly Troubleshooting

Wheel Shimmy

Probable Cause	Remedy
Loose wheel lug nuts	Tighten to 110 ft lbs
Loose or broken wheel bearing	Tighten spindle nut or replace and adjust wheel bearing
Wheel out of balance	Balance the wheel
Bent wheel	Replace the wheel
Improper axle alignment	Have axle aligned to manufacturer's specifications

Improper Tire Wear

Probable Cause	Remedy
Not rotating the tires	Rotate tires according to manufacturer's recommendations in owner's manual, or by an authorized mechanic at a trailer service center
Incorrect air pressure	Inflate the tires to proper pressure
Improperly acting brake	Correct as required (See "Brake" section)
Improper axle alignment	Align axle

Wheel Bearings

Maintenance of trailer wheel bearings is something that can be handled by anyone with a bit of automotive knowledge, sufficient and suitable wheel bearing grease, and a few basic tools such as a screwdriver and a pair of pliers.

Before handling the bearings there are a few things that you should try to remember to do and try to avoid.

REMEMBER TO DO THE FOLLOWING:

1. Remove all outside dirt from the housing before exposing the bearing.
2. Treat a used bearing as gently as you would a new one.
3. Work with clean tools in clean surroundings.
4. Use clean, dry canvas gloves, or at least clean, dry hands.
5. Clean solvents and flushing fluids are a must.
6. Use clean paper when laying out the bearings to dry.
7. Protect disassembled bearings from rust and dirt. Cover them up.
8. Use clean rags to wipe bearings.
9. Keep the bearing in oil-proof paper when they are to be stored or are not in use.
10. Clean the inside of the housing before replacing the bearing.

AVOID THE FOLLOWING:

1. Don't work in dirty surroundings.
2. Don't use dirty, chipped, or damaged tools.
3. Try not to work on wooden work benches or use wooden mallets.
4. Don't handle bearings with dirty or moist hands.
5. Do not use gasoline for cleaning, use a safe solvent.
6. Do not spin-dry bearings with compressed air. They will spin at a far greater speed than they are designed to withstand.
7. Do not spin unclean bearings.
8. Avoid using cotton waste or dirty cloths to wipe bearings.
9. Try not to scratch or nick bearing surfaces.
10. Do not allow the bearing to come in contact with dirt or rust at any time.

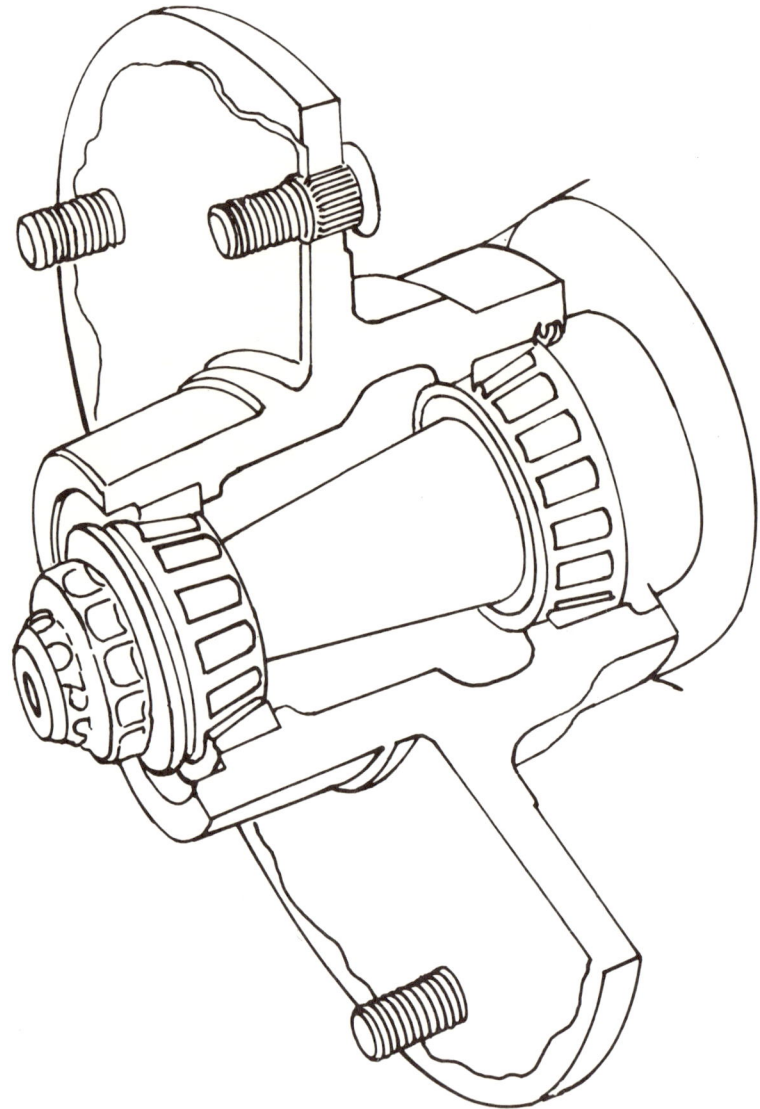

A cutaway view of a wheel bearing and hub assembly.

The procedure for checking and/or replacing the wheel bearings is as follows:

1. Jack the trailer up so the wheel is off the ground and can spin freely. Consult the owner's manual for proper jacking instructions and locations. It is easier to check all the bearings at the same time. If the equipment needed is available, raise the trailer off all its wheels through the use of stand jacks or blocks. Make sure the trailer is completely stable before proceeding any further.

2. Remove the hub cap and the dust cap with a heavy screwdriver. Some dust caps screw on, in which case a pair of water pump pliers will be needed to remove them.

3. Remove the cotter pin and discard it. Cotter pins should never be reused.

4. Remove the spindle nut and the washer behind it.

5. Wiggle the hub and wheel assembly so that the outer wheel bearing becomes loose and can be removed.

6. Remove the wheel and hub assembly from the spindle and place it on the ground with the outside facing up.

7. Place a block of wood through the spindle hole and tap out the inner grease seal. Never use anything made of metal to tap out the grease seal because of possible damage to the inner bearing. Tap lightly so as not to damage the bearing. When the seal falls out, so will the inner bearing.

Discard the seal. Perform the above procedures to all the wheels that are going to be serviced.

8. Place all of the bearings, nuts, washers, and dust caps in a container of solvent. Cleanliness is basic to wheel bearing maintenance. Use a light soft brush to thoroughly clean each part. Make sure that every bit of dirt and grease is rinsed off, then place each cleaned part on an absorbent cloth and let them dry completely.

9. Inspect the bearings for pitting, flat spots, rust, and rough areas. Check the races on the hub and the spindle for the same defects and rub them clean with a rag that has been soaked in solvent. If the races show hairline cracks or worn, shiny areas, they must be replaced with new parts. Replacement seals, bearings, and other required parts can be bought at any auto parts store or trailer service center. The old parts that are to be replaced should be taken along to be compared with the replacement part to ensure a perfect match.

10. Pack the wheel bearings with grease. There are special devices made for the specific purpose of greasing bearings, but, if one is not available, pack the wheel bearings by hand. Put a large dab of grease in the palm of your hand and push the bearing through it with a sliding motion. The grease must be forced through the side of the bearing and in between each roller. Continue until the grease be-

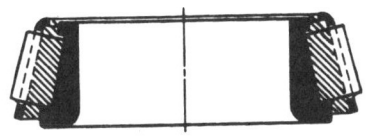

A cutaway view of a bearing. The shaded areas represent the positioning of the grease.

gins to ooze out the other side and through the gaps between the rollers; the bearing must be completely packed with grease. There is a special wheel bearing grease for trailers; it has longer fibers than the type used on cars. The reason for this is that when trailer axles are made, the spindle is machined before the axle is bent to the desired shape. In the bending process, the spindle is sometimes bent slightly out of round. Trailer bearings are, therefore, slightly more susceptible to failure than those on a car. To compensate for this unfortunate condition, special grease with longer fibers (to take up the gap that is created between the bearing and the imperfect surface of the spindle) is used. Be sure to use the special trailer bearing grease which can be obtained from any well-equipped trailer service center.

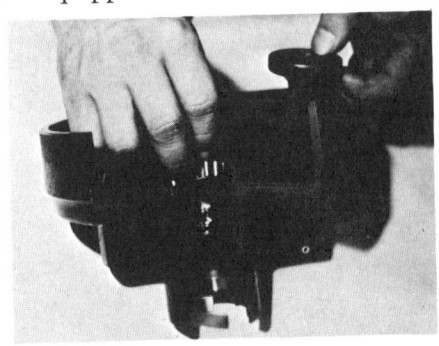

Replace the inner bearing and the grease seal. A cutaway view.

11. Turn the hub assembly over, making sure that it is perfectly clean, and drop the inner wheel bearing into place. Using a hammer and a block of wood, tap the new seal in place. Do not hit the race with the hammer directly. Move the block of wood around the circumference until it is seated properly.

Place the hub and drum assembly on the spindle.

12. Slide the hub and tire/wheel assembly onto the spindle, and push it as far as it will go, making sure that it has completely covered the brake shoes.

13. Place the outer bearing in place over the spindle. Press it in until it is snug. Place the washer on the spindle behind the bearing. Put on the spindle nut and turn it down until a slight binding is felt, then back it off to the nearest notch, place the new cotter pin up and over the end of the spindle, and cut off the other end with a pair of cutters.

156 RUNNING GEAR ASSEMBLY

Installing the outer bearing.

Install and adjust the spindle nut.

14. Replace the dust cap and the hub cap. The dust cap must fit snugly to protect the bearings from dust, water, and the like. If it looks as though it might not be able to seal the hub properly, replace the dust cap.

BEARING DIAGNOSIS

This section will help in the diagnosis of bearing failure. Such a diagnosis can be helpful in determining the cause of rear axle failure. The illustrations will help to take some of the guesswork out of deciding when to use an old bearing and when to replace it with a new one.

When disassembling a rear axle, the general condition of all bearings should be noted and classified where possible. Proper recognition of the cause will help in correcting the problem and avoiding a repetition of the failure.

Some of the common causes of bearing failure are:

    a. Abuse during assembly or disassembly;
    b. Improper assembly methods;
    c. Improper or inadequate lubrication;
    d. Bearing contact with dirt or water;
    e. Wear caused by dirt or metal chips;
    f. Corrosion or rust;
    g. Seizing due to overloading;
    h. Overheating;
    i. Frettage of the bearing seats;
    j. Brinelling from impact or shock loading;
    k. Manufacturing defects;
    l. Pitting due to fatigue.

To avoid damage to the bearing from improper handling, it is best to treat a used bearing the same as a new bearing. Always work in a clean area with clean tools. Remove all outside dirt from the housing before exposing a bearing and clean all bearing seats before installing a bearing.

CAUTION: *Never spin a bearing, either by hand or with compressed air. This will lead to almost certain bearing failure.*

RUNNING GEAR ASSEMBLY 157

Bearing Failure Chart

General Wear

Cause	Serviceability
Wear on races and rollers caused by fine abrasives	Clean all parts and check seals. Install new bearing if old one is rough or noisy.

Normal wear pattern. (© Chevrolet Div. G.M. Corp.)

Step Wear

Cause	Serviceability
Wear pattern on roller ends caused by fine abrasives	Clean all parts and check seals. Install new bearings if old one is rough or noisy.

Step wear. (© Chevrolet Div. G.M. Corp.)

Indentations

Cause	Serviceability
Surface depressions on races and rollers caused by hard foreign particles	Clean all parts and check seals. Install new bearing if old one is rough or noisy.

158 RUNNING GEAR ASSEMBLY

Indentations. (© Chevrolet Div. G.M. Corp.)

Galling

Cause	Serviceability
Metal smears on roller ends due to overheating from improper lubricant or overloading	Install a new bearing. Check seals and use proper lubricant.

Galling. (© Chevrolet Div. G.M. Corp.)

Etching

Cause	Serviceability
Bearing surfaces appear gray or gray-black with related etching	Install new bearing and check seals. Use proper lubricant.

Etching. (© Chevrolet Div. G.M. Corp.)

RUNNING GEAR ASSEMBLY

Bearing Failure Chart (cont.)

Cage Wear

Cause	Serviceability
Wear around outside diameter of cage and rollers caused by foreign material and poor lubrication	Clean all parts, check seals, and install new bearing.

Cage wear. (© Chevrolet Div. G.M. Corp.)

Fatigue Spalling

Cause	Serviceability
Flaking of surface metal due to fatigue	Clean all parts and install new bearing.

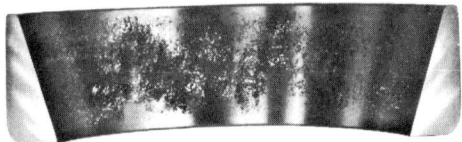

Fatigue spalling. (© Chevrolet Div. G.M. Corp.)

Heat Discoloration

Cause	Serviceability
Discoloration from faint yellow to dark blue due to overload or lubricant breakdown. Softening of races or rollers also	Check for softening of parts by drawing a file over suspected area. The file will glide easily over hard metal, but will cut soft metal. If overheating is evident, install new bearings. Check seals and other parts.

160 RUNNING GEAR ASSEMBLY

Heat discoloration. (© Chevrolet Div. G.M. Corp.)

Stain Discoloration

Cause	Serviceability
Stain discoloration ranging from light brown to black, caused by lubricant breakdown or moisture	Reuse bearings if stains can be removed by light polishing and no overheating exists. Check seals.

Stain discoloration. (© Chevrolet Div. G.M. Corp.)

Brinelling

Cause	Serviceability
Surface indentations in race caused by rollers under impact load or vibration while the bearing is not rotating	If the old bearing is rough or noisy, install a new bearing.

Brinelling. (© Chevrolet Div. G.M. Corp.)

RUNNING GEAR ASSEMBLY

Bearing Failure Chart (cont.)

Bent Cage

Cause	Serviceability
Improper handling	Install a new bearing.

Bent cage. (© Chevrolet Div. G.M. Corp.)

Bent Cage

Cause	Serviceability
Improper handling	Install a new bearing.

Bent cage. (© Chevrolet Div. G.M. Corp.)

Misalignment

Cause	Serviceability
Outer race misaligned as shown	Install a new bearing and be sure races and bearing are properly seated.

Misalignment. (© Chevrolet Div. G.M. Corp.)

Cracked Inner Race

Cause	Serviceability
Crack due to improper fit, cocked bearing, or poor bearing seats	Install a new bearing and be sure it is seated properly.

Cracked inner race. (© Chevrolet Div. G.M. Corp.)

Frettage

Cause	Serviceability
Corrosion due to small movement of parts with no lubrication	Clean parts and check seals. Install a new bearing and be sure of proper lubrication.

Frettage. (© Chevrolet Div. G.M. Corp.)

RUNNING GEAR ASSEMBLY

Bearing Failure Chart (cont.)

Smears

Cause	Serviceability
Metal smears due to slippage caused by poor fit, improper lubrication, overloading, or handling damage	Clean parts, install new bearing, and check for proper fit and lubrication.

Smears. (© Chevrolet Div. G.M. Corp.)

Electric Brakes

Electric brakes are operated by 12 V current supplied by the tow vehicle and are integrally connected with the tow vehicle's brake system. The controller, which is hooked up to the tow vehicle's master cylinder and battery, transforms surge pressure from the master cylinder into electrical current. The controller can be set to determine when the trailer's brakes will start to operate in relation to the amount of pressure exerted on the brake pedal. A selective resistor regulates the amount of current coming from the controller and going to the brake assemblies. It can be adjusted according to how much electrical power is needed at the brakes—based on the total trailer weight.

When the brake pedal is applied, surge pressure is received from the tow vehicle's master cylinder by the controller's hydraulic cylinder. The controller's hydraulic cylinder pushes down on a set of points which completes a circuit from the tow vehicle's battery to the selective resistor. The electric current flows through the selective resistor and is decreased to the desired amount, according to how the selective resistor is set up. The proper amount of current then flows through the electrical coupling between the tow vehicle and the trailer, and then on to the brakes. The electric current then activates the magnet assembly causing it to attach itself to a steel armature plate that rotates with the

Electric brake assembly.

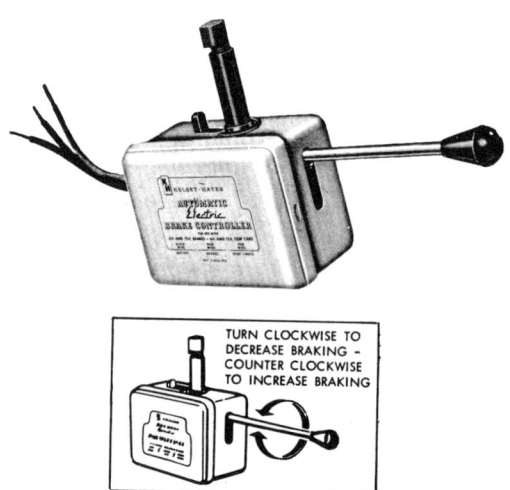

Electric brake controller. This type is usually mounted on the steering column.

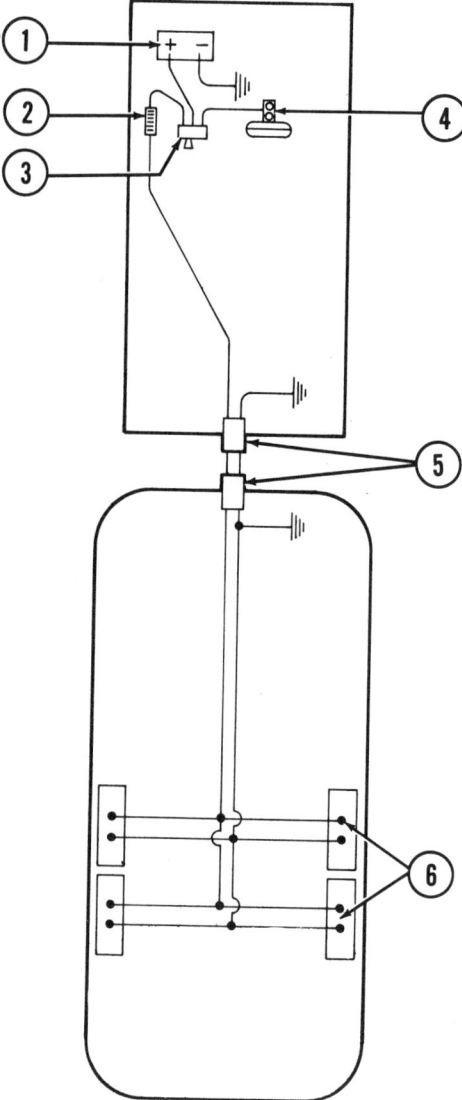

Location of electric brake components. (© Airstream Corp.)

1. Tow vehicle battery
2. Selective resistor
3. Controller
4. Tow vehicle master cylinder
5. Electrical connection between the tow vehicle and the trailer
6. Trailer brakes

brake drum. The magnet tries to rotate with the armature plate and, in fact, does move slightly, causing the arm, to which the magnet is secured, to move and expand the brake shoes against the brake drums.

There are various types of controllers available. The three basic designs, which all operate in a similar manner, will be discussed here. The completely automatic controller (in that the driver does not have to handle the controller in any way to operate it) is usually mounted under the dash or under the hood. This type of controller is hooked into the tow vehicle's hydraulic braking system and is activated automatically when the brake pedal is pushed. The only disadvantage to this type of system is that the trailer brakes cannot be applied separately without the tow vehicle's brakes also being applied. The completely manually operated controller (in that the driver has to operate the controller by hand every time the trailer brakes are needed) is usually mounted either on the steering column or dash where the controlling lever is convenient to the driver. When the driver wishes to stop, using both the car brakes and the trailer brakes, the brake pedal and the controller lever must be applied simultaneously. Needless to say, this is a slight inconvenience and the habit of reaching down for the controlling lever every time the brake pedal is pushed must be developed.

The third type of controller can be operated manually or left to operate automatically. It too is hooked integrally to the tow vehicle's brake system and is activated by pushing on the brake pedal. But it also has a controller lever which allows it to be operated manually. This allows the driver to apply the trailer brakes separately if so desired. This controller is also mounted on the steering column or dash to give the driver access to the controller lever.

The lever or handle protruding from the control unit serves two purposes: it initiates, at the correct time (according to the point gap setting), the flow of electric current from the tow vehicle's battery and on to the rest of the system; it also serves as the selective resistor adjustment. In controllers with levers, the selective resistor is usually incorporated into the control box. The system activation is accomplished by depressing the handle. The selective resistor setting is made by rotating the handle in either direction, thus increasing or decreasing the amount of current needed at the brakes.

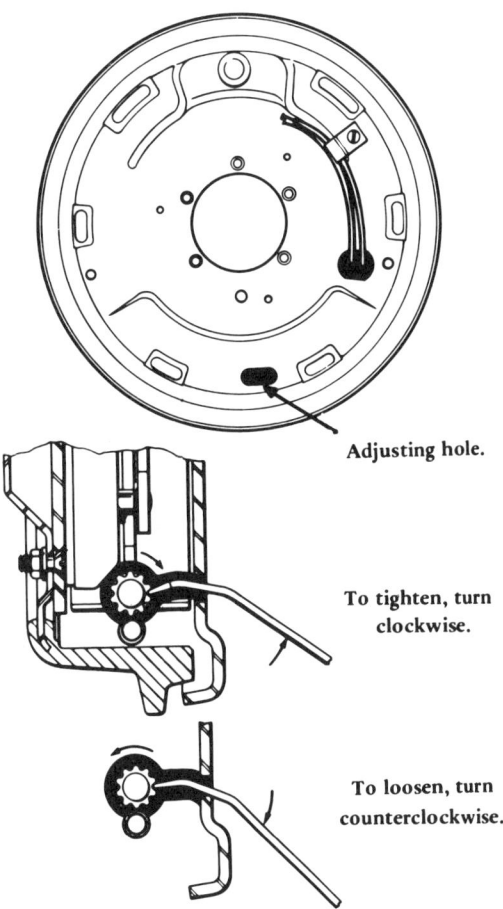

Brake adjustment. (© Airstream Corp.)

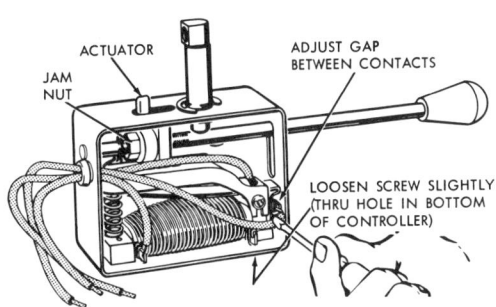

The internal components of an electric brake controller. Adjusting the point gap.

MAINTENANCE

Checking, Repairing, and Replacing Mechanical Components

Brake Adjustment

1. Electric brakes should be adjusted at least every 10,000 miles or every year, whichever comes first.
2. Block the wheels so the trailer won't move.
3. Jack the trailer at the proper location just high enough so the wheel clears the ground.
   NOTE: *It is extremely important to consult each individual trailer owner's manual for proper jacking instructions. Failure to do so could result in serious damage to the trailer.*
4. Remove the small rubber plug at the base of the backing plate.
5. While spinning the wheel, tighten the brakes by turning the star adjuster wheel. A brake adjusting tool or a screwdriver bent to a 90° angle will do the job properly. Turn the star adjuster until the wheel has a heavy drag, then back up the adjuster about 10 or 12 notches until the wheel turns freely. It is important that there is no drag present after the adjusting procedure is completed. Electric brakes on trailers must "hit" the drum fairly hard to be effective. To accomplish this they must travel farther, so the adjustment must be backed off more than would be common practice for an automobile.
6. Replace the rubber plug.
7. Repeat the above procedure on all trailer wheels.

Brake Assembly and Installation

1. Block the wheels so the trailer won't move.
2. Jack the trailer at the specified location high enough so that the wheel is off the ground. Once again be sure that the individual trailer owner's manual is consulted for proper jacking instructions.
3. Remove the hub cap and dust cap.
4. Remove the cotter pin.
5. Remove the spindle nut and washer.

166 RUNNING GEAR ASSEMBLY

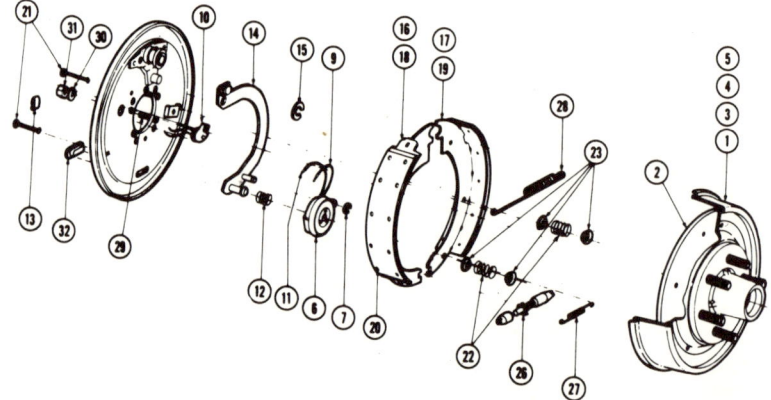

An exploded view of the brake assembly components. (© Airstream Corp.)

1. Drum assembly
2. Armature plate
3. Hub
4. Lug studs
5. Armature-to-drum attaching hardware
6. Magnet assembly
7. Retaining ring
8. Number 8 does not exist in the illustration
9. Terminal
10. Terminal connector
11. Terminal
12. Magnet spring
13. Cable clip
14. Actuating lever
15. Lever retaining springs
16+18. Primary shoe and lining assembly
17+19. Secondary shoe and lining assembly
20. Rivets
21. Hold down pin
22. Hold down spring
23. Hold down cup
26. Star adjusting wheel assembly
27. Adjusting wheel spring
28. Retractor spring
29. Backing plate mounting stud
30. Backing plate mounting washer
31. Backing plate mounting nut
32. Brake adjusting hole cover

6. Remove the outer bearing.

7. Remove the wheel, hub, brake drum, and inner bearing—all in one assembly.

8. Remove the brake shoes by removing all springs, retainers, and hold-down pins. Take note as to where they are located so they can be replaced in the same position. Special brake tools are available to facilitate the removal and installation of brake shoes. If none are available, such tools as a screwdriver and a pair of pliers can be used. Caution should be exercised when removing or installing springs because of their high tension.

9. Remove the star adjustment wheel from the bottom of the brake shoes. Make sure that the star wheel turns freely. A drop of light lubricating oil on the threads is recommended. When the star wheel is replaced on the new brake shoes, it should be adjusted to about the halfway point.

10. Apply a small amount of Lubriplate to the backing plate where the shoes rub.

11. To install, reverse the above procedure. Be sure the bearings and races are clean before installing. Tighten the spindle nut until it is snug, then back off one notch and install a new cotter pin. Adjust the brakes.

ARMATURE PLATES

Inspect the armature plates. Under normal conditions the plate should last indefinitely. If the plate shows excessive wear due to sand, mud, small stones, and so on,

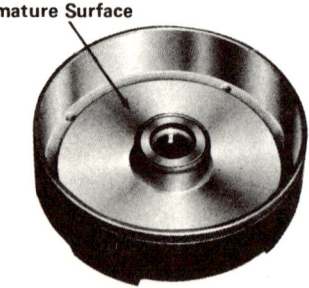

Armature plate surface.

however, it should be replaced. If only one armature plate is bad, replace only the one that is worn. If the armature plate is riveted in place, the rivets can be drilled out and the replacements parts installed with screws, nuts, and lockwashers.

NOTE: *Always inspect the magnet assembly when replacing the armature plate since the same condition that damaged it could also cause damage to the*

RUNNING GEAR ASSEMBLY

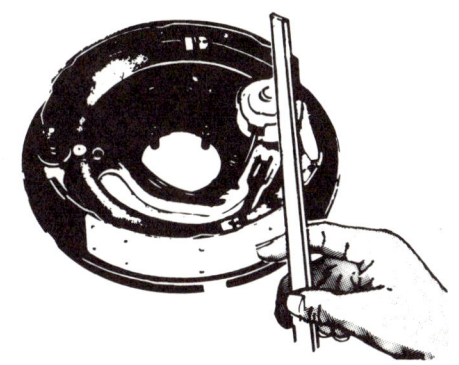

Use a straightedge to check the magnets for proper wear patterns.

magnet. If the magnet is wearing flat, there is no need to replace it unless it shows signs of wearing through to the magnet coil.

Brake Drums

Inspect the rubbing surface of the brake drum. It should be dull gray. One or two light score marks are no cause for alarm but if heavy scoring and excessive wear are present, the rubbing surface should be rebored or cut. Be sure that no more than the recommended amount is taken off the rubbing surface and the inside diameter of the drum is not extended beyond the recommended limits.

NOTE: *After cutting or reboring a brake drum, the brake lining may have to be ground to coincide with the new diameter of the drum. Some linings may even require shims between the lining and the shoe. Adjust the brakes after having the drum cut or rebored.*

Brake Lining

Inspect the lining for wear. If it is worn to the rivets or past the minimum thickness allowed, replace it. Uneven wear patterns indicate improperly located flanges or a bent backing plate. If the lining is badly contaminated with grease or oil, it should be replaced since this type of damage cannot be sanded or dissolved out of the brake lining.

NOTE: *Always replace brake linings in sets, both shoes on the same axle.*

Checking, Repair, or Replacing Electrical Components

When making any electrical tests, hook up the trailer to the tow vehicle.

The instrument for checking continuity is a test light. Tests should be made at three locations: inside the tow vehicle between the control box and the trailer power lead to the car-trailer electrical plug; at the trailer tongue between the breakaway switch and the power lead; at the brake assembly at each wheel.

Checking the Controller

Hook into the trailer power lead at the controller and operate the controller slowly. The test light should begin to glow and increase in brightness at a steady rate as the handle or brake pedal is depressed. If the test light operates, and increases and decreases in intensity smoothly, it can be assumed that the controller is operating correctly. If the test light does not perform as mentioned above, the controller should be checked for the following problems.

Circuit Check

1. Check the connector plug for proper contact and cleanliness.
2. Check all terminal points and splices in both tow vehicle and trailer for proper contacts and bare wires that might be shorting out the system.
3. Check for a blown fuse in the tow vehicle portion of the circuit.

Controller Check

Connect one lead of the test light to the trailer power lead and ground the other lead to the vehicle. Operate the controller. The current should vary smoothly. The test light should gradually get brighter as the controller lever is depressed. If the light does not brighten smoothly or there is no current present at all, remove the controller cover and inspect the resistor coil. If the coil, which should last indefinitely, is burned out, something is drastically wrong. (This can be detected visually.) The entire electrical system should be checked for a short circuit which could destroy any electric brake controller.

Be sure to set the prescribed gap clearance between the contactor strip and the resistor coil after replacing the coil. The gap can usually be adjusted by loosening one screw through an access hole in the bottom of the controller case. This setting is what determines when the electric brakes start to work after the pedal is pushed. The wider the setting, the farther the brake pedal has to be pushed before the brakes go down.

Inspect the hydraulic cylinder inside and its fittings outside for leakage while checking the controller. If leakage is present from the cylinder, it should be replaced. If leakage is originating at one of the fittings, try to tighten the fitting but if this does not help, the fitting should be replaced. After replacement of the hydraulic cylinder in the controller, the line is to be bled at the controller.

Checking the Breakaway Switch

The breakaway switch, which is located on the tongue of the trailer, serves as an emergency braking system for the trailer should it accidentally uncouple from the tow vehicle. This switch is usually connected to the tow vehicle by a small chain or cable. If the trailer becomes detached from the car, the cable pulls out a pin or activates the switch. The switch then draws current from its own power source (usually two or three dry-cell batteries or the trailer's self-contained power source) and activates the trailer brakes.

The breakaway switch can be checked by simply placing a test light in the circuit between the switch and the brakes and then activating the switch by pulling out the pin. If no current flows to the brakes, check the breakaway switch contacts for cleanliness and proper contact.

Another way of checking the breakaway switch is to jack the trailer up and have someone spin a wheel while the switch is activated. If the switch is operating correctly the brakes should lock the wheel.

Check the batteries or trailer battery for adequate charge. Replace the batteries if necessary.

Checking the Magnet Assembly

Inspect the magnet for wear and flatness. If the rubbing surface doesn't show signs of rubbing through and is wearing in the proper manner, it need not be replaced. To check the magnet for proper wearing pattern, lay a scale or straight-edge on the rubbing surface. The surface should be flat all the way across. If the magnet is not wearing properly it must be replaced because it is not working at its top efficiency if the entire rubbing surface is not making contact with the armature plate.

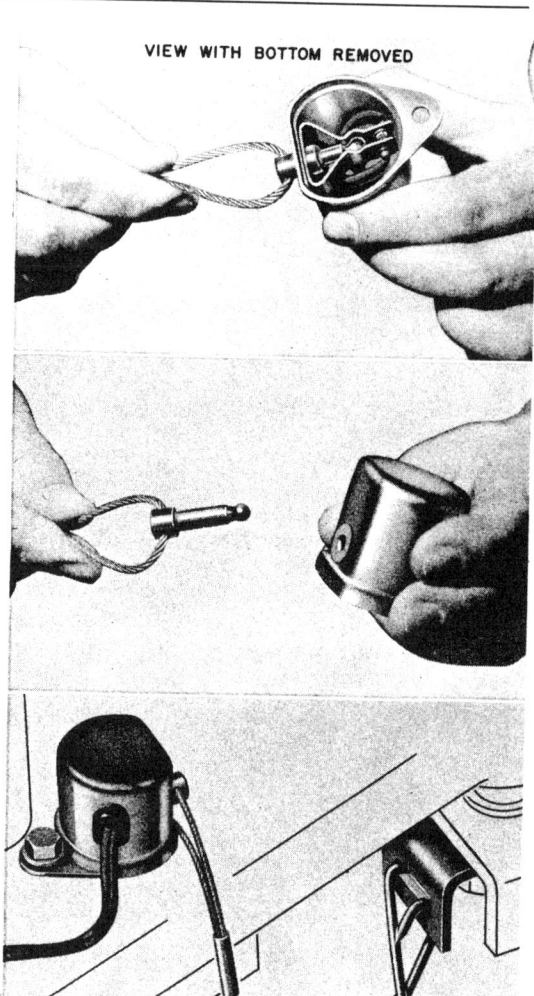

Breakaway switch.

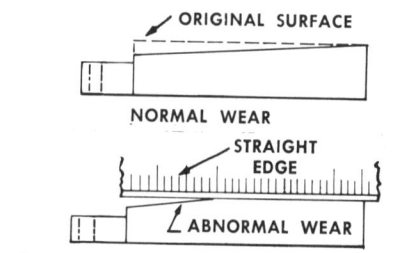

Checking the magnets for proper wear pattern.

Before replacing the defective magnet, determine the cause of the improper wear. Check the magnet lever pivot. A worn pivot can cause the magnet lever to cock, thus allowing the magnet to rest upon the armature plate unevenly. If this happens, the lever assembly should be replaced. Make sure that all wires are placed in such a way as not to get crimped or squashed and remember to allow ample clearance for movement of the lever and other moving parts whenever installing magnets.

To check for an electrical short in the magnet assembly, remove the magnet from the brake assembly and hook up a test light in a series with the magnet assembly and the tow vehicle's 12 V battery. Since the short may occur intermittently, move the lead ends and rap the magnet while checking it. If the light does not react or flickers, the magnet is defective and should be replaced.

THE SELECTIVE RESISTOR

As explained in the beginning paragraphs of this section, the selective resistor regulates the maximum braking capacity of the trailer brakes. Because of the wide ranges of axle loading, the rated maximum load braking capacity of the brakes may exceed the actual braking needs of a particular trailer. Thus the need for a selective resistor. The resistor has various settings according to the maximum trailer weight. Some resistors have setting diagrams to follow, but if no diagram is present, a qualified trailer mechanic should make the correct setting on the resistor. After the resistor is installed on the tow vehicle and set according to the proper specifications, check application of the trailer brakes with the controller fully applied. With the controller fully on, the brakes should provide firm braking action just short of the tires skidding on dry pavement.

Surge Brakes

Surge brakes are similar to car brakes in that they are operated by hydraulic pressure. There is a master cylinder that compresses brake fluid in the lines which in turn expands wheel cylinders at the brakes and presses the brake shoes against the drums. The only difference between surge brakes and electric brakes is the way in which they are activated. Though electric brakes seem to be more popular at the present, this does not mean that hydraulic brakes are not as effective. In fact it is said that hydraulic brakes operate more smoothly than their electric counterparts.

The master cylinder that operates the trailer brakes with a surge system is located on the tongue of the trailer. When the tow vehicle slows down, the momentum of the trailer pushes or "surges" against the hitch ball and activates the master cylinder. Pressure is then sent through the brake lines to the wheel cylinders which press the brake shoes against the drums.

The breakaway switch on surge brakes operates in a manner similar to those on electric brakes. The purpose is the same: to provide emergency braking for the trailer in case of an accidental disconnection of the tow vehicle and the trailer.

The breakaway switch is connected to the tow vehicle by a chain or a cable. When, and if, the trailer becomes disconnected from the tow vehicle, the cable pulls on a lever which is hooked to a tooth bar so that it cannot return without being released by hand. The lever pushes in on the master cylinder thus activating the brakes.

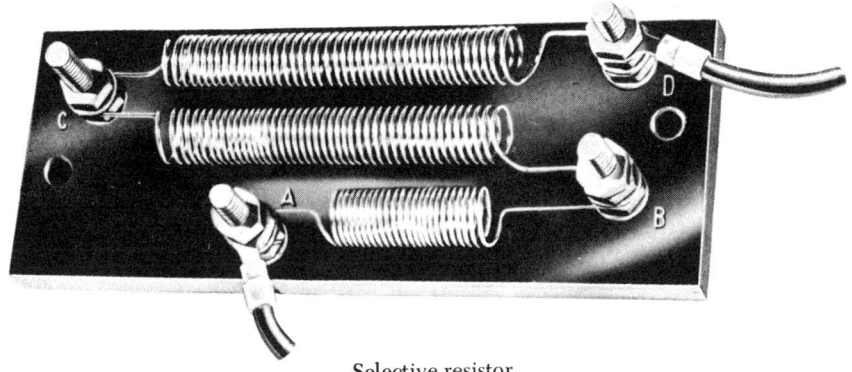

Selective resistor.

170 RUNNING GEAR ASSEMBLY

Position of a hydraulic brake assembly on the tongue of a travel trailer when being towed forward.

Position of a hydraulic brake assembly on the tongue of a travel trailer when decelerating.

A hydraulic brake assembly with its cover installed.

MAINTENANCE

Maintenance procedures for hydraulic brakes are similar to electric brakes in many ways. The procedures for removing the brake shoes and installing them, checking for proper wear patterns on the brake shoes and drums, and having the drums cut are all the same.

The Master Cylinder

The master cylinder is to be inspected frequently for leakage and to ensure that the proper level of brake fluid is maintained in the reservoir. If the cylinder does show signs of leaking, it should be replaced. There is a leak somewhere if the fluid level in the reservoir is below the prescribed level and continues to drop after being refilled. To check for a leak, inspect all connections in the brake lines. To check the wheel cylinders, the wheel assembly and brake drum must be removed. Refer to the section on electric brakes to remove the wheel assembly and drum. Once the wheel cylinder is exposed, look

Hydraulic brake assembly at the wheels.

for surfaces coated with brake fluid. If the brake shoes are soaked with brake fluid, they have to be replaced. If there is no evidence of leakage immediately visible, pull back the dust covers on the wheel cylinder itself. If there is fluid present just inside the dust cover, the wheel cylinder is leaking and must either be rebuilt or replaced.

Rebuilding the Wheel Cylinders

1. Assuming that the trailer has been jacked up properly, the wheels have been blocked, and the wheel assembly and drum have been removed, remove the

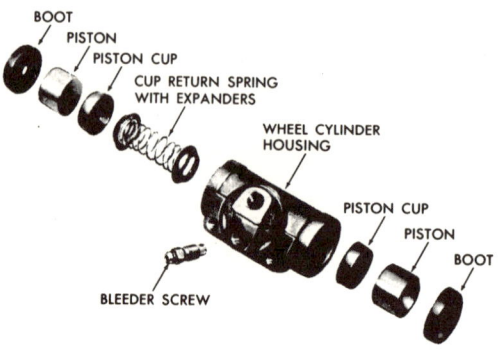

Wheel cylinder components.

brake shoes. (Refer to the section on electric brakes in the owner's manual for information on jacking.)

2. Remove the dust covers or boots from the cylinder ends and discard them. Remove the pistons, remove and discard the seal cups, and remove the expanders and spring.

3. Inspect the bore and pistons for damage or wear. Damaged pistons should be discarded as they cannot be reconditioned. Slight bore roughness can be removed by using a brake cylinder hone or crocus cloth with a fine grain. The cloth should be rotated in the bore under finger pressure. Do not slide the cloth lengthwise.

4. Clean the cylinder and internal parts with brake fluid.

5. Insert the spring expander assembly. Lubricate all rubber parts with fresh brake fluid.

6. Install new cups with the seal lips facing inward.

7. Install the pistons and rubber boots.

8. Replace the brake shoes and the wheel/drum assembly.

9. Bleed the system at the wheel cylinder.

Bleeding the Brakes

1. Fill the reservoir of the master cylinder with brake fluid.

2. While pressure is being applied to the master cylinder by pushing the breakaway switch lever against the master cylinder, loosen the bleed screw on the wheel cylinder about a quarter of a turn. This will allow air in the line and the wheel cylinder to escape.

3. Refill the master cylinder with brake fluid and repeat the above procedure until no more air—just brake fluid—comes out of the bleed screw.

4. Top off the master cylinder with brake fluid.

NOTE: *If the wheel cylinder is completely replaced, the system still has to be bled at the wheel cylinder.*

Brake Adjustment

The brake adjustment procedure for hydraulic brakes is very similar to that of electric brakes. The only difference is that when the star adjuster wheel is backed off it should only be backed of enough so that there is still a slight drag of the brakes when the wheel is spun by hand. Make sure that each wheel is adjusted so that there is approximately the same amount of drag on each wheel. (Refer to the "Electric Brakes" section for the exact brake adjusting procedures.)

Brake Troubleshooting Chart

Problem: Locking or Grabbing Brakes

Probable Cause	Solution
Controller not modulating	Check wiring for worn covering, broken wires, and wires that may be shorting out the system. Check with a test light.
Grease or brake fluid on the lining	Replace the seals or dust caps and replace the brake lining.
Wrong brake lining	Change the linings to all the same brand and material.
Rust in the armature plate and/or brake drums	Drum and armature may rust from non-use; condition is usually corrected by continued normal use.
Loose parts	Remove the hub and look for broken springs or loose rivets jammed in the brakes.
Excessive braking power	Install or adjust the selective resistor.

Brake Troubleshooting Chart (cont.)

Problem: Weak Brakes

Probable Cause	Solution
Improper adjustment	Adjust the brakes to compensate for wear.
Poor connections	Check to be sure that all connections are clean and tight.
Defective magnets	Replace the magnets.
Selective resistor is set incorrectly	Check for correct resistance setting to avoid too much resistance.
Grease or brake fluid on the brake lining	Replace the seals or dust caps and the brake lining. Check for a leaking wheel cylinder.
Misaligned or bent backing plate	Straighten or replace the backing plate.
Unlike voltage systems	If the tow vehicle has a 6 V electrical system, then use 6 V magnets.
Short circuit in the electrical system	Check the electrical system with an ammeter.
Poor ground	Check for correct grounding in the tow vehicle, trailer, and connector. Install a ground wire between the tow vehicle and the trailer.
Use of the trailer brakes only	Use of the trailer brakes only can cause early fade which is loss of friction due to excessive heat. Synchronize the braking through the resistor or controller adjustments and settings.
Wrong wire	Install heavier gauge wire.
Extreme trailer loading	Lighten load, or add a four-brake system to tandem-axle trailers.

Problem: No Brakes

Probable Cause	Solution
Bad magnets	Check with a test light. Replace if necessary.
Defective resistor	Check for loose connections or replace.
Poor brake adjustment	Adjust the brakes.
Open circuit	Check for broken wires, loose connections, improper grounding, and a faulty connector plug between the car and the trailer.
Improperly wired or inoperative controller	Check the controller operation with a test light.
Short circuit	Check the electrical circuit.
Loss of brake fluid	Check for leaking connections and wheel cylinders. Also look for a possible hole in the brake line.

Problem: Intermittent or Surging of the Brakes

Probable Cause	Solution
Out-of-round drums	Rebore the drums if they are more than 0.015 in. out of round.
Loose wheel bearings	Adjust the wheel bearings; replace if they are defective.

Brake Troubleshooting Chart (cont.)

Problem: Intermittent or Surging of the Brakes

Probable Cause	Solution
Deficient trailer ground	If the ground is through the hitch, install a ground wire.
Broken or loose magnet wires	Check the magnets with a test light and replace if necessary.

Problem: Dragging Brakes

Probable Cause	Solution
Brakes are adjusted incorrectly	Check the brake adjustment.
Electrical defect in the controller	Not enough gap between the controller contactor strip and the coil may cause the brakes to be on continuously.
Hydraulic defect in the controller or the master cylinder of the tow vehicle or the trailer (surge brakes)	Too much residual pressure in the tow vehicle hydraulic system or a gummed-up controller cylinder may cause the controller to be held "on" slightly. Also a gummed-up master cylinder on the tongue of a trailer equipped with surge brakes would have the same effects as mentioned above.
Corroded brake unit	Check the operation of all unit parts to be sure that they all move freely. Clean and lubricate brake assemblies.
Broken or weak shoe return springs	Check and replace if necessary.
Bent backing plate	Straighten or replace.

Problem: Noisy Brakes

Probable Cause	Solution
Loose parts	Check springs, rivets, bolts etc.
Improper bearing adjustment	Check for damaged or worn bearings. Replace if necessary. Adjust the bearings.
Grease, oil, or brake fluid on the brake linings	Replace the lining and clean the drum.
Lining is worn to the rivets	Replace the linings.
Bent backing plate	Straighten or replace.
Brake release, poor adjustment	A certain amount of noise is normal when the brake releases. Proper adjustment will minimize this noise.

7 · Routine Maintenance

The following is a list of routine maintenance procedures that should be performed frequently to avoid mishaps and inconveniences.

1. Lubricate the locking mechanism on the trailer coupler. Also lubricate the hitch ball with a small amount of light grease. This prevents noise and possible wear that could take place while you are towing.
2. Inspect the tires for wear and dry rot. Inflate them to the proper pressure; do not overinflate them.
3. If your travel trailer is equipped with canvas awnings or an enclosed porch, remember maintenance for the canvas. (See the section on "Canvas Care" in this chapter.)
4. Keep metal zippers lubricated. They are usually aluminum and, in the open air —especially near salt water—the aluminum will anodize and cause rough operation. Frequently lubricate the mechanism with either special zipper lubricant or candle wax. Never use oil; it will stain the fabric and smear your fingers.
5. Check the torque on the wheel lug nuts of the trailer before any extended trip. It is common for these nuts to loosen and, sometimes, come off. It is difficult for the operator of the tow vehicle to hear any odd noises coming from the trailer that might give him a clue that his wheels are coming loose.

Check them before you leave. The manufacturer of your trailer or your owner's manual can supply the correct torque specifications of the lug nuts. (Most require 110–115 ft lbs.)
6. The trailer bearings should also be examined at least once a year and more frequently if the trailer is used often. (See

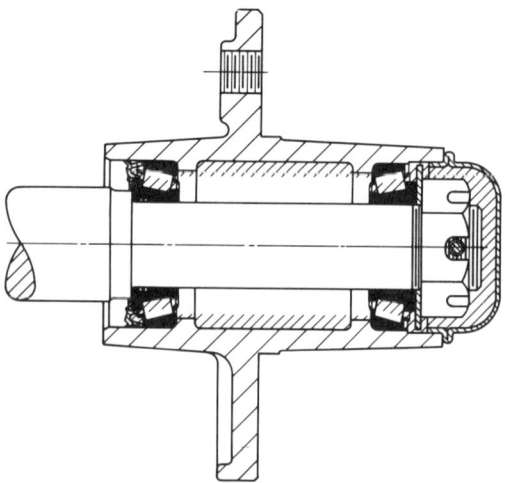

Lubricate the inner and outer bearings. This is a cross-section that shows where the grease is to be packed (black areas).

"Chassis Maintenance.") Use the correct type of grease when repacking the wheel bearings. Examine them for improper wear patterns before reinstalling them.
7. Some trailers have bolts that hold

ROUTINE MAINTENANCE 175

the coupler to the tongue. Check these to make sure they are tight.

8. Examine the path of the wiring under and through the trailer to guard against short circuits. Check the wire insulation and the condition of the rubber grommets that separate the wiring from the metal surfaces of the trailer frame.

9. Check the condition of the gas lines and the security of their connections. Look for places in the lines that might have

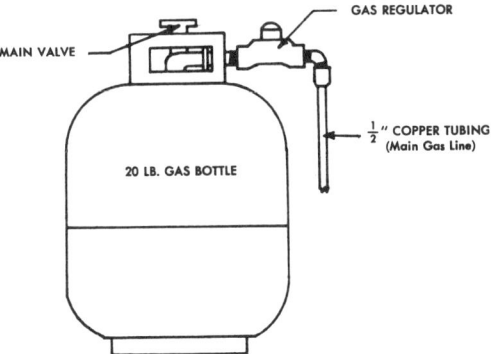

Check all gas lines and their connections for leaks.

rubbed against the trailer frame and partially penetrated the lines. Replace these sections and protect them by inserting rubber grommets into the hole or wrapping the line with electrical tape.

10. Know the dimensions of your tow vehicle and trailer when they are hooked together. Know the height of your trailer and don't forget to include the air conditioner in your measurements. You wouldn't want to get caught under a low bridge, would you? The length of your trailer is important because some states have laws governing the combination length of a tow vehicle and trailer. There are also regulations regarding single-vehicle lengths in some campgrounds due to terrain and campsite limitations. These laws apply to travel trailers and ignorance is no excuse.

11. Before starting out, test your brakes. Listen for squealing, chatter, or any other suspicious noises that might indicate that there is something going wrong. Don't let an obvious sign of trouble go too long without investigating. By catching a malfunction early and correcting it, you can avoid great expense and possible accidents. Adjust the parking brake frequently to make sure that it will hold both vehicles when necessary.

12. The trailer must have a good spare tire; it should be mounted securely on the tongue of the trailer or in a place where it can be reached easily. If the spare is in open view, chain it and lock it to prevent theft. Carry the key in the trailer.

Since spares are rarely used, check the air pressure frequently to make sure yours isn't flat.

It is a good idea to make a checklist which can be applied to the trailer before each outing. It is common for trailer owners to forget all maintenance; to just hitch and go. Travel trailers, because of their basic mechanical simplicity, require only a

Know the dimensions of your trailer and tow vehicle when they are hooked together.

limited amount of periodic maintenance, but don't forget it because it is necessary. hanging tree limbs or power tension lines—for obvious reasons.

Canvas Care

This is an important part of the regular maintenance of the trailer. Without maintenance, the canvas may wear out in a relatively short period of time. For example, if you have to pack the canvas while it is still wet, or even damp, don't forget to unpack it when you get home. The canvas should be allowed to dry or else mold will form, causing the fabric to deteriorate. If spots of mold or mildew appear on the canvas, scrub them with soap and warm water and allow the fabric to dry in direct sunlight. Make sure that the surface is completely dry before repacking.

If your canvas awning begins to leak, brush or spray waterproofing compound on it. Follow the manufacturer's directions. To be sure of a good job, you might want to apply a double coating. These waterproofing compounds can be found at any well-equipped camping supply store.

If the canvas rips, fix it immediately because it can only grow. There are two types of patch available; the conventional sew-on type which works best when applied with a heavy-gauge sewing machine, and the new iron-on type which can be applied in the manner the name indicates. In either case, after the patch has been applied, a coat of water-repellent should be sprayed on both the inside and outside of the canvas. In fact, it is a good practice to carry a container of this sealer with the trailer.

When packing, do not allow the canvas to be situated near any sharp edges where road vibration can cause possible contact and rips.

Do not stretch canvas when it is being used for shelter because the tighter the surface becomes, the harder it is to close the side zippers. It is possible to break the zipper this way.

Canvas without a vinyl outside covering has a tendency to leak when you brush against it. If this happens, the only cure is to use spray waterproofing on both sides of the material.

Avoid parking your trailer under low-

Vinyl Care

Vinyl is possibly the easiest thing to keep clean. Soap and water will help to keep the original luster for many years but cleansers can cause a loss of shine and color.

Glue-on repair patches are specially made for use on vinyl.

Interior Maintenance

Fabric Upholstery: Use a foam cleaner. Soap and water will leave water marks in the fabric.

Carpeting: Most of the newer travel trailers use indoor-outdoor carpeting; it needs only limited care. A small 12 V vacuum cleaner is a good investment for keeping these carpets clean at all times. Foam cleaners can be used to remove stains.

Vinyl: Use soap and warm water. Heavy industrial cleaning agents are not necessary. For small spills, a damp cloth will work well.

Drapes: Either dry clean trailer drapes or consult the manufacturer for their recommendations. Most fabrics, however, are machine washable.

Counter Tops: Use a mild soap solution for cleaning tables and counter tops. Never use an abrasive cleaner because it will dull the finish.

Common-sense maintenance of your travel trailer, the same as for your home or car, will generally provide years of trouble-free trailering.

Exterior Maintenance

Preserving the outside finish of the trailer is just as important as the finish of the tow vehicle. The trailer can be washed in the same fashion as the car. If a scrub brush is used, make sure that the trailer surface is wet and the brush is dipped in a soapy solution. No harsh detergent should be used on the trailer since the abrasives in it will scratch the finish. Any oil spots can be removed with Naphtha. Never use lacquer thinner on any painted surfaces.

For preserving the finish, any type of good automotive wax will do a good job. There are special aluminum cleaning and waxing compounds available for those trailers with bare aluminum exteriors.

Aluminum Care

Many newer trailers use aluminum for their exteriors. Several manufacturers use bare aluminum, after the fashion of Airstream, without even painting it. This bright surface keeps the interior of the trailer cooler since it reflects heat and the added weight of paint is saved too. Furthermore, aluminum won't rust and it is light and reasonably strong.

Cracks may appear in a trailer's aluminum skin due to road vibration and trailer stress. If the crack is small, it can be stopped by "stop drilling." This is done by finding the very end of the crack and drilling one hole at each end with a $3/32$ in. twist drill. If the crack is large, the same procedure is used except that the larger crack should be caulked liberally. A doubler plate can be applied over the crack and pop-riveted to the skin. The edges of this plate should be caulked as well.

If the trailer is painted, and defects show up in the aluminum, sand the spot until it is smooth and remove all foreign material. Only paint which is made for use on aluminum should be used; other paints will not bind to an aluminum surface.

Pop Rivets

Pop rivets are used on most current aluminum repairs and they are far easier to install than the conventional rivets which have to be bucked. The pop rivet gun listed is the ordinary type which can be purchased at a good hardware store. The rivets are available in various sizes.

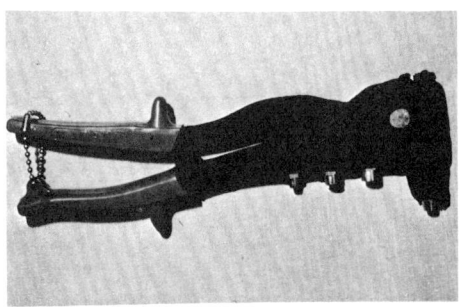

Pop rivet gun.

To use a pop rivet gun, first drill a hole (of the same diameter as the rivet) where the rivet is to fasten. Insert the rivet into the gun with the spiked end entering the gun first. (It is sometimes necessary to lift the handle of the gun when inserting the rivet in order to allow the rivet to catch.) Once the rivet is in the gun, it should stay by itself and the gun handle should be in the cocked position.

Place the rivet into the hole where it is to be inserted. Press down on the rivet gun and, at the same time, press down on the gun lever. This will compress the rivet and break off its end so it is flush with its head. If the end does not break off, open the handle of the rivet gun and take another

Drilling out pop rivets.

"bite" of the rivet shaft. Push down on the handle until the end of the shaft breaks. Make certain that the rivet is secure because it must be drilled out and another must be inserted if it isn't tight.

Drilling Solid Rivets

Solid rivets, which are used to hold aluminum panels together, are standard

equipment on most trailers. If it becomes necessary to remove the panels to gain access to an inner part of the trailer, these rivets must be removed. This procedure is not as simple as it might seem.

First of all, take your time, and if at all possible, use a variable-speed ¼ in. drill.

Insert a twist drill, of the same diameter as the rivet, into the drill and carefully tap a centering mark in the middle of the rivet's head with a center punch and hammer. Place the tip of the drill into this punch mark and start the drill on a very slow speed, applying a reasonable amount of pressure. Be careful that the drill does not slip from the head and mark the aluminum skin. *Do not drill all the way through.* Drill only far enough to spin the head off the rivet. If you do drill all the way through, you will enlarge the rivet hole and necessitate the use of an oversize replacement rivet. Once the head is removed, the remainder of the rivet can be removed from the skin by punching it out with a small drift pin.

Solid rivets are usually replaced with pop rivets because they are so easy to install. This procedure is highly recommended. For pop rivet installation procedures, see the preceding section.

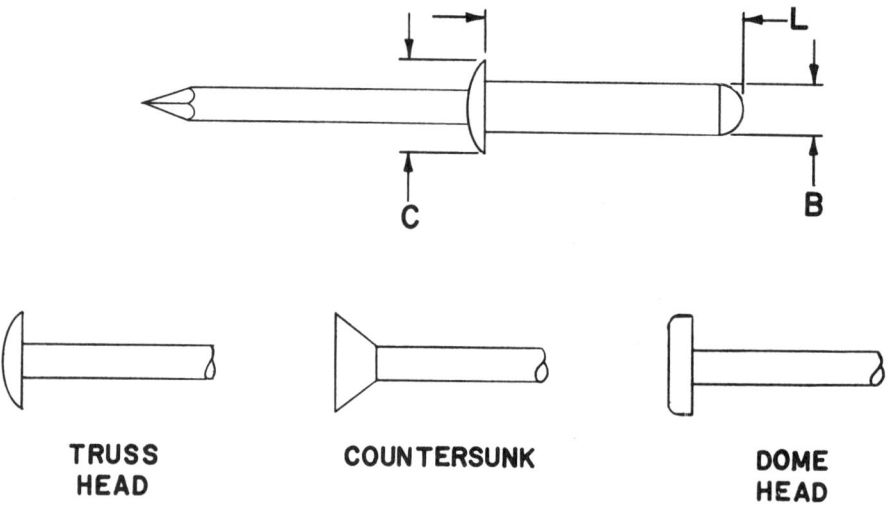

BODY DIA. "B"	HEAD DIA. "C"	HEAD TYPE	LENGTH "L"	GRIP RANGE	HOLE REQ'D.	TYPE
3/16	.342	DOME	.720	.187 — .437	.199	ALUM.
3/16	.336	DOME	.530	.062 — .250	.199	ALUM.
5/32	.255	DOME	.470	.046 — .250	.166	ALUM.
3/16	.625	TRUSS	.656	.250 — .500	.199	ALUM.-GOLD
3/16	.625	TRUSS	11/16	.375 — .500	.199	STL.
1/8	.250	TRUSS	.419	.251 — .312	.129	STL. MAN. ALUM.
5/32	.245	CS	.530	UP TO .312	.166	ALUM.
1/8	.205	CS	15/32	.093 — .250	.136	ALUM.
3/16	.375	BUTTON	25/32	1/2 — 5/8	.199	ALUM.
5/32	.255	DOME	.470	.046 — .250	.166	ALUM.-GOLD
1/8	.215	DOME	.400	.031 — .187	.136	ALUM.-GOLD
3/16	.625	TRUSS	.968	.500 — .781	.199	ALUM.
3/16	.625	TRUSS	.968	.500 — .781	.199	ALUM. DARK

Rivet chart.

Fiberglass Repairs

Many trailers have various fiberglass components which, under the stress of towing, either crack or break. It is not always necessary to replace the entire section. The following sections give detailed outlines of how to repair both major and minor fiberglass defects.

Fiberglass repair kits with resin, hardener, thixatrope, fiberglass cloth, and other essentials are available from auto shops which specialize in fiberglass car bodies or boating supply outlets which do fiberglass boat repairs.

Loose-strand fiberglass is used in resin preparation. Since both resin and spun fiberglass can be irritating to skin, apply protective cream to your hands and arms when making fiberglass repairs.

If the fiberglass must be sanded after it is applied, work in the open air or see that the sander being used has a vacuum attachment to collect all of the fiberglass dust.

NOTE: *When working with the resin, mix and apply it in a well-ventilated area; the fumes can be toxic.*

For the repair of minor damage, remove all paint and other coating from the damaged area. Follow the directions, mixing

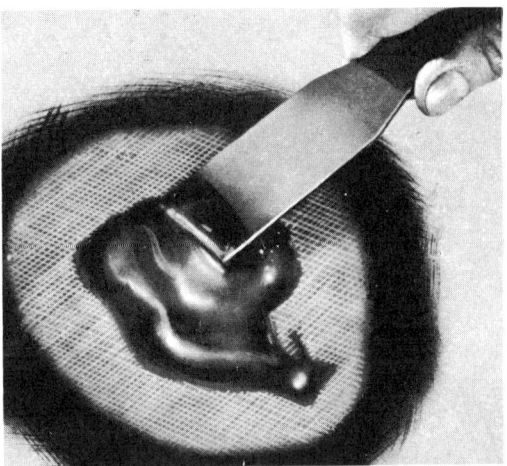
Applying the resin to the damaged area. (© Chevrolet Div. G.M. Corp.)

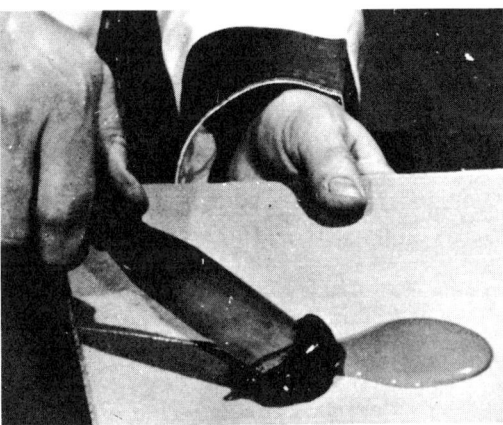
Mixing the resin with the hardener. (© Chevrolet Div. G.M. Corp.)

Finishing the damaged area. (© Chevrolet Div. G.M. Corp.)

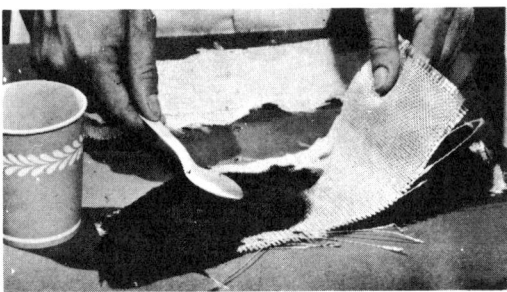
Mixing the finished resin with the fiberglass mat. (© Chevrolet Div. G.M. Corp.)

only enough fiberglass to be used in a half hour. Apply the resin with a rubber squeegee or a putty knife. Fill the damaged area, smoothing the fiberglass to the contour, and finish by sanding the area smooth and then repainting it.

Completely cracked or broken panels are classified as major repairs. Before mixing the resin, which is done in the same manner as for a minor repair, remove all the paint from the area surrounding the damage. Grind the edges of the damaged area so that they form a wide "V." This

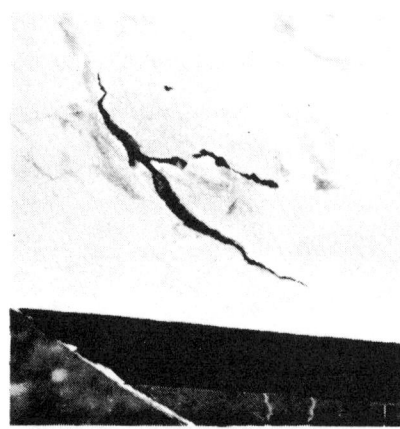

A break in the trailer skin.

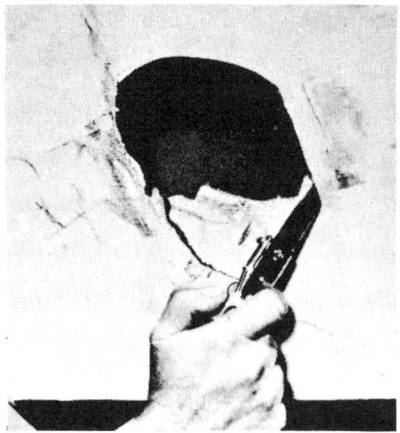

Cutting loose pieces from the damaged area.

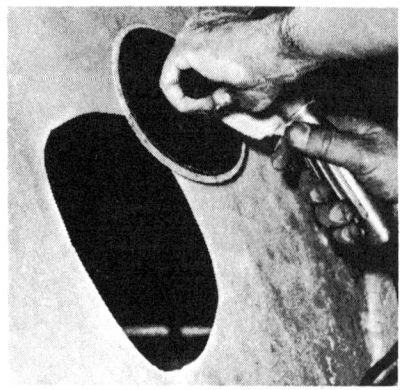

Roughing the area with a sander.

Reinforcing the damage from the inside of the trailer.

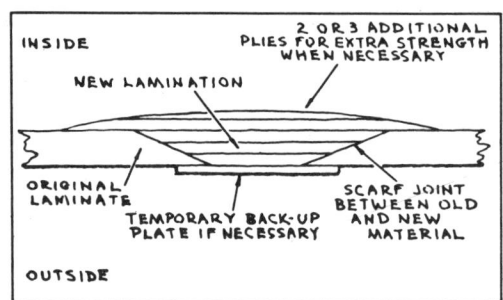

Fiberglass repair construction.

will provide a good bonding surface for the resin. For severe damage, coat a layer of sheet fiberglass in the resin and bond the damaged area on both sides.

For scratched panels or spot repairs which have gone through to the fiberglass, it is necessary to remove the paint from the surrounding area. Feather sand the damage with no. 220 or 230 wet sandpaper until it is smooth and level. Do not sand into the fiberglass mesh.

For cracked panels, it is best to work with the temperature of the work area at least 70–75° F. This will ensure sufficient hardening of the resin. To be certain of the conditions recommended, check the resin container for the exact instructions. Use lacquer thinner to remove all paint and foreign material from both the surface and the underside of the fractured section. Rough the surface of the fiberglass to afford a better bonding surface and remove all jagged edges from the fracture, applying a 30° angle to the broken edges. Align the broken panels. This can be done with C-clamps. Follow the outlined procedures under the "Major Repair" paragraph.

STRENGTH OF THE REPAIR

If the fiberglass repair is done correctly, the finished product will be as strong, or stronger, than the original surface. Extra strength may be added, as listed in the preceding section, by inserting reinforcing panels constructed of mesh fiberglass that have been dipped in the resin solution and applied to the rear portion of the damage.